"Whoever excels in what we prize appears a hero in our eyes."

Thomas Carlyle
"On Heroes and Hero Worship"

Legends of the Mat

by

MIKE CHAPMAN

CULTURE HOUSE BOOKS
(641-791-3072)

LEGENDS OF THE MAT

A publication of Culture House Books – November 2006

Copyright – 2006 by Mike Chapman
All rights reserved.

No part of this book may be reproduced or transmitted in any form or by any means, electronic or mechanical, including photocopying, recording, or by any information storage and retrieval system now known or to be invented, without permission in writing from the publisher, except by a reviewer who wishes to quote brief passages in connection with a written review for inclusion in a magazine, newspaper, or broadcast.

For information, address: Culture House Books
P.O. Box 293
Newton, Iowa 50208

Library of Congress Cataloging-in-Publication Data
Chapman, Mike, 1943 -
    Legends of the Mat.

    1. Wrestlers – United States – Biography. 2. Wrestling – United States – History.
    3. United States – University – Wrestling – History.

ISBN 978-0-9676080-9-9

PRINTED IN THE UNITED STATES of AMERICA

First Edition

Acknowledgements

A book such as this requires the cooperation of a number of people, and their efforts are greatly appreciated. Foremost among those who contributed their time and knowledge are Kyle Klingman, associate director of the International Wrestling Institute and Museum, in Iowa, and Bev Chapman, the best proofreader I have ever worked with. Jim Duschen, a lifelong friend and hall of famer, also provided valuable input on various levels.

You will notice that many of the pictures in this book were taken by Steve Brown, one of the nation's leading wrestling photographers; I thank him for his generosity in allowing me to use so many superb images.

I am also indebted to the scholarship of many other wrestling writers and historians, men who care deeply about the sport and have worked hard through the decades to insure that its greatest memories are preserved. Finally, I want to thank the great wrestlers profiled in this book, many of whom I have become friends with along the way. I truly believe they are among the finest athletes ever produced in this country and their stories deserve to be told.

Legends of the Mat

(Listed in chronological order)

1. Earl Caddock – *Paving the Way*
2. Robin Reed – *He Liked It Rough*
3. Jack VanBebber – *Three-Time NCAA Champion to Olympic Hero*
4. Stanley and Josiah Henson – *A Great Brother Act From Oklahoma*
5. Henry Wittenberg – *The Longest Winning Streak*
6. Bill Koll – *The Master of the Mental Game*
7. Glen Brand – *The Wrestling Engineer*
8. Bill Smith – *King of the Whizzer*
9. Dan Hodge – *Terrifying Power*
10. Doug Blubaugh – *The Epic Journey*
11. Terry McCann – *Small Body, Huge Heart*
12. Gray Simons – *Seven Times a Collegiate King*
13. Bobby Douglas – *Champion at All Levels*
14. Rick Sanders – *A Maverick Who Excelled*
15. Wayne Baughman – *Owner of 16 National Titles*
16. Dan Gable – *Obsession and Domination*
17. Chris Taylor – *The Gentle Giant*
18. John and Ben Peterson – *In the Footsteps of Jacob*
19. Wade Schalles – *Mr. Excitement*
20. Lee Kemp – *As Good As it Gets*
21. Bruce Baumgartner – *King of the Big Men*
22. Ed and Lou Banach – *Never-Say-Quit Battlers*
23. Dave and Mark Schultz – *Iron Sharpens Iron*
24. Randy Lewis – *It's All About the Pin*
25. Ken Monday – *Tough As a Puma*
26. John Smith – *Six Times King of the World*
27. Kevin Jackson – *Precision in a Singlet*
28. Tom and Terry Brands – *Twin Tornadoes*
29. Rulon Gardner – *The Impossible Dream*
30. Cael Sanderson – *All-Time College King*

Preface

To be a legend, says the dictionary, is to be "a very famous or notorious person."

In the world of sports, legends are ubiquitous. Perhaps no other field of endeavor creates legends as quickly, or as imperiously. Very few who obtain legendary status ever lose it. In fact, the passage of time is generally of no consequence to the enduring popularity of a sports legend.

Babe Ruth played his final game of baseball in 1935 and today, over seven decades later, he is as big a legend as sports has ever produced. Every time a Roger Maris or a Barry Bonds pounds a baseball into the upper deck of some baseball stadium, the memory of Babe Ruth is reborn. The legend swells, and creeps forward like a glacier, unstoppable and magnificent in its hugeness.

Baseball, it seems, produces legends at a faster pace than any other sport. The list began at the turn of the 20th century, and is almost endless. Included are such icons as Cy Young, Shoeless Joe Jackson, Ty Cobb, Christy Matthewson, Ted Williams, Hank Aaron, Willie Mays, Mickey Mantle, Cal Ripken Jr., Roger Clemens....the list goes on and on.

Jack Dempsey, one of the most ferocious boxers to ever climb into a ring, joined the ranks of the sports immortals when he knocked out Fred Fulton, a much bigger man, in 18 seconds, and then faced the huge champion, Jess Willard. Again, Dempsey struck like lightning, sending Willard to the canvas seven times in the first round alone. On that hot July 4th day, in long ago 1919, Jack Dempsey became a legend that will endure for all time.

Whenever a new track sensation rockets into the national spotlight, the exploits of Jesse Owens are revisited. In its March 31, 2002, issue, *Sports Illustrated* ranked the performance by Owens in 1935 as the No. 1 collegiate sports event of all time. What the indefatigable Mr. Owens did that autumn day of long ago was participate in four races – and set four world records! That is truly the stuff of which legends are made.

And so it goes with most sports. Legends explode onto the national scene and seldom fade away completely. Maybe Jim Thorpe and Red Grange aren't as well known today in football circles as are Dan Marino and Barry Sanders, who came many decades later; perhaps the names of Stanley Ketchel and Gene Tunney don't slip off the tongue of today's boxing fans as easily as do the names of Muhammad Ali and Sugar Ray Leonard, but their names can at least be read in the numerous books of boxing history, which themselves are relatively easy to find.

It is also necessary to point out that to be a legend in sports doesn't necessarily mean to be the very best. To be a legend means to be the type of athlete that people talk about consistently, and to be remembered as being among the best, either because of the tremendous record that was fashioned or by virtue of the excitement that the athlete generated while performing at a high level.

Sadly, very few sports forget their legends as easily as amateur wrestling. It's not the fans that are to blame. Wrestling enthusiasts place their heroes on pedestals, just like the fans of every other sport. Much of the problem resides within the world of journalism – from newspapers to magazines to books, and with the companies that publish them. Sadly, the men and women who write for general consumption publications prefer sports with balls, and are loath to report on sports they don't fully understand, like wrestling.

The power of books is often overlooked. Books are the permanent record of a society, and of a culture. Abraham Lincoln will never be forgotten because there are over 10,000 books covering the life of this great man. Neither will the deeds of Babe Ruth fade from the scene. At last count, there were an estimated 200 books about baseball's greatest star.

But precious few books have been written about the heroes of the sport of wrestling. Most of those that are written about this sport are technique books, or coaching books. Very few deal with the great personalities of the sport, or make an effort to record the deeds of these great American athletes.

The primary purpose of *Legends of the Mat* is to establish a permanent record of the exploits of some of the greatest wrestlers in American history. This volume does not presume to include all of wrestling's legends but, rather, to provide a basic overview of the sport over the past century, as seen through the careers of some of the best wrestlers to ever step on a mat. The stories are presented in chronological order and if a person reads the book as written, they will also be seeing an overview of the history of the sport, as seen through the careers of some of its greatest stars.

Certainly, there are other wrestlers that could have been included; there are many more legends of the mat than just those found in these pages. But everything has a finite limit, and so it is with this book. Perhaps there will be more such books as time goes on.

Until then, I hope you will enjoy the stories of these particular legends of the mat. For what they accomplished in the noble pursuit of their goals, they are worthy of your praise and your time. And they deserve to be remembered in the pantheon of America's greatest sports heroes.

                              Mike Chapman
                              Newton, Iowa

Earl Caddock
Paving the Way

To Earl Caddock goes the honor of being the first great amateur wrestler to become the world heavyweight professional champion, back when the professional game was still a genuine athletic contest. Handsome, well-built, tremendously skilled, articulate and deeply religious, Earl Caddock truly was one of the greatest athletes of his generation, and one of the finest technical wrestlers who ever lived.

Beyond that, he was a legitimate war hero and successful businessman, and a superb role model to a generation of young athletes across the nation. Like Pat Tillman nine decades later, Caddock volunteered to serve in the United States Army during a time of war. He was a doughboy in World War I and fought in the trenches in France, suffering lung damage from mustard gas. He returned home after the war to briefly resume his wrestling career, and then moved into the business world, becoming highly successful and raising a family of devout Christians who, in turn, became highly successful athletes and businessmen.

And yet today, Earl Caddock is a name scarcely recognized by even the most devout amateur wrestling fan.

Like most of the great wrestlers of the early 20th century, Earl spent his formative years on a Midwestern farm. He was born February 27, 1888, in a small cabin near Huron, South Dakota. When he was very young, his family moved to Chicago, where his father found work as a fireman. Shortly after the move, his father was killed in an accident, and the children were dispersed to relatives. Earl went to live with his uncle Ike, on a farm near Anita, in southwestern Iowa.

As a teenager, Earl worked hard on the farm, and looked forward to weekend gatherings with other rural families in the area. The young men would play baseball, race against each other, and engage in friendly but highly-competitive wrestling matches. His local reputation grew as he became the best young wrestler in the area. Though he loved farm life, he moved back to Chicago late in his teen years to help bring in more money to support his mother, three brothers and a sister. He worked as a mail clerk on the Rock Island Railroad and was also employed briefly by Western Electric.

In the Windy City, he was introduced to formal wrestling through a chance encounter with the Cherry Circle Athletic Club and began competing in organized matches. He took to the sport like a duck to water, and won the national AAU freestyle title at 175 pounds in 1914. The next year he won two national titles – repeating at 175 pounds, and also claiming the national AAU heavyweight championship. At the time, he was representing the Chicago Athletic Association and Hebrew Institute.

After winning three AAU national titles, Earl Caddock turned professional and in 1917 captured the world heavyweight title. He later fought in World War I.

Legends of the Mat – 10

Earl Caddock was one of the most skilled wrestlers to ever climb into a ring. Here he shows his famous head scissors.

Earl was undefeated in all of his 50 matches as an amateur, and his skills attracted the attention of Frank Gotch, the man many consider the greatest professional wrestler of all time. Also an Iowa farm boy, Gotch earned worldwide renown with his dramatic victory over the famed Russian Lion, George Hackenschmidt, in Chicago in 1908. When Gotch repeated the victory over Hackenschmidt on September 8, 1911, in the brand new Comiskey ballpark in front of 30,000-plus fans, he became the best-known athlete in America. Thousands of Midwest farm boys – including Earl Caddock – grew up with dreams of becoming the heavyweight wrestling champion of the world.

Caddock had earned the nickname "Man of a Thousand Holds" for his tremendous command of wrestling holds and maneuvers, and Gotch was suitably impressed. He worked out with Caddock, and helped land him a spot as a training partner for Gotch with the Sells-Floto Circus Athletic Show. Gotch and Jess Willard, the world heavyweight boxing champion, were the star attractions, taking on local toughs in bouts for money; but Caddock earned invaluable experience in how to wrestle the professional style, where submission holds were allowed.

Convinced that he could earn considerable wealth, Caddock decided to become a professional like Gotch. Matches then were very similar to a college match today, with double-leg takedowns, single-leg takedowns, foot sweeps, cross faces, reverses and half nelsons all common. A wrestler could win via a three-second pin, or by forcing the other wrestler to either submit or just plain quit. Bouts could go as long as two hours, with considerable time spent on the mat working for a joint-lock submission or a pin hold.

As a professional, Caddock wrestled all over the Midwest, winning match after match with relative ease. The drums began beating for a championship bout between Earl and Joe Stecher, the new world heavyweight champion.

After Gotch's retirement, a brawny Chicago wrestler named Charlie Cutler won the vacant title, in 1914. Less than a year later, Cutler journeyed to Omaha to face the unknown Stecher, and was defeated easily. Stecher, though just twenty-one years of age, was a wrestling marvel. His leg strength was phenomenal and was developed by squeezing bags of wheat on his father's farm, near Dodge, Nebraska. His body scissors quickly became the most feared maneuver in all of wrestling.

Long and lanky, Stecher had a warrior's heart. He was unbeaten in 60 matches when he and Caddock climbed into the ring on April 19, 1917, before a sell-out crowd of 10,000 fans in Omaha. Caddock had never lost as an amateur or a professional, and was riding a combined winning streak of nearly 80 in a row! It was billed as a Nebraska-Iowa rivalry, and Gotch was in Caddock's corner, drawing even more attention to the match.

Stecher had a slight height advantage, and weighed 205 to Caddock's 188 pounds. Stecher took the first fall in one hour and 22 minutes, with a pun-

Earl Caddock

ishing body scissors and half nelson. It was the first time Caddock had ever felt his shoulders held to the mat in 72 amateur or professional matches. But he fought back to take the second fall in one hour and 40 minutes, with a crotch hold and half nelson.

The rules called for a ten-minute break between falls, and both wrestlers were bone tired after nearly three hours of wrestling. Caddock walked down the aisle amid a chorus of cheers and shouts of encouragement, and climbed into the ring to battle for the third and deciding fall. But Stecher failed to appear and his manager sent word from his dressing room that he was too exhausted to continue.

Earl Caddock, a three-time AAU national champion and the nation's best-known amateur wrestler, had just become the professional heavyweight champion of the world!

With his clean-cut looks and pleasing personality, Caddock was one of the biggest attractions in sport. He was in constant demand and traveled the nation. His matches were front-page news on sports sections everywhere; when he defeated Wladek Zbyszko in Des Moines on February 9, 1918, the Des Moines newspaper carried two huge headlines on the front page: "Caddock Wins Over Zbyszko" was the top headline, and beneath it was "Separate Peace in Ukraine." Shockingly, a story about professional wrestling had received top billing over a major World War I story.

Three months after beating Stecher to win the title, Caddock married Grace Mickel, an attractive schoolteacher, and moved to her hometown of Walnut, a tiny Iowa community just thirty miles east of Omaha. They raised three sons and a daughter. Earl Jr. attended the University of Iowa and played on the same Ironman football team with the legendary Nile Kinnick, 1939 Heisman Trophy winner. Robert and Richard both played football at rival Iowa State University, and Joan was a beauty queen at Colorado Women's College.

Caddock made front-page news around the nation when he joined the United States Army in September of 1918. "Of all the great sports figures in this country, only the world heavyweight wrestling champion, Earl Caddock, has demonstrated true courage and leadership by showing his willingness to fight for his country," wrote a sportswriter in the East, lauding Caddock. It was the same type of courage and patriotism that NFL player Pat Tillman exhibited nine decades later and resulted in his death in Afghanistan.

Caddock turned down an officer's commission in the Army and entered as a private, saying he wanted to be just like everyone else. He was promoted to sergeant in March of 1918 and was shipped overseas six months later. He saw considerable front-line action while serving in France, and his lungs were injured in a mustard gas attack.

Just before sailing for home when the war ended, he was forced against his wishes to enter the Allied Expeditionary Games. He won the heavyweight wrestling championship with ease, adding another prestigious amateur title to his resume.

Upon his return to the States, the nation was primed for a return match between the two handsome farm champions – Earl Caddock and Joe Stecher. The two warriors met for the second time on January 20, 1920. New York's famed Madison Square Garden was sold out, with 14,000 fans on hand. Caddock was escorted into the ring by soldiers, and Stecher, who had served in the navy during the war, was escorted by a crew of sailors.

The match was a one-fall affair, and was a grueling bout between two of the finest wrestlers in history. It lasted two hours and five minutes. Excerpts from the bout are preserved on video and can be seen at the International Wrestling Institute and Museum in Iowa.

"Wrestling people, even amateur champions, are shocked by the high quality of the wrestling," said Kyle Klingman, the museum's associate director. "It is obvious to one and all that this is a pure scientific match between athletes of tremendous skill."

Olympic champions John Smith, Ben Peterson, Dan Gable, Doug Blubaugh and Bill Smith are among the many great amateur stars who have seen the film and come away with a new perspective on professional wrestling in that era.

"It looked like a college match. Those guys could really wrestle, no doubt about it," said Blubaugh, 1960 Olympic champion.

Caddock's lung condition affected his performance, and he visibly wore down during the long bout. Stecher, twenty pounds heavier, spent most of the last hour on top, working for his famed scissors hold. At

Legends of the Mat – 12

Earl Caddock

last, Stecher secured a very tight body scissors and arm bar, and pinned Caddock. It was the first loss for the champion in nearly 100 official matches, covering seven years of both amateur and professional competition.

Caddock's last bout came in May of 1921, but already professional wrestling was being taken over by promoters who wanted pre-arranged matches. Earl Caddock would have none of that. He decided it was time to move on.

He homesteaded a cattle ranch in Wyoming, and then operated a Ford and Farm Implement Agency in Walnut. He loved the West and took his family on long trips, as far away as California. Hotels and motels were rare and they often camped out under the stars. He eventually formed the United Petroleum Corporation in Omaha, and served as the company's president.

All three of his boys served in World War II. Earl Jr. was on the front lines of a medical unit, and died in 1953, as the result of injuries suffered during the war. Robert was a captain with an artillery unit and won the Bronze Star. Richard was a B17 pilot and earned the Distinguished Flying Cross.

In his later years, Caddock loved to talk about the values of amateur wrestling, and was often called upon to be the guest speaker at Iowa high school banquets. Finn Erikson, the man who is credited with starting the great tradition at West Waterloo High School, said Caddock was a legendary figure who all Iowa prep coaches looked up to.

Earl Caddock died in 1950 at his home in Walnut, after a long struggle with cancer. He was sixty-two years old. The sports world mourned his death from coast to coast, and the accolades flowed in.

"No finer man ever graced a roped square than Earl," wrote Nat Fleischer, the most respected boxing and wrestling writer of his era, in his book, *From Milo to Londos*. "He was far superior to the majority of matmen in both technique and intelligence.

"He was an inspiration to the youth of America. During his entire career he exemplified the best in America sports tradition." Fleischer added that Caddock should be at the very top of the list "as the man who had done the most for the uplift of wrestling in this country." *(1)*

His greatest foe, Joe Stecher, was full of praise:

"I thought I was wrestling against five men at the same time," he said.

Caddock was voted into the Iowa Sports Hall of Fame shortly after his passing, and was inducted into the George Tragos/Lou Thesz Professional Hall of Fame at the International Wrestling Institute and Museum in 2000. Members of his family came to the museum and met members of Joe Stecher's family in a remarkable reunion.

Earl's legacy has lived on in the memory of wrestling scholars and through his sons, who revered him.

"He was the finest man I ever met," said Richard Caddock of his father, in 1998. "I owe whatever success I have had in life to him." Richard was a very successful businessman and owned an international company at the time of his death in 1999.

"Earl was above all a Christian," said Bob in 2000. "He was faithful in passing on to his children his high moral values, integrity and Christian faith."

Sec Taylor, who covered sports for the Des Moines Register newspaper for over 50 years, was Caddock's friend and knew him well.

"He was a champion, not only in wrestling but in every other way," wrote Taylor at the time of Earl's death. "Modest, reliable, loyal, a Bible student and religious; square jawed, handsome and with a vibrating, contagious personality; home loving and at heart a small-town farm boy."

Earl Caddock was a Christian, patriot, family man, war hero, businessman and wrestler of extraordinary accomplishments, a legend for the ages.

Highlights – Earl Caddock won the AAU national title at 175 pounds in both 1914 and 1915, and was AAU national champion at heavyweight in 1915. He won the heavyweight title at the San Francisco Exposition, in 1915 and also the Allied Expeditionary Games, at the end of World War I. His estimated number of amateur bouts is 50, with no losses. He won his first 43 professional matches in a row before going off to fight in World War I and suffering lung damage due to mustard gas attacks. He was world heavyweight professional champion from April 9, 1917, until January 20, 1920. He recorded an overall record of 73-4 as a professional, retiring in 1921.

Robin Reed
He Liked It Rough

Robin Reed never lost as an amateur, and had a long and distinguished professional career. He is shown here in the 1930s with his world welterweight professional championship belt.

As an amateur wrestler, the record book is very clear when it comes to Robin Reed: He never lost a match at any time, at any place, to anybody. Period.

"There are lots of legends and stories about Reed, and I would guess most of them are true," said Dale Thomas, longtime coach at Oregon State University, when discussing Reed in the 1990s. "He was a strange man, really a different breed. But one thing is certain: he was a tremendous competitor, and a ruthless wrestler. Maybe the meanest guy to ever step on a mat."

Reed grew up in Portland, Oregon, and was on his own at an early age. He also roamed the streets and learned how to defend himself. Small and rangy, he had lightning reflexes and a strength that belied his skinny frame. He also harbored a fierce pride, and a burning rage inside him, a rage that made him dangerous on and off the mat.

Professional wrestling was popular in the Pacific Northwest area when Reed was growing up, and he most certainly heard of the exploits of the top pros of the era. This style of professional wrestling was a far cry from the theatrical world of today; many of the men Reed would have read about, and heard stories of, were tried and true warriors who were experts in a style of wrestling known as catch-as-catch-can – men like Frank Gotch, Earl Caddock and Joe Stecher. They were not interested in scoring points, they were interested in pinning their foe flat, or in making him surrender by the application of dangerous joint locks and choke holds. Ad Santel, one of the wrestlers who worked the area during the late teens and early 1920s, was feared far and wide for his submission moves. It was a style of wrestling that fascinated Reed all of his youth and into his early adult years.

By the time he reached Franklin High School in Portland, Reed was dabbling in wrestling at the local YMCA, and in gym classes. He was also on his own, separated from his family, and struggling to earn a living as a day laborer.

Robin Reed (left) squares off against Russell Vis after both men won gold medals in the 1924 Olympics. Reed won his title at 134 pounds while Vis won at 145 pounds.

"I needed gymnasium credits to graduate from high school, but I didn't want any gym because I was already getting all the exercise I needed operating an air hammer in the shipyards," Reed once said. "I was only 125 pounds and could barely hold onto that air hammer."

Reed took to wrestling very quickly, and won the Oregon state high school championship at 121 pounds. He also learned how to make an opponent go straight to his back. The hold he favored was a double wristlock, a very painful joint-lock made popular by the top professional wrestlers, and that was still legal in amateur circles. The move put tremendous pressure on the opponent's elbow, and forced him to make a quick choice between having his elbow dislocated or turning his back to the mat. According to those who knew him, Reed thoroughly enjoyed using the move and causing excruciating pain to his foes.

Some time in the 1920s, Reed traveled to Ames, Iowa, to seek a spot on the Iowa State College squad, which was coached by Hugo Otopalik. Reed was impressed by the quality of wrestlers, both amateur and professional, that were being produced in the Midwest and wanted to test the waters for himself. He hitchhiked all the way to Ames to face the fine college men of Iowa.

According to sources, Reed showed up at the Iowa State practice room unannounced, and in scraggly attire. He sought out the coach and asked if he could try out for the team. Otopalik sized him up and expressed doubt that he could make the squad.

Angered by the coach's statement, Reed said he would like to wrestle the members of the team when they arrived for practice. Otopalik agreed – and Reed reportedly defeated every member of the varsity squad, and all by pin! When the stunned coach saw what Reed was capable of, he tried to make amends and offer him a spot on the team. But Reed was no longer interested, and stalked out of the room.

Returning to the West Coast, Reed went on a tear. There was no official organized college national tournament at the time, but while attending Oregon Agricultural College (now known as Oregon State University), he was undefeated in all sorts of local and national competition. He won

Robin Reed

national AAU freestyle titles in 1921, 1922 and 1924. Entering the Pacific Northwest Olympic trials in 1924, he ripped through the field, winning championships in four different weight classes – 135, 147, 160 and 174 pounds!

He made the U.S. Olympic team, in the 134-pound class with no difficulty. On the long ocean voyage en route to the Olympic Games in Paris, he worked out with every member of the United States team, except Russell Vis, the 145-pounder. Vis was also a fierce competitor with a long string of victories and titles, and the two mat warriors avoided each other, for whatever reason. But Reed punished the other members of the team with his feared wristlock maneuver. It is accepted as a matter of fact that he could pin both the 191-pounder and the heavyweight, and yet both of those men won gold medals in Paris!

Underlying the Reed ability was an attitude that made him feared far and wide by wrestlers anywhere near his own size. Earl Conrad was a world lightweight champion in the Reed era, somewhat smaller than Reed but very feisty and competitive. He worked out with Reed on numerous occasions.

"Robin Reed had a real mean streak. There was never any doubt that he would just as soon break your elbow as put you on your back," said Conrad in 1990. "He was really something, just a fierce, fierce wrestler who enjoyed beating up and pinning his foes."

The Olympic Games of 1924 were not near as large and multi-national as they were to later become, and Reed had little trouble winning the gold medal. He pinned all four of his foes, including his teammate, Chester Newton, in the finals. In fact, Newton was not only a fellow American, but he was also a teammate of Reed's at the Multnomah Athletic Club.

After the Paris Olympics, Reed returned to Oregon to coach, both in the high school ranks and at Oregon Agricultural College. According to the Oregon State University wrestling press guide, he compiled a 7-0 dual meet record in his two seasons as coach, going 4-0 in 1925 and 3-0 in 1926. His teams won the Pacific Coast conference title both years, and he also coached his team to the national AAU freestyle title in 1926.

Eager to apply his knowledge of submission-style wrestling, Reed turned to professional wrestling and stayed with it for nearly a decade. As a welterweight, he was a top attraction wherever he appeared, and was American champion for a period. The real pros harbored a very healthy respect for him due to his great amateur background, while the showmen were quick to realize they were not in the same class with Reed, and tried to stay on his friendly side.

"I never met him, but I heard about him for years, back in the days when I was just starting out," said legendary world heavyweight professional champion Lou Thesz, who wrestled in over 6,000 matches. "Reed had a reputation as a wrestler who could really hurt a foe, or cripple an opponent, if he wanted to."

Always interested in learning all he could about submission holds, Reed sought out two of the top professionals of his era, Farmer Burns and John Pesek. Burns was the sport's most respected trainer, having developed both Frank Gotch and Earl Caddock, and even helped train world heavyweight boxing champion James Jeffries. Pesek, on the other hand, was the most feared submission wrestler of the 1930s, an expert in joint locks and choke holds.

Journeying to Nebraska to meet Burns and Pesek, Reed discovered a whole new and very painful style of wrestling. According to professional historians, Pesek, who outweighed Reed by at least thirty pounds, administered a sound beating to his Oregon visitor. Both Pesek and Burns took a liking to Reed and showed him many secrets of the trade.

Many years later, in an interview with wrestling historian Don Sayenga, Reed expressed his profound respect for his two mentors: "My greatest discussions were with John Pesek and Farmer Burns. Ah! Those were the masters," he gushed.

Mary Lee Pesek, the daughter of John, recalled seeing Reed at the family home when she was growing up.

"Robin visited our farm quite a bit and dad

Legends of the Mat – 16

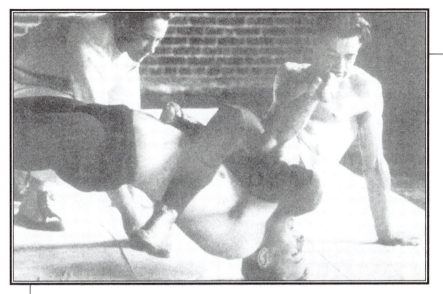

In this amazing photo from the 1920s, Robin Reed (top) executes a short arm scissors hold on a training partner.
(Photo courtesy of Oregon State University)

really enjoyed spending time with him," said Mary Lee. "Dad liked and respected Robin Reed and taught him a lot of tricks."

When Reed left professional wrestling, he turned to real estate, where he met with great success. He and his wife, Vivian, built a beautiful home on a cliff overlooking the Pacific Ocean. They had no children. He stayed busy with real estate and hunting, and remained a mythical figure in the wrestling pantheon for decades.

"When I first took over as head coach at Oregon State, I wanted to meet him," confided Dale Thomas. "I called his house many times, but he wouldn't return my calls. Finally, his wife set up a meeting between us at his home. After I got there, he kept me waiting for three hours in the living room, before finally showing up. When he walked into the room, he looked at me hard, and said, 'Well, what do you want?'

"I said I just wanted to meet him, because he was such a legend. We had a nice talk then, but he didn't open up too much. He was a very private person."

Thomas coached at Oregon State for 34 years (from 1957-1990) and saw his teams win or tie for the conference championships 22 times. With a record of 616 wins, 168 losses and 13 ties, he holds the NCAA record for the most victories ever by a wrestling coach. As a wrestler, he won six AAU national titles and was one of the most respected wrestlers of his era. Yet, he regarded Reed with a sense of awe. So did most others who came in contact with him.

"He was a real legendary figure, that's for sure," said John Dustin, an All-American wrestler at Oregon State in the 1950s, who later was a top official at the national AAU headquarters. "Dale put Robin in a position to talk to the coaches and tried to honor him, to let the coaches and wrestlers know that this was a great man.

"I enjoyed meeting him. He was fascinating to listen to, with all of his stories of wrestling in the 1920s and '30s."

"I had the privilege of meeting Robin around 1980, shortly before he died," wrote Wayne Baughman, a man who won 16 national titles and coached several world and Olympic teams. "He was still very tough and ornery."

No one knows how many amateur matches Reed participated in, but it was probably in the neighborhood of 120. What is certain is that he never lost an amateur match, ever. He was a student of the sport, at all levels.

Reed passed away on December 20, 1978, at the age of 79. He left a large estate, and a reputation as being one of the greatest and most feared wrestlers who ever lived, a true legend for the ages.

Highlights – Robin Reed won AAU national titles in 1921, 1922, 1924, the last two at 135 pounds. He also won titles at four weight classes in the Northwest Regional Olympic trials of 1924, and won the Olympic gold medal in 1924, at 134 pounds. His number of amateur bouts is unknown, but is estimated at 120, without a single loss. Reed also wrestled as a professional for nearly a decade, holding the American welterweight championship for some time.

Jack VanBebber
Three-Time NCAA Champion to Olympic Hero

Jack VanBebber has the honor of being the first three-time NCAA champion to win an Olympic gold medal in wrestling.

From the first day he became acquainted with wrestling, Jack VanBebber was on a mission. He loved the sport at the very outset and dreamed of becoming a state champion in his hometown of Perry, Oklahoma. But the odds were stacked against him. Being born into a large, poor family meant he would have to work his way through his high school years, and through college. And he was a sickly youth, who seemed too often get in the way of serious injury.

When he was just six years old, he fell off the back of a wagon being driven by his dad and a huge, metal-rimmed wheel ran over his chest. His breastbone was pushed against his spinal cord and there was great concern that his heart and lungs had been severely damaged. It was feared that he might be crippled for life.

The young boy fought back, and overcame the physical setback. Though he was still often ill, he began to dream of being a great athlete. One day, he and a larger boy got into a fight, and the coach made them put on boxing gloves to settle the matter. The larger boy knocked Jack out, and he was humiliated. He began to find solace in his own private retreat, an isolated spot called Black Bear Creek, where he fashioned dreams of a bright future.

"I would think about my physical fitness and how wonderful it would be if someday I was able to defend myself like the coach said, and perhaps one day even be one of the school's athletes," he confessed in his autobiography, *A Distant Flame*. "The picture in my mind was always that of a wrestler." *(2)*

His wrestling goals crystallized in ninth grade when he was given a writing assignment by an English teacher. Not knowing what to write about, he at last settled on the Olympic Games. He began to research the Olympics, and became fascinated by the subject. He read about Milo of Crotona, the mighty wrestler who won six Olympic championships in ancient Greece. He also read about the exploits of the great Jim Thorpe, like Jack a native of Oklahoma. Thorpe was not only an All-American football player in college, but he won gold medals in both the decathlon and the pentathlon in the 1912 Olympics in Stockholm, and won acclaim as the

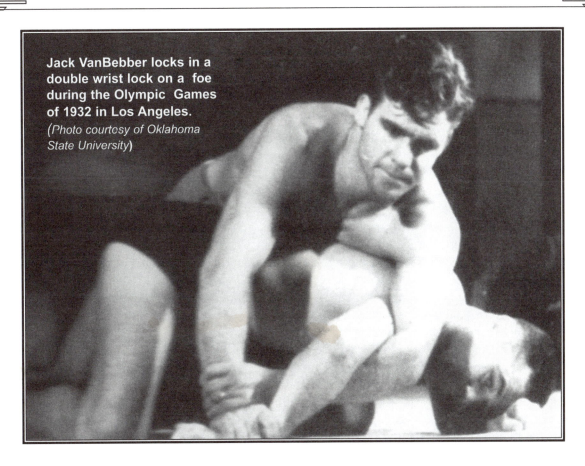

Jack VanBebber locks in a double wrist lock on a foe during the Olympic Games of 1932 in Los Angeles.
(Photo courtesy of Oklahoma State University)

greatest athlete in the world.

Jack's goals began to grow from just being a member of the Perry High School team to actually becoming an Olympic champion. The vision became "a distant flame" for Jack VanBebber.

But there was an even greater problem than just his ill health for Jack to overcome. He was one of seven children on the poor farm, and his labor was required at home. He worked long hard hours on the farm, sandwiched around his school time, but through persistence talked his parents into letting him try out for the wrestling team.

The young VanBebber seemed ideally suited for the sport of wrestling, both physically and emotionally. He had a long, lean build with sinewy muscles, and he was an extremely hard worker. He ran up and down the country road leading to his farm, day and night, in bad weather and good. He figured out early that to reach his goals he would need to outwork boys with greater natural abilities, and he was not hesitant to put that belief into action.

Making the high school team, he won all his dual meets his last two years and won two high school state championships. He was also voted Perry High School's most outstanding athlete as a senior, an honor that shook him to his core and cemented his determination to keep wrestling in college.

Entering Oklahoma A&M in the fall of 1927, Jack VanBebber was about to embark upon one of the finest amateur athletic careers of the first half century. But there was a ton of work ahead of him before he could claim his spot in wrestling history. With no scholarships available from colleges in those days, athletes had to either have enough money from home or plan on working their way through. Jack was in the latter category.

As soon as he arrived for classes on the campus in Stillwater, he began looking for jobs. He

Legends of the Mat – 19

Jack VanBebber

landed one job as a janitor in a college dorm for thirteen dollars a month, and then took another at nighttime in a diner called Lynn's Beanery, where he worked for his meals.

As if that wasn't enough, he found a third job delivering milk for a dairy. His work ethic is what would make the difference.

"My day began at 3:45 in the morning when I left for the dairy barn," he said. "That milk delivering turned out to be challenging work. Some mornings I felt like I couldn't lift another bottle, but on those mornings the coming freshman wrestling tryouts and the district Olympic tryouts popped into my mind. I wasn't just there delivering milk, but grappling to win." (3)

After delivering the milk, he ran to classes, then to the diner for a quick bite to eat, then back to class, and an hour of wrestling practice. He'd study for a few hours in the evening before going to the diner to wash dishes and clean tables, closing out a long and tough day. It was a routine he stuck to through four years of college. He even worked for a funeral home for a while, and actually went out late one night to pick up a body from an auto accident.

But his determination saw him through. He won NCAA championships at 155 pounds in 1929, and at 165 pounds in both 1930 and 1931. The national tournament his senior year was held at Brown University in Providence, Rhode Island, and he pinned both his semifinal and finals foes. When it was over, he decided to give himself a rare treat and call his mother back in Perry to tell her the news. Incredibly, it was the first long-distance phone call he made during his entire four-year college career!

But he had learned to get by on next to nothing while going to college. That meant watching every penny. Phone calls were a real luxury, and so was an automobile.

"There was a story Jack used to like to tell," said Dan Hodge, who followed VanBebber out of Perry to make wrestling history himself some twenty-five years later. "One Friday after practice at A&M, he told a teammate he was going home to Perry (about twenty miles from Stillwater) for the weekend. The friend asked if he could come along.

"Jack said, 'Sure, glad to have you. Meet me outside the gym.' When the other fellow showed up, looking forward to a weekend in Perry, he asked Jack where his car was. Jack said, 'Heck, I don't have a car. I just run home.'

"Well, the other fellow made it about halfway to Perry, then hitched a ride back to Stillwater," said Dan, chuckling. "Jack said the other fellow never asked to go home with him again."

VanBebber ended his college career without a single loss, winning 47 consecutive matches. He also captured three AAU national titles during his college years. He won his third AAU title in 1932 in New York City with eight consecutive pins. Those wins sent him to the final Olympic trials in Columbus, Ohio, in the 158.5-pound division. He won his first four matches there by pin, but then lost a decision to George Manoli of the Boston YMCA, his first loss in over four years. But Manoli was pinned in the next round by Carl Dougovito, and VanBebber decisioned Dougovito to make the team.

Being on the U.S. squad for the 1932 Los Angeles Games was a huge thrill for the young wrestler from Oklahoma. He got to briefly meet Jim Thorpe, one of his childhood idols, and Mildred "Babe" Didrickson, perhaps the greatest female athlete of all time. At the Olympic Village for the American team, "Babe" even challenged him to an impromptu wrestling match (he pinned her in mere seconds), then she went out and won two gold medals and a silver medal in the Games.

On the Olympic mat, Jack pinned his foe from Mexico, and scored decisions over wrestlers from Denmark and Canada. The Canadian wrestler, Daniel McDonald, actually punched VanBebber in the face during their match in an effort to break his focus; Jack responded with a jab, knocking the Canadian to his knees. The close, hard-fought victory over McDonald put Jack in the finals against Eino Leino of Finland, who was a three-time Olympian, winning a gold medal in

Legends of the Mat - 20

— Jack VanBebber —

1920, a silver in 1924 and a bronze in 1928.

A tremendous mix-up on the day of the final Olympic match almost ruined VanBebber's dream forever. Told his finals match was at 6 p.m., he returned to the Olympic Village for a nap, to try and settle his nerves. Shortly after falling asleep, he was awakened by a pounding on his door. Opening it, he was told he had to wrestle at 3 p.m. He had just one hour to travel the six miles to the arena.

Jack began to panic. He pulled on his Olympic uniform and ran out into the Olympic Village, looking for a ride. But the place was deserted. There was no bus available, or even a taxi. And so he took off running, out onto the main highway leading to the Olympic Auditorium.

"A fist-like knot gripped my arms and legs," he wrote years later. "I slowed to a fast walk. On other days, the stretch to the auditorium would've been a pleasurable training stint. Today it tortured my body throughout. I felt deserted by the rest of the world." (4)

Miraculously, a car finally stopped, with the driver on his way to the wrestling arena. He drove Jack right to the door, and he ran into the arena just in time to hear his name being called for the match. VanBebber outscored Leino 2-0 during the twelve-minute match and won a referee's decision. He was now an Olympic champion, fulfilling a dream that had been born on a small farm in Oklahoma by a near-crippled boy ten years earlier.

He coached for a brief spell at Texas Tech University and even wrestled professionally for a while. But the pro game was not to his liking, and he soon embarked upon a long and successful career as an executive with the Phillips Petroleum Company. He saw combat duty with the 136th Infantry during World War II in the Philippines. He and his wife, Julia, returned in their retirement years to live in Perry. They had no children.

In 1950 a large collection of sports writers and coaches selected the top ten amateur athletes of the first half-century for the Helms Foundation. Of course, Jim Thorpe made the list… and so did Jack VanBebber! It was truly an outstanding climax to an incredible athletic career.

Murl Thrush, who coached at the New York Athletic Club and elsewhere for a total of forty-two years, once wrote that he had known hundreds of top American wrestlers through the years. He rated VanBebber the best he ever saw.

"His style was so unorthodox that there's never been anybody that would come close to executing certain moves the way Jack did. I think that he is the best 160-pound wrestler that ever lived," said Thrush. (5)

Jack VanBebber was inducted into three major halls of fame during his lifetime. He died on April 13, 1986, and is remembered today as one of the greatest amateur wrestlers in American history.

Highlights – Jack VanBebber was an undefeated, three-time NCAA champion for Oklahoma A&M, winning titles in 1929, 1930 and 1931. He also won three straight AAU national titles. He pinned 13 consecutive foes during the Olympic trials of 1932 and lost just one match during his final four-plus years of wrestling. He won the gold medal at 158.5 pounds in the 1932 Olympic Games, and in 1950 was voted by the Associated Press as one of the top ten amateur athletes in American history of the first 50 years. His estimated overall record was 60-1.

Stanley and Josiah Henson
A Great Brother Act From Oklahoma

The discussion about who is the greatest college wrestler in American history has been held thousands of times, at various wrestling events and in out-of-the-way spots as fans gather to talk about their favorite sport. The same dozen or so names crop up, over and over. And among the older group of fans, the name of Stanley Henson is always high on the list, often in the top spot.

Stanley Henson was a three-time NCAA champion for Oklahoma A&M, winning titles in the years 1937, 1938 and 1939. He was voted the outstanding wrestler at the NCAA tournament as a sophomore, and might have won it a couple of more times, but the award was a new one (having been initiated in 1932) and the coaches were hesitant to give it to the same man more than once.

Henson brought tremendous natural attributes to the sport, and had a solid education to fortify his God-given abilities. He was a two-time state champion at Tulsa Central High School, under the direction of Art Griffith, one of the sport's finest coaches. Henson was also voted the outstanding wrestler at the Oklahoma high school state meet his senior season.

Moving on to Oklahoma A&M in Stillwater in the fall of 1936, Henson was immediately subjected to the coaching genius of Ed Gallagher, the man responsible for building the foundation of the tremendous Aggies/Cowboys wrestling empire. Gallagher was a keen student of the sport who had even traveled to Vermont at the start of his career to consult with legendary collar-and-elbow experts there. They were a breed of professional wrestlers who understood the dynamics of applied leverage and position, and their knowledge of wrestling techniques was second to none.

An extremely intelligent person, Henson was the perfect student for coaches like Griffith and Gallagher. He studied wrestling in the same fashion they taught it. Henson then applied what he learned with precision.

But he had more than just an intelligent

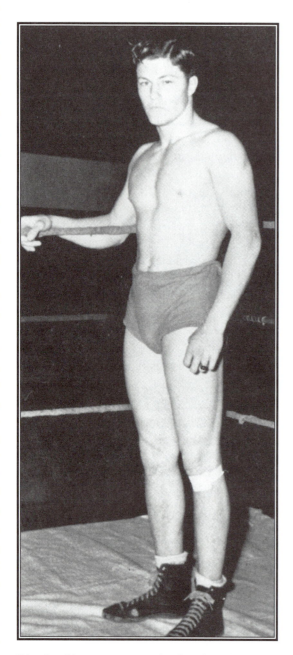

Stanley Henson poses in the ring during his senior year at Oklahoma A&M. Henson was a three-time NCAA champion for the Aggies. *(Photo courtesy of Oklahoma State University)*

Joe Henson was undefeated during his collegiate career at the Naval Academy and won a bronze medal in the 1952 Olympics. He later became one of the most influential Americans in amateur wrestling history.

approach to the sport. He was also a hard worker and deceptively strong on the mats. In the hot, dog days of summer, he had forged lean, strong muscles by toiling on the oil rigs high above the Oklahoma plains. It was very demanding physical work, and the wrestlers who worked the oil fields found that the experience served them well in the long wrestling seasons.

"We did rig building, on a 136-foot derrick, working summers and vacations," he said decades later. "It was very difficult work, back in the Depression, working from sunup to sundown. Putting this steel together, up high, walking on scaffolds, with all the steel you could possibly carry.

"This, I think, is what gave me the strength, which was much more than people thought I had. Mr. Gallagher once said, pound for pound, I was the strongest man he had ever seen and yet I didn't look like I had much muscle, like some of the other fellows.

"Joe McDaniel (also a three-time NCAA champion for the Aggies) and I both worked for my dad in the oil fields and both of us attributed that to the endurance and strength that we had.

"One year, 1938, Joe and I and Karl Kitt (All-American from Weatherford State Teachers College who coached for many years at the Air Force Academy) were using a 16-pound sledge all day, seven days a week. We didn't lift weights in those days, but we worked very hard at what we did."

Henson's favorite takedowns were a whip-over maneuver, a technique that took the foe straight to his back, and a heel pick that was virtually unstoppable. He wrestled at 155 pounds much of his sophomore season, and lost an overtime decision to a powerful wrestler from arch-rival Oklahoma named Bill Keas. It would turn out to be his only loss in six years. Because he was only weighing 145 pounds, Gallagher wanted Henson to wrestle at that weight for the rest of the season, but Stanley wanted the rematch with Keas and told Gallagher he would agree to wrestle at 145 only after taking on Keas again.

During the second match, Henson suffered a shoulder separation when he tossed Keas to his back. Action was halted while the team doctor pushed Henson's shoulder back in and the match went into overtime. Henson won the match by riding Keas for three minutes and escaping in just two seconds of his "down" period.

However, the injury would bother Stanley off and on the rest of his mat career.

At the end of the year, Henson won his first NCAA title, breezing to the 145-pound championship. He was slick, deceptively powerful and indefatigable. He was so impressive that he was voted the Outstanding Wrestler Award, as a sophomore! The Aggies won the team title by a 31-13 margin over runnerup Oklahoma. Keas captured the 155-pound title for the Sooners, but the Aggies had three other champs besides Henson.

In 1938, Henson repeated as NCAA champion, and again helped the Aggies win the team title,

Legends of the Mat – 23

Stanley and Josiah Henson

but by a much slimmer margin, 19 to 15 over second place Illinois of the Big Ten. He moved up to 155 pounds as a senior, not cutting a pound along the way. But the shoulder dislocation continued to plague him during his final season.

Improvising, he devised a shoulder strap that held his injured left shoulder in place. While the strap offered protection, it also severely hampered his range of motion.

"I could no longer use the head-and-heel pickup that that I had developed in high school but I could use the double-leg takedown with a half nelson and crotch, and I could use the whipover to good advantage," he said.

Despite the handicap, he had little trouble winning his third individual NCAA championship and his Aggies also copped the team title. A&M scored 33 points to 12 for Lehigh, far behind in second place.

Harold Nichols, who would go on to one of the finest coaching careers in history, won the title at 145 pounds, the spot Henson had vacated. After leading Iowa State University to six NCAA team titles, Nichols told a reporter that he would not have been an NCAA champion if Henson hadn't moved up a weight.

"Stanley Henson was the best wrestler I had seen up to that point," said Nichols. "He was head and shoulders above the rest of us."

During his three years of college wrestling, Henson was so dominant that he never surrendered a single offensive point. The only way an opponent could score was if he let them escape, with the intent of taking them down again into a pinning position.

A top student in pre-medicine, he placed an extremely high priority on his studies but still found time to wrestle a little outside of college. He won the prestigious Pan-American Exposition Games in 1937 and the national AAU freestyle title in 1938.

In 1936, as a freshman, Henson had entered the Olympic trials held at Lehigh University and made it to the final round-robin. His only loss came on a referee's decision to Frances Millard, the eventual Olympic team member at 134 pounds. Millard wound up with the silver medal in Berlin.

In 1940, Henson was considered the clear choice to make the United States Olympic team at 145 pounds, and probably would have been the nation's top candidate for a gold medal. But the Games, scheduled for Tokyo, were cancelled when World War II erupted in Europe. Like hundreds of thousands of young Americans, Henson was forced to forget about athletic pursuits while the Allies fought against the tyranny of Nazi Germany and the Axis powers of evil.

Henson spent five years in the United States Navy, first at the Naval Academy in Annapolis, Maryland, as assistant wrestling coach and physical education instructor, then on board ship as a commissioned officer. When the war ended, he entered medical school at the University of Maryland, graduating in 1950.

He then spent four years at the famed Mayo Clinic on a fellowship in surgery and obtained a masters degree in surgery from the University of Minnesota in 1956. He began his practice in Fort Collins, Colorado, and became one of the most respected surgeons in his field. He also took an active interest in sports medicine, and was in demand as a lecturer all across the nation.

For many years, he would come into the wrestling room at Colorado State University when Jim Kinyon, a fellow Oklahoma A&M graduate, was head coach, and work with the team.

"It was a real honor to have Stan Henson in our room, the guys really looked up to him," said Kinyon. "He had a tremendous dignity about him, but when it came time to wrestle you could see that he was something special. He could still work that heel pick on guys less than half his age."

Because his wrestling career was relatively short, and because World War II denied him an opportunity to wrestle for Olympic glory, it's hard to evaluate Stanley Henson as a wrestler except for the opinion of the other wrestlers and coaches who saw him compete. Many of the best wrestlers of his era regarded him with a respect that borders on awe.

LEFT: Joe Henson works over a foe from North Carolina during Henson's college days at the Naval Academy.

RIGHT: Stanley Henson demonstrates a hold with a teammate during his senior year at Oklahoma A&M.

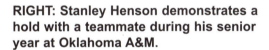

"I had never seen wrestling like that," recalled Olympic champion Henry Wittenberg, of watching Henson in the 1939 NCAAs. "He was just so good and so slick. He was definitely one of the greatest technique wrestlers of all time, maybe the best."

Port Robertson, the legendary coach at the University of Oklahoma, a bitter rival of Oklahoma A&M, once said he felt Stan Henson was the best collegiate wrestler he had ever seen. Certainly, few wrestlers could control a match the way Henson could. In five national tournaments – three NCAA and two AAU – he never let a man go behind him.

"Stanley was a great wrestler, and a very slick wrestler," said Paul Scott in 2002. Scott had a keen perspective as he attended nearly fifty NCAA tournaments and led Cornell College to the team title in 1947. "Many old-timers think he was the best ever."

His younger brother, Josiah, also was a superb wrestler. Five and half years younger than Stanley, he struggled valiantly to live up to the high standards that Stanley had set. He also wrestled for Coach Griffith in Tulsa but was a late bloomer and never made it to the state tournament. He surprised everyone in the spring of 1940, after his senior year in high school, by placing second in the AAU senior national freestyle meet at 112 pounds. He selected the Naval Academy to continue his education, where his brother was serving as assistant coach.

Joe went through his three years unbeaten (he graduated early to serve in World War II). He was captain of the undefeated 1944 team that was ranked No. 1 in the nation, but he and the team

Legends of the Mat – 25

Stanley and Josiah Henson

never had the opportunity to defend that position in an official NCAA championship as the tournament was cancelled from 1943 through 1945 due to the global conflict.

While training at the Baltimore YMCA, Joe developed a lightning quick move on his feet that seemed virtually unstoppable. Billy Martin, Sr., the legendary coach at Granby (Virginia) High School, asked Joe to show it to him and dubbed it "the Henson Takedown." Later, it became known as the shrug.

In 1952, Josiah entered the AAU national championships and was voted the outstanding wrestler of the freestyle event. He didn't give up a single point during the entire tournament. Shortly after, Joe made the 1952 Olympic team without a close match in the trials and was on his way to Helsinki, Finland. Despite suffering a broken nose and concussion in the early rounds, he earned the bronze medal at 136.5 pounds. He also earned the distinction of becoming the first American to defeat a Soviet wrestler in top-level competition.

Two of his teammates, Bill Smith (who won the gold medal at 160.5 pounds) and Dan Hodge (at 174 pounds), consider him one of the finest wrestlers they have ever seen.

"He was terrific, one of the best technicians of his era," said Smith. "He was an instinctive wrestler and had a great feel for where he was on the mat, all the time."

"He was a wonderful wrestler, just a pleasure to watch wrestle," said Hodge. "When we were on the 1952 Olympic team together, I was just a wet-behind-the-ears kid of nineteen. Joe was about the best I had ever seen at that time, way ahead of everyone else. He impressed me as a wrestler and because he was a naval officer."

Wittenberg, who won a gold medal at 191.5 pounds in the 1948 Olympics, also was on the 1952 team and earned a silver medal. He had high words of praise for his Oklahoma teammate.

"Joe was the most courageous wrestler I knew," said Wittenberg. "He actually broke his nose but continued in the Games despite medical recommendations to withdraw. We did not have all the gadgets in those days and he fought along with just some tape on his nose."

Henson retired from active competition after Helsinki's Olympics to concentrate on his career as an officer in the United States Navy. After a four-year layoff, he came back to try and make the 1956 Olympic team and fought his way to the final round-robin before losing a close decision. But he still played a role in the success of the American team. Remembering the problems that the U.S. team had faced in 1952 because they were so unfamiliar with the rules, he became involved with officiating and produced the first written international rules to ever appear in English.

Joe Henson has a long string of accomplishments both on and off the mat, and has been a leader on the American and world wrestling scene on a number of levels. He helped impact international rules and was largely responsible for FILA abandoning the rolling or touch fall and adopting the control fall. He is the first American referee to earn an international ranking from FILA, the sport's international governing body.

He worked as a referee, judge and mat chairman at four Olympic Games and was awarded a FILA gold star for outstanding contributions to international wrestling. Long-time FILA President Milan Ercegan once called Henson "the most influential American wrestler in international sports," an incredible compliment to his decades of service to the sport he loves.

Like his brother Stanley, Josiah was extremely successful away from the mat. He attained the rank of captain in the United States Navy and took part in the largest sea battle in history, at Surigao Strait, during World War II. A decorated war veteran, he also commanded air anti-submarine squadron 31 during the Cuban Missile Crisis. Henson served as assistant Chief of Naval Personnel in Washington, D.C., helping to supervise over 500 civilian and military personnel of the government agency that oversees the entire U.S. Navy.

He was executive director of the "People to People Sports Committee," founded by President

— Stanley and Josiah Henson —

Dwight Eisenhower to coordinate international sports exchanges, and was invited to serve on boards of a wide variety of other high-level associations. For two decades, he was senior vice president of the World Taekwondo Federation. He was on the board for the U.S. Modern Pentathlon and received a special commendation from President Ronald Reagan for his contributions to American sport.

Joe was a member of the U.S. Olympic Wrestling Committee for 16 years and was elected chairman for the period 1965-1968. He served as president of the Amateur Athletic Union for four years, as well. He founded The Henson Company, a manufacturer of sports goods under the BRUTE wrestling label and LIGA football/soccer label. Under his leadership and that of John Purnell, his former partner and now owner, the company has made many donations of time and equipment to sports programs all around the world.

His sons, Jeff and Josh, were successful wrestlers who later served as French translators and interpreters at international meetings of the highest level.

In reflecting back upon his career in 2004, Joe gave considerable credit for his successes to his parents and to the impact of his older brother, Stanley.

"My parents taught us the value of hard work," he said. "That was always stressed in our home, as well as being the best you can be. And of course Stanley had a big influence on me. He was such a tremendous wrestler and student, and I was proud to be his brother. I wanted to try and follow in his footsteps as best I could."

Stanley Henson was voted into the National Wrestling Hall of Fame in the third class, back in 1978. In the summer of 2006, Joe joined his brother as a distinguished member of the hall.

On and off the mat, the brothers Henson were extremely successful and have brought considerable honor to the sport through their character and their careers.

Stanley's Highlights – Stanley Henson was a three-time NCAA champion, posting a 36-1 record in college. He was also AAU national champion in 1937, and Pan-American Exposition champion in 1938. He defeated three of Europe's best wrestlers on an overseas trip in 1939. His overall record is hard to determine but is probably close to 70-1.

Joe's Highlights – Joe Henson was undefeated during his collegiate career at the Naval Academy, and won the national AAU title in 1952 without surrendering a single point. He won the bronze medal at the 1952 Olympics at 136.5 pounds and later became one of the most influential Americans ever in the circles of international wrestling. His total record is unknown.

Henry Wittenberg
The Longest Winning Streak

Henry Wittenberg offered a formidable sight to foes of the 1940s. He won eight national titles and an estimated 400-plus straight matches during his sensational career.

Long streaks are one of the cornerstones of athletic legend. Few examples of excellence in performance are as revered by the nation's sporting public. For instance:
- The University of Oklahoma football team's 47-game winning streak;
- Joe DiMaggio's 56-game hitting streak in major league baseball;
- Rocky Marciano's 49-0 record as heavyweight boxing champion;
- Cael Sanderson's 159 straight wins in college wrestling.

And then there is the amazing streak turned in by Henry Wittenberg, 1948 Olympic wrestling champion at 191.5 pounds. The streak is very long. In fact, it is so long that no one is certain what its true length really is. In his National Wrestling Hall of Fame biography, it is said Wittenberg "wrestled more than 300 matches without a loss." Actually, it was far more than that, according to the man who should know.

"Well, no one was keeping records back then, and neither was I," said Wittenberg in 1999, speaking from his home in Somers, New York. "All I know is I wrestled a lot of matches, and I didn't lose for many, many years. I would guess it was somewhere between 400 and 500 in a row."

That's an amazing record, under any circumstances. But when one realizes Wittenberg didn't even wrestle in high school, and only took up the sport as a sophomore in college, the record becomes astounding.

"I went to a high school in Jersey City (New Jersey) which didn't have wrestling, and I didn't participate in any sports," said Wittenberg. "I was kind of a book worm. And my parents were poor Jewish people who didn't know anything but hard work."

Henry's father wanted him to earn a college education, and told his son he would move the family to New York City if Henry wanted to attend the City College of New York. Henry said yes, and the family moved to New York. Shortly after, Henry discovered wrestling.

"There were a lot of basketball players at City College, and this wrestling coach named Joe Sapora," recalls

Henry Wittenberg crushes a foe during the 1948 Olympic Games in London. Wittenberg won the gold medal in the 191.5-pound class, and came out of retirement to win a silver medal in the 1952 Olympics.

Wittenberg. "He had been an NCAA champion at Illinois (115 pounds in both 1929 and 1930). He had a sign-up one day looking for wrestlers, and I decided to give it a try."

To say Wittenberg caught on fast is a vast understatement. In his second year, 1938, he placed third in the NCAA tournament at 165 pounds. His senior year, he finished second at 175 pounds. But the best was yet to come. Henry was just getting warmed up!

Shortly after graduation, he and five teammates from the New York West YMCA hopped in a car and drove all the way to Ames, Iowa, for the 1940 national AAU meet. Henry won the title at 191 pounds and two others placed high… and they drove back to New York City with the team trophy in the car.

"Lots of Iowans were there, and guys from Oklahoma," said Wittenberg. "It was a great experience for us. We were so happy we won."

World War II halted many young men from wrestling; Wittenberg joined the army and was made a hand-to-hand combat instructor. He was stationed in Norfolk, Virginia, and when the war was over he returned to New York City and joined the city's police force. There, he met Edith, a young policewoman who was also an expert fencer.

Within a very short time, they were married, and Henry was back in the wrestling room.

"There were at least 15 clubs in the city and we had dual meets on Friday nights, and tournaments on Saturday," said Henry, who combined police work with his love of wrestling for most of the next decade. "The YMCAs had teams, and there were just a lot of wrestling matches going on, all the time. It was a lot different back then."

The Wittenberg streak continued to climb. He won the AAU nationals eight times in all. And then one day he decided to go to the next level.

"I said to my wife, 'I think I'll try out for the Olympics.'"

Henry Wittenberg

He made the team, defeating a young University of Minnesota star, Verne Gagne, in a very close match in the finals. At the Games in London – resumed after World War II forced the cancellation of the 1940 and 1944 Olympics – Henry won six straight matches (three by fall) to earn the gold medal. Iowa State's Glen Brand also won a gold medal at 174 pounds, while Gerald Leeman earned a silver medal at 125 and Leland Merrill took a bronze at 160.5.

"He was my idol," said Brand in 2006. "He was the spokesman for our team and a real gentleman. He was someone that we all looked up to."

With a gold medal in his pocket, Wittenberg retired from wrestling, at least for a while. He enjoyed oil painting and chess, and even considered wrestling a sort of chess match with a physical twist to it.

But in 1951, he decided to make a comeback, and earned a spot on the 1952 Olympic freestyle team. In the trials, his long winning streak was halted when he lost a close decision to Dale Thomas. But in the final trials, he came back to make the freestyle team with two hard-fought wins over the powerful Thomas.

In Helsinki, Wittenberg won four of five Olympic matches and earned the silver medal. In the championship bout he lost a narrow decision to the eventual champion, Bert Palm of Sweden. "This match was so close that it could have gone to Henry, as well," said coach Ray Swartz in his official report.

At that point, he was only the second American to ever win two Olympic medals in wrestling (George Mehnert was the first, in 1904 and 1908).

"Henry is without doubt one of the greatest wrestlers of all time," said Bill Farrell, a long-time friend who coached the 1972 Olympic team to three gold medals. "He was tremendously strong and always in great shape. The Midwest fans didn't like him, because they saw him as a mean, arrogant Jewish boy who came and beat up on their guys. He was just so physical.

"He had a front headlock where he would pull the other guy down, then grab his ankle and take him to the mat. Once on a trip to Oklahoma, he was being booed by the fans just for being from the East. He snapped his foe down and grabbed his knee so hard he broke the guy's leg. That really set off the booing.

"I think he would have won a couple of more Olympics if it wasn't for World War II canceling the Olympics. He was at his best in the early and mid 1940s."

After the 1952 Olympics, Wittenberg continued to stay involved with the sport. He was one of the founding fathers of the Macibbiah Games, a contest for athletes of Jewish descent. Entering the wrestling competition, he captured gold medals in 1949 and 1953.

Wittenberg spent 13 years on the New York City police force, and then moved into the printing business for several years. But when his alma mater called and offered him the positions of professor of physical education and wrestling coach, he jumped at the chance to return to his roots. He coached the United States Greco-Roman team at the 1968 Olympics in Mexico City, and also informally coached his son, Mike, who just missed making an Olympic team.

But Henry's affection for international athletics was given a severe test in 1972. He was at the Olympics in Munich when 13 members of the Israeli team were massacred. He and Edith left Munich the next morning, stunned and dismayed.

"I knew every one of the Israeli athletes and coaches who were murdered," he said solemnly. "We were in a room right next to where it happened. I said to Edith, 'If this is what the Olympics have become, I'm just not interested anymore.'"

By 2002, Henry and Edith were long retired. They traveled extensively, and had seen many parts of the world. He doesn't dwell on his wrestling accomplishments unless some writer calls to ask him to do so.

"Wrestling was very important to me for a long time, but it's like a big circle, it's come and gone," he said in 2002. "It was great, but it's ended. It was like having two different lives – the

Henry Wittenberg

wrestling part and then the rest."

When asked to reflect back on his years in the sport, he attributed much of his fantastic success to his running routine and to his love of weight training.

"I was one of the first weightlifting wrestlers," he said, with a touch of pride in his voice. "I lifted because I felt strength gives wrestlers an edge. I had weights at home and lifted very seriously, several times a week."

Not everyone agreed with weight training back then, but Wittenberg wouldn't budge on his formula for success. He knew weights were very important.

"Art Griffith (the long-time coach at Oklahoma State University) was the coach of the 1948 Olympic team, and he told the team he didn't want any of us lifting weights because it would make us muscle bound," said Wittenberg. "I told him I was going to lift anyway, and he said, 'Okay, but don't let the other guys see you doing it.'"

Wittenberg also was a proponent of hard running. He liked to run the stairs in the football stadium back at City College of New York. It was revolutionary training back in the 1940s.

"Matches were 15 minutes long back then. I did a lot of stair climbing. I didn't just run the steps, I ran over the seats," he said. "That made me lift my legs higher and work harder."

"Henry Wittenberg is one of the finest wrestling minds and one of the greatest people I have ever had the privilege to know," wrote Wayne Baughman in his book, *On and Off The Mat*. "I believe he was far ahead of his time as far as wrestling is concerned in every respect: technique, training methods, strategy, diet and sports psychology. His accomplishments were amazing for any era, but to have done it in his era in the way he did it is truly phenomenal." *(6)*

As the years go by, memories of great accomplishments tend to fade. But the long winning streak of Henry – somewhere between 400 and 500 – should be remembered for as long as men and women wrestle. It is one of the finest accomplishments in all of sports history.

Highlights – Henry Wittenberg was an Olympic champion in 1948 and Olympic silver medallist in 1952. He placed second and third in the NCAA Championships and won eight national AAU freestyle championships. Though his records are not verifiable, it is estimated that he won around 400 consecutive matches in post-college competition. His overall record could be in the neighborhood of 450-5.

Bill Koll
Master of The Mental Game

Bill Koll was undefeated during his three-year varsity career at Iowa State Teachers College in the late 1940s. He won three NCAA titles and was twice voted the Outstanding Wrestler of the tournament.

World War II played a pivotal role in the lives of millions of men and women all around the world, changing forever the way they viewed society and the way they chose to live their lives. For Bill Koll, the war was a huge factor in his transformation from a good high school wrestler to one of the most intimidating and punishing wrestlers in collegiate history.

The stories of Bill Koll's accomplishments are endless, stretching from coast to coast. It seems that no one who ever saw him wrestle ever forgot him; his impact was felt for decades, particularly in the state of Iowa, where great wrestlers are looked upon with the same awe as a Babe Ruth or a Rocky Marciano.

Koll was a skinny, scrappy kid when he enrolled at Fort Dodge High School, a town of 20,000 in north central Iowa, a hotbed of wrestling. He made the team his junior year, and proceeded to lose every single dual meet he participated in. But he was making progress nonetheless. By the end of the season, he managed to place third in the Iowa State Tournament of 1940, at 125 pounds.

As a senior in 1941, Koll went undefeated and won the state title at 135 pounds. But the Depression had ravaged his family's finances, as well as much of the rest of the nation, and college didn't seem possible. Yet, he scraped up enough money to enroll at Iowa State Teachers College (ISTC) at Cedar Falls in the fall of 1941. Dave McCuskey was the head coach, and was early in a career that would stamp him as one of the finest wrestling mentors of all time.

But World War II intervened and

Known for his aggressive, non-stop style of wrestling, Bill Koll fashioned a reputation as one of the most feared wrestlers of all time. He was credited with being the reason the slam was outlawed in college wrestling. *(Photo courtesy of University of Northern Iowa)*

— *Bill Koll* —

grabbed most of the nation's able-bodied men. First, McCuskey left for the war, and then the wrestlers followed, including Koll, just as he was beginning to find the form that would make him a legend.

"I was inducted into the Army on February 9, 1943, and never saw a wrestling mat for 34 months," said Koll. "As a combat engineer, I spent 24 months in Europe where our amphibious engineers landed at Omaha Beach at 6:15 a.m. on June 6."

His unit also saw action at the Battle of the Bulge and was involved in the final drive across the Rhine, into the Rhur Valley. He was awarded the Bronze Star, and returned to the Iowa State Teachers College campus as a far more mature man, both physically and mentally.

Wrestling with an entirely different mental approach, forged in the difficult war years, Koll won the NCAA championship at 145 pounds in 1946. In the finals, against Edgar Welch of Oklahoma State, he gave up a takedown en route to a 7-2 win. It was the only takedown he ever gave up in his entire college career!

As a junior in 1947, Koll won the NCAA title again, without a close match all season. He defeated Roger Snook of Cornell College in the finals 7-2, and was also voted the Outstanding Wrestler (O.W.) of the tournament. He repeated again in 1948, in sensational fashion. Since 1948 was an Olympic year, the tournament was held under freestyle rules, and Koll was 7-0, with all pins! Navy's John Fletcher finished second, but was pinned by Koll in the fourth round in one minute and 42 seconds. Koll was voted the Outstanding Wrestler award again, the first wrestler to ever win the honor twice.

Throughout the years, stories about Koll and his workouts were favorite topics of conversation in the wrestling world. He could walk the length of the football field on his hands, and was often seen going up the steps of the football stadium on his hands. On occasion, he was spotted running to class backwards, or moving in a duck waddle between classes, his textbooks strapped to his back, exercising his legs.

After the 1948 college season, Koll sailed through the final Olympic trials, made the team at 145, and was voted the O.W. award. His physical, punishing style of wrestling was known far and wide, and he was the most feared wrestler of his generation. His swooping double-leg takedown was nearly impossible to stop, and he would elevate his foe and slam him hard to the mat, often dazing his opponent, and some times knocking him senseless.

"Bill's philosophy was simple," said Bill Nelson, also a three-time NCAA champion at ISTC and a 1948 Olympian. "If you were willing to go out on the mat with him then you were going to have to pay the price. He prepared himself better mentally than any wrestler. I don't think he was ever satisfied with himself unless he pinned his opponent." (7)

Bob Siddens is one of the most successful high school coaches of all time. He led West Waterloo High School to 11 state team titles, 88 straight dual meet victories, and coached such stars as Dan Gable and Dale Anderson in high school. He also roomed with Koll while in college.

"He had very powerful hips, and hip action is the key to the whole thing," said Siddens. "But he also had a fierce attitude. He could be nasty on the mat, though he was a really sweet guy off the mat. I can still remember he wore saddle shoes in those days, and I would actually see him skipping from class to class. Honestly!"

But Bill Koll transformed himself when it came time to wrestle.

"He was a gentleman off the mat, but it was a different story on the mat," said Siddens. "Slamming was allowed in his era,

Bill Koll

and they put a rule in that if your knee touched at the same time as your foe came down, you could slam. Well, I can remember clear as a bell this one time Bill slammed a foe to the mat so hard the fellow was nearly unconscious. Bill shook him when he was on top, so it looked like the guy was trying to escape, and the referee called a pin. The referee raised Bill's hand, but the poor guy just laid on the mat. They had to carry him off.

"They changed the slam rule after that; they changed it because of Bill Koll."

Koll also believed the rule was changed after officials saw him in action at the NCAA tournament that season.

"Keep in mind that slams were legal then," said Koll in an interview many years later. "I was blessed with some quickness and had some power in my hips. This enabled me to pop guys into the air and drive them into the mat before they could counter. I still believe that most guys are looking for a reason to lose. I tried to make it easy for them to find a reason.

"In the national tournament my senior year, I had a couple spectacular slams. Because they were in the national tournament, everybody saw them. The next year, slams were illegal."

Writing a chapter in 1981 for the book *From Gotch To Gable*, Koll confided that he had developed a mental outlook early in his college career, and it was an approach that he continually honed and perfected.

"....when I was working against outstanding talent in the practice room, I also realized that directing and controlling one's arousal to competition could be as important as learning skills. I discovered that if I would focus my anger towards some incident, object, event or person that my state of readiness and overall performance was increased. My strength, speed and ability to think were increased tremendously by just sitting apart from the action prior to the match and getting into a state of controlled anger. The key is that I was always in control of the arousal and never allowed it to control me." *(8)*

Few athletes in any sport have ever mastered the art of arousal as effectively as did Koll. Almost six decades later, Siddens still recalled some of the techniques that his roommate would use to prepare himself mentally for a match.

"If we were wrestling on a Friday or Saturday night, he would pull the shades down in the windows of our room, and sit in the dark for hours, getting mentally ready for the match that night," said Siddens. "He really would work at getting psyched up for the matches."

While winning three NCAA titles, Koll also captured three AAU national freestyle titles. He was the catalyst behind the great Iowa State Teachers College teams of the era, leading the Panthers to NCAA team finishes of second, second and fourth in his three seasons (1946, 1947 and 1948).

Despite his enormous talents and abilities, Koll had trouble adjusting to the much different international style of wrestling, and placed fifth in the 1948 Olympics at 147.5 pounds, winning two matches and losing two. Even though he held a large edge in takedowns during his match with Atik of Turkey, in 1948, no points were given for takedowns. Koll lost by fall when the two athletes were not even touching, but because Koll had rolled through on his shoulders after breaking a hold.

"I was very surprised that Bill didn't win the gold medal in London," said Glen Brand, who won the 174-pound Olympic championship that year. "Everyone was expecting him to win. But he fell victim to some bad officiating. I feel he was the best wrestler in his weight."

Eager to begin earning a living, Koll left competition behind and began coaching. Considered an exceptionally intelligent man

Bill Koll

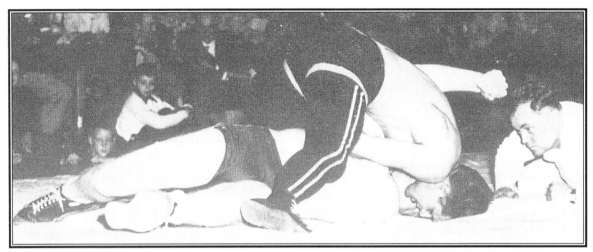

In one of the most dramatic photos ever seen of a pinning move, Bill Koll flattens a foe during his senior season at Iowa State Teachers College. Koll is one of the greatest pinners in collegiate history.

by all who knew him, he earned a master's degree in psychology and then a doctorate. He coached for one year each at the University of Chicago and at Cornell College in Mount Vernon, Iowa, and then eleven years at his alma mater, which is now known as the University of Northern Iowa.

His impact was felt in the wrestling room at Iowa Teachers for a generation. New wrestlers would enter the room in awe, after hearing stories about Koll. Iowa Teachers was one of the nation's top powers, placing in the top five in the nation for nearly a decade. Under McCuskey, the Panthers won both the NCAA and AAU national titles in 1950. The program also produced three men who were three-time NCAA champions (Koll, Bill Nelson and Keith Young) an Olympic champion (Bill Smith), and such respected NCAA champions as Gene Lybert, Jim Harmon and Bill Weick.

While all of them consider McCuskey a superb coach, much of the credit is also given to the enduring impact of Bill Koll.

"He was the leader by his actions all the time he was around the program," said Siddens. "He was very intent in everything he did. He beat Keith Young up every day in the room, and that's what made Keith a three-time NCAA champion himself, because he had to work out with Bill Koll every day."

In 1965, Dr. Koll moved to Penn State University, where he was head coach for 14 seasons, compiling a dual meet record of 127-22-7, for a winning percentage of .852. His best NCAA team finish was fourth in 1971, and he enjoyed five undefeated dual seasons. During his long career, Dr. Koll also taught tennis and lacrosse and developed a strong affection for both sports.

His son, Rob, was NCAA champion at 158 pounds for North Carolina in 1988, and then became a highly-successful coach at Cornell University in Ithaca, New York.

After retiring from coaching following the 1978 season, Dr. Koll faded from the college wrestling scene. But his legacy remained firm. His name is always called up when wrestling aficionados gather to discuss the truly great American wrestlers of all time.

Two of his biggest fans were Olympic champions themselves.

"Bill was incredible on his feet," said Henry Wittenberg, 1948 Olympic champion

Bill Koll

at 191 pounds. "He had great timing and speed, and would swoop under his foes and lift them incredibly fast. I think he was one of the most outstanding wrestlers of all time."

"He was the key to the great Iowa Teachers teams of the 1940s and '50s," said Bill Smith, a two-time NCAA champion after Koll and 1952 Olympic champion. "He administered beatings to all of us in the room, no matter what weight we were. He manhandled everybody, and made us all tougher. He was lightning quick, strong and mean.

"I probably wouldn't have been an Olympic champion without Bill Koll," said Smith. "I owe a great deal of my success to him, and so do all the other ISTC champions who followed after him."

Bill Koll died of a stroke in 2003 at the age of 80. His passing marked the end of an era for wrestling and wrestling fans.

Highlights – Bill Koll was an undefeated three-time NCAA champion at Iowa State Teachers College in the years 1946, 1947 and 1948, and also won three AAU national freestyle titles in those years. He posted a 72-0 record during that time span, with over 50 percent pins. He was named Outstanding Wrestler at the NCAA tournament twice, and was fifth in the 1948 Olympic Games. His overall record, in all styles, is estimated at 74-2.

Glen Brand
The Wrestling Engineer

In April of 2002, when Tom Brands was being inducted into the Glen Grand Wrestling Hall of Fame of Iowa in Newton, Iowa, he looked over at Glen Brand, sitting in the front row with his wife.

"When I first read about Glen Brand as I was growing up in Sheldon (Iowa), I was so impressed that I went to my mom and asked her if we could drop the 's' from the end of our name," said Tom. "I wanted to be a Brand, just like Glen Brand."

The crowd laughed and Glen Brand cracked a wide smile. But the fact of the matter is that many young wrestlers in the Midwest grew up wanting to be like Glen Brand, and in more ways than one. Not only was he a champion wrestler in both college and on the international scene, but he was a member of what Tom Brokaw called "The Greatest Generation," serving in World War II. He also became a very successful businessman, eventually owning his own companies.

"Glen Brand has always set a very high standard of excellence in anything that he does," said Bill Farrell, CEO of TW Promotions, and America's representative for Asics. "They just don't come any finer."

Like many self-made men, Glen's wrestling career got off to a slow start, in Clarion, Iowa. But his disappointments taught him a valuable lesson about sports and preparation that he would carry with him for the rest of his competitive career, and throughout life.

"The first year I wrestled, I wasn't in very good condition," he recalled in 2006. "I lost a couple of matches and I was so pooped I could hardly move. I made up my mind that I was going to either quit, or get in such good shape that I would never get tired again."

It was a lesson he never forgot: "You have to be prepared," he said firmly. "Preparation is the key to all success, in any field."

Glen Brand had a sensational year in 1948, winning an NCAA title for Iowa State College and claiming an Olympic gold medal in London.

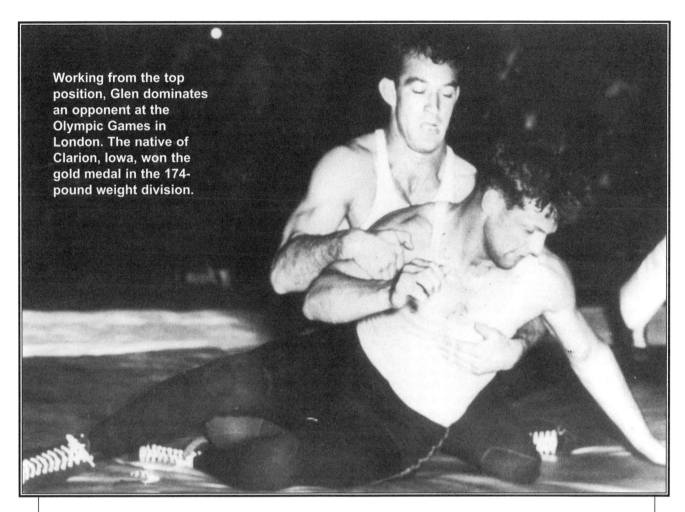

Working from the top position, Glen dominates an opponent at the Olympic Games in London. The native of Clarion, Iowa, won the gold medal in the 174-pound weight division.

Glen stuck with the sport and lettered in wrestling three times and twice each in football and track. He also had a superb role model and source of inspiration right in his own family.

"My dad left when I was two years old," said Glen. "I lived for the next four or five years with my grandmother. Also living there was my cousin, Howard McGrath. He was a lot older than me but we used to roll around on the living room floor doing wrestling moves. He went to Cornell College and did very well there. He was an inspiration to me."

McGrath was state champion for Clarion (Iowa) at 145 pounds in 1932, and NCAA runnerup at 155 pounds in 1935 for Cornell, and having that quality of wrestler in the family was a real boost for Glen. When Glen reached high school, his wrestling coach was Dale Brand, another cousin who was also an NCAA champion for Cornell College. Dale captured the NCAA title at 126 pounds in 1936, and was an alternate on the 1936 Olympic team.

Glen qualified for the state tournament twice but did not place. Hardly anyone at the time realized he was on the path to wrestling stardom, of the highest order. But before he could enter college and take his mat career to the next level, there was World War II. He was drafted at age 18 and served 33 months in the Marine Corps. Most of the time was spent on Guam in the South Pacific, working as a radio communications operator.

"I remember after boot camp, the commander told everyone whose last name began with A, B or C that they were going to radio communications, and the rest were going into the infantry," said Brand. "It was my good fortune that my name began with B.

"I was on Guam for two and a half years straight. The action was heavy for two months after I got there, then the Japanese were pretty

Legends of the Mat – 39

Glen Brand

much gone."

He was discharged November 15, 1945, and less than two months later he was on campus at Iowa State College in Ames. He was still considering which sport to devote his energy to, football or wrestling. But Hugo Otopalik, the wrestling coach, influenced him to forsake the gridiron in favor of the mat. Otopalik told Brand that if he concentrated solely on wrestling, he could be an Olympic champion.

Brand followed Otopalik's advice and made the wrestling team as a freshman, weighing just 190 pounds at the start of the season and wrestling heavyweight. His only loss in a dual meet that year came to Nebraska's Mike DiBiase, who weighed in at 230 pounds and had to hang on for a 5-4 win. In the NCAA tournament in Stillwater, Oklahoma, Glen lost to Indiana heavyweight Morris Chitwood, who outweighed him by 90 pounds. He still wound up in third place at the NCAAs.

With an All-American tag placed behind his name, Brand entered his sophomore season with high expectations. One of his biggest wins ever came that season in a dual with the University of Minnesota. The meet was scheduled before a sold-out basketball game in the Gopher arena with nearly 10,000 fans on hand to see the two powerhouse teams collide. The sportswriters were excited about the prospects of Brand tangling with Verne Gagne, who was destined to become Minnesota's greatest wrestler and a legendary world heavyweight champion in the professional ranks.

Fresh from the football team, Gagne wasn't in top shape. He scored the first takedown, then wilted. He spent most of the third period bridging off his back, fighting desperately to stave off a pin by the inspired Cyclone. Brand won, 6-3; it was the only dual meet Gagne ever lost in college, en route to two NCAA titles.

Years later, the two wrestling champions enjoyed discussing the match and teasing one another.

"I always wanted to get revenge and wrestle Glen again," said Gagne in 2002, "but he went down to 174 and I won my titles at 191 and heavyweight. We never had the chance to compete again. He was a great wrestler, no doubt about it."

Brand won every match his sophomore year until the finals of the NCAA. There, he lost to Iowa's Joe Scarpello in a close, hard-fought bout. Gagne placed third at heavyweight

The 1947-48 season was destined to be one of the greatest seasons a Cyclone wrestler – or any American wrestler, for that matter – would ever fashion. Brand was undefeated in 11 dual meets, including three at heavyweight. He won the Big Seven title with two pins, then entered the NCAA championships at Lehigh University in Bethlehem, Pennsylvania. Because 1948 was an Olympic year, the rules committee voted to use freestyle rules. Brand won all four of his matches, including three by fall.

But the season was far from over. Riding a winning streak of 24 in a row, he won seven matches in the Olympic trials, beating Scarpello along the way.

Years earlier in Clarion, Brand had learned that conditioning was a key component of an athlete's success, and he was diligent in that regard. He was always in top shape and that commitment played a key role in his win over Gagne; it was a lesson he never forgot the remainder of his career.

"The minute I get on a mat, I try to wear my opponent out, make him run out of gas, by making him work every minute," he said back in 1948. "I finally exhaust him and the last two minutes of the match are mine."

Scarpello was an alternate on the Olympic team and also made the trip to London. On the ship that carried the American team to London, mats were spread on the top deck. Brand and Scarpello engaged in many spirited workouts, along with the other members of the team. By the time the Olympic Games began, the U.S. team was in prime condition, both mentally and physically.

In London's Empress Hall, Brand won all four of his matches. He scored a decision over Abbas Hariri of Iran in the first round, drew a bye in the second round, then pinned R.B. Arthur of Australia and Achil Candenir of Turkey. Meeting

Glen Brand

Erik Linder of Sweden in the finals, the Iowan posted a decisive victory to claim the gold medal. Candenir took the silver and Linder the bronze.

Forty years later, Brand recalled his experience in London and the way he analyzed the competition.

"At the weigh-ins, I got to see the other 174-pounders for the first time," he said. "World War II had cancelled the 1940 and '44 Games, so we hadn't seen or heard anything about any of these people."

With his analytic engineering mind, Brand surveyed the field and saw that it was composed of ordinary guys, just like him. The insight made his confidence grow considerably.

His first match was the last bout in the weight class, so he sat in the top of the bleachers at the arena and watched the other 174-pounders compete. And he grew even more confident.

"The first two guys came out and started, and right away I said to myself, 'I can beat both of them!' I crossed them off. Two more came out: 'Shoot, they're worse than the first two.'" Then two more: 'I can beat these guys.'

"It just kept going that way. Wrestlers can usually tell by seeing people if they can beat them or not. And all of these people I was seeing I knew I could beat.

"All of a sudden, it's the match before mine and I'm still saying the same thing and I started getting goosebumps all over my body. I started to tremble and shake, and I found myself thinking, 'By God, I'm a world champion right now!'

"And I didn't just think it, I knew it. I had to have a little argument with myself to not get over confident, but I knew I was good enough to beat them all." *(9)*

A writer from the Chicago Tribune sought out Brand after his gold medal bout. The newspaper printed the following headline: "Glory small but sweat – We're tops: Brand." In the story, the writer quoted Glen thusly:

"We're not the glamour boys of this Olympics. We haven't had to worry about flashbulbs popping in our faces or duchesses at ringside. But I bet we sweat the most!"

Otopalik was on hand in London to see his star pupil win the gold medal in a huge outdoor stadium, which seated nearly 75,000 fans. After he returned to Iowa, Brand was given the star treatment everywhere he went. In his hometown, an estimated 7,000 people showed up for Glen Brand Day, which included a parade, street dance and festive atmosphere.

Although he was the second native Iowan to win a gold medal from Iowa, he was the first wrestler from an Iowa college to win gold. A native of Marshalltown, Allie Morrison wrestled in college at the University of Illinois before winning the gold meal at 134 pounds in 1928. Ironically, Morrison was Joe Scarpello's high school coach in Omaha!

The Cyclone program would have benefited immensely from having an Olympic champion in the lineup in 1949, but Glen missed the entire season with a severe shoulder injury. With eligibility still remaining in 1950, he tried to come back after a long layoff. He pinned four straight foes, including a heavyweight from Denver University who was considered one of the top men in the Rocky Mountain area. But he was hit by an emergency appendix operation just before the NCAA tournament and had to bow out.

He finished 51-3 in college, with 34 consecutive wins. He was also a great pinner, scoring 30 during his career. One foe was flattened in 23 seconds and another in 59 seconds.

Many sports fans at Iowa State felt that the Clarion star was the primary reason for a resurgence of wrestling interest on campus during his career. Crowds of 3,000 became commonplace his final two seasons. Otopalik and sportswriters who covered the Cyclone sporting scene said he was one of the most popular athletes in the history of Iowa State. In the late spring of 1950, Brand was one of the featured attractions at the annual Veishea Day activities on the ISU campus. The school newspaper glowed in its column about Brand:

"Ever since this sensational mat ace came to

Legends of the Mat – 41

Glen Brand

Iowa State, he has been a popular and colorful wrestler among sports writers and sports fans. Brand is a favorite among these spectators because he has reached the point of near perfection as a wrestler. Not only has he reached near perfection in wrestling itself, but he has reached near perfection in sportsmanship. If you don't think so, ask anyone who has seen him wrestle.

"Coach Otopalik is forced to admit that Brand is the most colorful wrestler he has coached since he came to Iowa State more than 25 years ago. And don't think Otopalik hasn't seen a lot wrestling. And coached a lot of champions."

After graduating with a degree in civil engineering, Brand went to work at a farm implement firm, and continued his interest in wrestling as a referee, and by coaching a YMCA team for nearly 14 years. There was even some talk of him trying out for the 1952 Olympic team, but the old shoulder injury came back to end the dream.

"I wanted to try out in '52," he said in 2006. "I was driving over from Omaha to Iowa State and working out with the team on a regular basis. But the shoulder went bad again. It just got worse and worse until I had to finally forget about it."

Otopalik credited Brand's wrestling success to four factors: (1) his natural ability, (2) his hard-work ethic, (3) unusual speed for a man his size, and (4) superior wrestling knowledge.

In an article written when he was 74 years of age, Brand said the key factor in wrestling success is the mental resolve of the athlete himself.

"There is nothing more important than determination," he told Dan McCool of the Des Moines Register. "You won't work hard if you don't have determination. If you have determination, you can accomplish just about anything you want to."

It was a philosophy that he carried over into the business world. By 1983, he was owner of two businesses in Omaha, Brand Hydraulics, Inc., and Brand Fluid Power, Inc. The companies had over 40 employees and 50 distributors all around the world. Glen himself designed many of the products that were produced and sold.

When he entered business for himself, he said he had two primary goals other than succeeding at work: he wanted to be able to go fishing and to attend the NCAA tournament every year.

The awards have flooded in through the decades. He is a member of every conceivable wrestling honors court, including the National Wrestling Hall of Fame, the Helms Athletic Hall of Fame and the Iowa State University Athletic Hall of Fame. In 2002, the International Wrestling Institute and Museum of Newton, Iowa, opened its own Iowa wrestling hall of fame, and voted to name it after Glen.

"We wanted to honor someone who was not only a great wrestler, but was successful in other walks of life and would be a superb role model," said Mike Chapman, the executive director. "Our board of directors settled on Glen Brand almost immediately and he was gracious enough to let us use his name."

There are two wrestling tournaments in Omaha that are named for Brand, as is the annual high school tournament in his hometown of Clarion. In addition, visitors to the Clarion gym are greeted by a larger than life photo of the school's most famous athlete.

Yet another honor came from *Sports Illustrated* magazine in 1999 when it announced the Greatest Sports Figures of the 20th Century in all 50 states. Brand was selected 34th on the list of all-time sports figures in the history of the state, ahead of many football, baseball and basketball stars of the past.

Bill Farrell, coach of the 1972 Olympic freestyle team that won three gold medals in Munich, and one of the most influential leaders in wrestling history, regards Glen with tremendous respect. He likes to tell a story about their first meeting, in Omaha in the mid 1950s.

"After I graduated from college, I had a business trip to Omaha," said Farrell. "I was a pretty tough college football player and when I was at the Omaha Y, I started wrestling with some big fellows. I was throwing them around pretty good.

"One day, I noticed this rather dignified fellow, a bit older than me, watching from the side-

Legends of the Mat - 42

Glen Brand

lines. I asked him if he'd like to wrestle, and he said, 'Sure, why not.' Well, I received the worst pounding of my life. Though I was heavier and bigger, he did whatever he wanted to, and with great ease. I was so humbled that I didn't come back to that Y for several weeks.

"Then, I finally came back and saw him again. I shook his hand and asked him if he'd show me some wrestling technique. He was happy to do so, and I later found out that he was an Olympic champion, that it was Glen Brand. That started me on my wrestling career and my long association with wrestling."

Farrell had a message that he wanted read to the first class of inductees at the Glen Brand Wrestling Hall of Fame of Iowa, in Newton.

"Please tell Glen and everyone there that it is a great honor for them to be inducted into a hall of fame named for such a great man, both on and off the mat."

Few wrestlers have ever enjoyed the success of Glen Brand or had as big an impact on their sport. He truly is one of the sport's legendary figures.

Highlights – Glen Brand was Olympic champion in 1948 and NCAA champion, as well. He was a three-time All-American at Iowa State University. He compiled a record of 51-3 in college, winning his last 34 matches in a row. He was 7-0 in the Olympic trials and was 4-0 in the 1948 Olympics, for an overall competitive record of 62-3.

Bill Smith
King of the Whizzer

Long and lanky, Bill Smith became one of the greatest wrestlers in American history.

When Bill Smith first went out for wrestling at Thomas Jefferson High School in Council Bluffs, Iowa, in 1942, he was a small, skinny kid with one goal: He wanted to earn a letter to impress his friends.

By the time he hung up his singlet nearly fifteen years later, he had accomplished, far, far more than that: Smith had fashioned a reputation as one of the finest wrestlers in American history, and would eventually be recognized as one of the best coaches. In addition, he developed a reputation for being the master of the whizzer, and turned that normally defensive technique into a superb offensive weapon that was talked about in awe in wrestling circles for decades.

"I went out for basketball in ninth grade, but wasn't doing too well there," said Bill Smith in 2003. "Then I heard some guys talking that the wrestling team needed a 103-pounder. I thought that if I wrestled on varsity, I could earn a letter… and I sure wasn't going to get one in basketball. So that's when I decided to try wrestling."

Actually, he could have come by the sport naturally. Prior to moving to Council Bluffs when Bill was ten years old, the Smith family lived in a small town in Kansas. His father, Frank, liked both boxing and wrestling so much that he put up a ring on his farm and would challenge anyone to contests in either boxing or wrestling.

"He just liked to tangle with anybody," said Bill. "He taught me and my brothers how to box and wrestle. I can remember fighting other kids my age in 1940 for money, when I was ten years old!"

When Frank Smith took a job with the railroad in Omaha, the family moved east and settled in Council Bluffs, a city named after the councils that Indians used to hold on the bluffs overlooking the Missouri River. Young Bill continued with his boxing even after making the wrestling team in ninth grade.

"I would go from wrestling practice right to an old boxing gym, not even stopping to eat," he said

Bill Smith (top) was a master technician in all phases. Wrestling for Iowa State Teachers College (now the University of Northern Iowa), he was unbeaten during his entire career and won two NCAA titles. Only a technicality kept him out of the NCAAs his senior year. *(Photo courtesy of University of Northern Iowa)*

with a chuckle. "But after so many weeks of that, I was getting pretty run down and had to make a choice. I decided to stick with wrestling because of that letter thing."

Though he lost his first match by pin, Bill learned quickly. He wrestled all four years in high school, and played quarterback on the football team. He never won a state title, but laid the foundation for greater things to come by twice placing in the Iowa state meet. He was third at 105 pounds in 1944 and second at 123 pounds in 1946.

Smith arrived on the campus of Iowa State Teachers College (ISTC) in the fall of 1947 as a tall and gangly 155-pounder. In the practice room, he ran into the great Bill Koll, in the midst of winning three NCAA titles at 147 pounds, and became a teammate of two more three-timers, Bill Nelson and Keith Young. In fact, the room was filled with exceptional wrestlers. Iowa Teachers, under the direction of coach Dave McCuskey, was one of the nation's top four wrestling powers for nearly a decade.

ISTC was second in the NCAA Championships in 1946, by a one-point margin (25-24) to Oklahoma State; in 1947, the Teachers finished second, ahead of the Aggies but behind in-state rival Cornell College. ISTC

— Bill Smith —

was fourth in the NCAA tournament in 1948, second in 1949, and finally claimed the NCAA team championship in 1950.

Smith made the team as a freshman, but the NCAA did not allow freshmen to participate in the national tournament. Though he couldn't compete in the 1948 tournament, he claimed the NCAA championship at 165 pounds in 1949, finishing an undefeated season. He defeated Melborne Flessner of Oklahoma State in the finals, 6-1.

In 1950, ISTC hosted the NCAA tournament and romped to the team title. Keith Young (145), Bill Nelson (155) and Smith (165) won the middleweights, while Floyd Oglesby (136) and Fred Stoeker (heavyweight) finished second. They lost close matches in the finals to a pair of three-timers, Lowell Lange of Cornell College and Dick Hutton of Oklahoma State, respectively. Smith defeated tough Jim LaRock of Ithaca College in the finals, 10-7. ISTC rolled up 30 points to 16 for runnerup Purdue.

Midway through his senior season, Smith was riding a 54-match unbeaten string and owned two NCAA titles. Out of nowhere, ISTC received word that he had been declared ineligible for the 1951 NCAA tournament because he had wrestled in a few matches as a freshman.

"It was a real blow," Smith said many years later. "Dave (Coach McCuskey) was caught off guard by the ruling, too. I had wrestled a couple of meets as a freshman but back then freshmen were eligible. The NCAA changed the rules and knocked me out of the NCAAs my senior year. It was a tremendous shock, to me and to Dave."

Hugely disappointed, he decided to play football his senior season.

"It was fun, but it sure didn't take the place of wrestling," he candidly admitted. Without Smith in the lineup, the Teachers slipped to fourth in the NCAA Championships held at Lehigh University in Bethlehem, Pa. A first place finish by him would have given ISTC enough points to win a second straight team title.

Poised and confident, with great leverage and a solid understanding of mat position and technique, he had very few close matches and was one of the finest wrestlers of the era. He went through his entire collegiate career without losing a single match, finishing with 52 wins and two ties.

He gives considerable credit to his performance to the men he wrestled daily in the workout room, stars like Koll, Nelson and Young, all three-time NCAA champions.

"You take a guy who has something in him, the potential to be good, and then put him in there with all those great champions, and they'll find a way to improve," said Smith fifty years later. "I really didn't think about progress at the time, you just do what you have to do to survive. I was beating NCAA placewinners as a freshman but didn't really think that much about it.

"Koll was the toughest person I ever wrestled – he would just chew you up. And Nelson would crunch you on the mat. It was either toughen up or get killed in that room. The room made me a collegiate champion, working out every day with people like Nelson, Young and Fred Stoeker, the heavyweight."

Coach McCuskey stressed conditioning and Smith felt the Iowa Teachers were always in better shape than anyone else they wrestled.

"Dave always had a very hot practice room and that kept our weight down, as well as helping us from getting injured. He stressed endurance and conditioning."

Wrestling meets were very popular on the campus, located in Cedar Falls, which was next door to Waterloo, long a hotbed of wrestling. The local newspaper, The Waterloo Courier, devoted a great deal of space and attention to high school and college wrestling and helped to make ISTC wrestling a big-time sport.

"People were going to our wrestling meets because everyone on campus was talking about it," said Smith. "The gym could seat about two

Bill Smith

thousand people and it was always packed. Athletes in the other sports looked up to us, too. Other sports were competing for honors in the small conference we were in but the wrestling team was going against schools from the Big Ten and Big Seven and earning national honors. We were a big deal on campus back then."

In the summer of 1951, with his eye on the 1952 Olympic Games, Smith worked at the large John Deere tractor plant in Waterloo while his wife, Bonnie, taught school. Smith had won three AAU national freestyle titles during his college days, and between collegiate and AAU action had gone 128 consecutive matches without a loss.

He won the Olympic trials at 160.5 pounds, and flew to Finland with the United States team. He won four straight matches in Helsinki to go into the round-robin round. There, he lost a scoreless, split referee's decision to the Swede, Per Berlin, and then watched as the Iranian, Abdullah Modjabavl, defeated Berlin. Smith scored a decisive decision over the Iranian and wound up with the gold medal under the bad-mark system. At first, he walked up to the awards platform and took the third-place position, and then was directed by officials to the gold medal stand.

"I wasn't sure what I had won until the last moment, under those rules," said Bill. "We had a very good team. I think Tommy Evans should have won the gold medal, too. He took his foe down seven times and never received a point for any of them."

Smith was the only champion for the United States team, but Evans (147.5) and Henry Wittenberg (191.5) won silver medals, while Josiah Henson (136.5) earned the bronze medal.

"Bill had a very unusual style and was very strong, even though he didn't look like it," said Wittenberg, who won a gold medal in 1948 to go with his silver medal in 1952. "Some guys had a style that made them very difficult to wrestle, and Bill was one of those. Bill was very tough, and very tough to score on."

Smith gives much of the credit to his summer training partner, Bill Weick, who had won the NCAA championship at 157 pounds that spring.

"Back then, the coaches didn't know anything about the international rules and there weren't many guys around to work out with," said Smith in 2004. "Weick would work with me and I developed a strategy whereas I would underhook guys and lift them up, then trip them backwards. Takedowns didn't count but back points did. I scored all of my victories in Helsinki by taking guys straight to their back."

Returning to a hero's welcome in Iowa, Smith soon accepted a position as wrestling coach in Rock Island, Illinois. Though out of competition, he stayed in shape by working with his team, and in 1956 decided to enter the Olympic trials again, this time at 174.5 pounds. That decision put him on a collision course with one of the sport's biggest legends and led to one of the most-talked about matches in American history.

As a raw youngster of nineteen, Dan Hodge was on the 1952 Olympic team with Smith. He won two of his four matches but did not earn a medal at 174 pounds. During his college career at Oklahoma, Hodge went on a rampage. He pinned almost eighty percent of his foes, and in 1956 pinned his way through the NCAA championships, the AAU national freestyle tournament and the AAU national Greco-Roman nationals – winning three national titles with 13 consecutive pins.

Smith had lost a match to Don Vonk of the Navy in the AAU nationals at 174 pounds, with Hodge pinning Vonk en route to the title. Several weeks later, the two were on a collision course at the 1956 Olympic trials in Los Angeles. Smith won his first five matches before dropping a decision in the round-robin to Wenzel Hubel of Army. Hodge roared through the trials without a blemish, defeating Hubel in the round-robin. Finally, Smith had one last

Legends of the Mat – 47

Bill Smith

Bill Smith upends an opponent during the 1952 Olympics in Helsinki. Smith won the gold medal in the 160.5-pound weight class. *(Photo courtesy of Bill Smith)*

chance; he needed a pin over the pinning sensation Hodge to make the squad.

"It was one of the most highly-anticipated matches ever," said the late Gary Kurdelmeier, a NCAA champion at 177 pounds for Iowa who went on to become the architect of the great Hawkeye program. Kurdelmeier was pinned twice by Hodge in college and had worked out with Smith many times, so he took great interest in the match.

"A lot of people thought Dan Hodge was absolutely unbeatable," said Kurdelmeier. "He was perhaps the strongest wrestler of all time, but Bill Smith is one of the smartest wrestlers of all time. It was a very intriguing matchup, one that caught everyone's attention"

The match ended when Hodge shot in at the 2:35 mark for a takedown, and Smith hit him with his favorite move, the whizzer. The unbeaten Sooner went to his back for a touch fall.... and it was suddenly all over! The match was of such magnitude that it was still being talked about in elite wrestling circles fifty years later. In 2004, when asked to select the single highlight of his entire career, Smith picked the win over Hodge above all else he had accomplished, including winning an Olympic gold medal.

"I think that would have to be the highlight, in view of all that Dan accomplished in wrestling and the way people have talked about if for so long," said Smith.

Smith had made his second United States Olympic freestyle team, and Hodge went on to earn a spot on the Greco-Roman Olympic team. But Smith was declared ineligible because he was earning his living by teaching and coaching at Rock Island High School. Hodge was awarded the freestyle spot, and won the silver medal in Melbourne.

Bill Smith's fabulous mat career was over, but his coaching career was just beginning. He turned his energy to teaching mat skills to others and became one of the sport's most respected tutors. He coached Rock Island to the Illinois state team title, then coached a year in Ann Arbor, Michigan. Smith left Michigan to take a position as head wrestling coach at the University of Nebraska, where he was also golf coach and assistant football coach.

In 1960, he moved to the San Francisco

Bill Smith

Olympic Club and took over the wrestling job at that prestigious institution. He led the Flying O wrestlers to seven national AAU team titles, including three in freestyle and four in Greco-Roman. He was asked to coach the 1968 U.S. Olympic team, but the San Francisco club wouldn't give him the time off. Frustrated, he took a job in Canada and wound up coaching the 1968 Canadian Olympic team.

He coached one year at San Jose State College and another season at San Francisco State, and then returned to the high school ranks. In 1977, he led the Clayton High School team in Concord to the California state team title – when there was only one class for all 800 schools!

In 1990, Bill lost his wife to cancer and he decided to return to Iowa. He lives with his son in the tiny town of LuVerne, Iowa, farming a bit, spending time with his grandkids, and attending various wrestling events from time to time.

"There has always been a certain aura about him," said Ron Pineda, a talented wrestler who met Smith when Pineda was in the Marines in the early 1960s, and wrestled for him at the Olympic Club. "In the 1960s, Bill Smith was like Dan Gable was in the 1980s, a legendary figure who commanded great respect everywhere he went. Everyone who wrestled for Bill Smith through the years idolized him. He was not only a great coach, he is a great person."

His reputation even spread all the way to the United States Congress. In May of 2002, Jim Leach, a member of Congress for twenty-six years, visited the International Wrestling Institute and Museum in Newton, Iowa. When he saw a large photo of Bill Smith in the Olympic pavilion, the Congressman had to stop and tell his friend: "There is one of the greatest wrestlers of all time. He took one hold, the whizzer, and made it a terrific offensive weapon. Others knew how to use it, but Bill Smith took the whizzer to a whole different level."

Leach was a state champion wrestler in high school at Davenport, Iowa, and wrestled at Princeton University. Throughout his political career, he has stayed close to his wrestling roots, and he knew that Bill Smith was one of the greatest matmen of all time.

There are many legends in the sport, but Bill Smith stands near the very top in the opinion of many. He is a member of half a dozen halls of fame and is one of only a handful who has excelled as both an athlete and a high-level coach. And it all started because a small, scrappy kid simply wanted to win a varsity letter!

Highlights – Bill Smith was NCAA champion at Iowa State Teachers College in 1949 and 1950, with an overall 52-0-2 college record. He also won AAU national titles in 1949, 1950 and 1951. Between the years of 1947 and 1952, he wrestled 128 matches without a loss. He won the Olympic gold medal at Helsinki Games of 1952 in 160.5-pound class. Bill made the 1956 Olympic team but was ruled ineligible because he was coaching high school at the time. He coached the San Francisco Olympic club to seven national titles. He had an estimated overall record of 134-4.

Dan Hodge
Terrifying Power

He came out of Perry, Oklahoma, in the 1950s to blaze a trail across the wrestling landscape that was unparalleled at the time. What Dan Hodge accomplished in a relatively brief amateur career has marked him as one of the greatest wrestlers of all time.

Hodge was known primarily for his incredible strength, particularly in the hands. Stories of him crushing apples and snapping the handles off pliers catapulted him into a legendary status that few wrestlers have ever matched. In the State of Oklahoma, he was a folk hero of epic proportions for decades, taking on a near-mythical status.

What really set him apart from the crowd was not just the overpowering style of wrestling, but the records he set, all in a relatively short amount of time.

Dan Hodge came from a broken home and lived above the fire station in Perry his last two years of high school. Wrestling became his passion, and he captured an Oklahoma state championship his senior year. Shortly after, Hodge entered the United States Navy and was stationed in the Great Lakes. He tried out for the Navy team, and made it; he also made the United States Olympic team, at the tender age of nineteen, becoming at that time the youngest Olympic wrestler in American history. Knowing nothing about international wrestling, he won two matches in Helsinki, but failed to earn a medal.

After two years in the Navy, he enrolled at the University of Oklahoma in Norman and set about re-writing the college record books.

In his first collegiate dual meet, he faced a former NCAA champion, Ned Blass of Oklahoma State, and defeated him 6-0. He wound up the season without a close match, winning the NCAA title at 177 pounds in 1955 with a pin in 4:23 over Joe Krufka of Penn State.

Dan Hodge poses with one of the numerous trophies he won during his great career. Hodge was an undefeated three-time NCAA champion for the University of Oklahoma at 177 pounds.

Legends of the Mat – 50

Known for his incredible hand strength, Hodge pinned 15 of 16 wrestlers his senior year in college. Once he was in the top position, it was almost impossible to escape. In 1956, he won the NCAA, national freestyle and national Greco-Roman championships with 13 consecutive pins.

As a junior in 1956, he shocked the wrestling world by winning three national titles in less than one month's time, and winning every single bout by pin! He pinned all four opponents in the NCAA championships at 177 pounds, including Gary Kurdelmeier, who would become NCAA champion two years later for Iowa, in the semifinals. Hodge then entered the national AAU freestyle tournament at 174 pounds, and registered five more pins. To top it off, he entered the AAU Greco-Roman nationals the day following his freestyle victories, and scored four more pins! It was a stunning feat – 13 consecutive pins, three national titles.

No wrestler had ever won all three major national tournaments the same year, let alone with all pins. It's a record that was still standing in 2005, almost half a century later.

At the 1956 Olympic trials, he was the heavy favorite at 174.5 pounds despite the presence of 1952 Olympic champion Bill Smith in his weight class. Several weeks prior at the AAU nationals in Tulsa, Smith was pinned by Don Vonk in the second round, and Hodge pinned Vonk two rounds later en route to the championship!

In the Olympic trials in Los Angeles, Hodge, Smith and Wenzel Hubel all entered the round-robin undefeated. There, Hubel decisioned Smith in the first match, and then Hodge defeated Hubel. That set the stage for the showdown.

In one of the most highly-anticipated matches of the century, the two legends squared off. At the 2:35 mark, Hodge shot in for a takedown. Smith used his famous whizzer maneuver to tilt Hodge on his back and score a stunning touch fall. Shocked but unbowed, Hodge turned to Greco-Roman in an effort to gain a spot in the Olympics, and won the trials in that style. But when Smith was declared ineligible because he had been coaching at a high school in Rock Island, Illinois, Hodge was re-instated on the freestyle team. He decided to pass up the Greco-Roman spot and it was given to the alternate, Jim Peckham.

When the Olympics began in Melbourne, Hodge was one of the two favorites in the 174-pound class, along with defending world champion Nikola Stanchev of Bulgaria. Hodge started off his quest for a gold medal with a lop-sided victory and three pins. That put him in the semifinal round against Stanchev. The American took a commanding lead over the defending world champion midway through the match and then something strange happened. The two wrestlers were locked in a tight grip when they flew apart, going separate ways. Hodge landed on his side and rolled through on his back, not even touching the Bulgarian wrestler.

Seconds later, the referee brought them together. "I thought it was to raise my hand as the winner," said Hodge many years later. "But he raised the Bulgarian's hand. I was shocked."

With two seconds left in the period, the Russian mat judge had called a rolling fall against the American! Twenty years later, an Australian official touring the United States said it was the worst call he ever saw in international wrestling.

"I was right there, at matside, and Hodge was winning easily. There was no way a fall should have been called," said the official. "It was all political."

Devastated, Dan still had to wrestle for the silver medal. He faced Georgy Skhirtladze of the Soviet Union, and punished him with a three-quarter nelson before pinning him.

"They said you could hear the Soviet wrestler screaming in the fifth row," said Wayne Baughman, one of America's top wrestlers and coaches. "Right after that, the international committee held a meeting and outlawed the three-quarter nelson."

In his official report, U.S. Coach Dave McCuskey wrote that Hodge "was, in my estimation, one of the outstanding wrestlers of the tournament."

With the Olympic Games behind him and a silver medal in his pocket, Hodge entered his senior year at the University of Oklahoma. He soon made history by being placed on the cover of *Sports Illustrated* on April 1, 1957. To this day, he is the only amateur wrestler to ever make the cover of the nation's most respected sports journal. On the mat, he resumed right where he left off as a junior, pinning foe after foe. At one point, he had 22 straight pins, setting a NCAA record that stood for fourteen years, until Dan Gable pinned 24 in a row for Iowa State University.

Hodge pinned his way through the entire dual season and Big Seven Conference tournament. He had pinned his way through the NCAA tournament as a junior and was determined to do it again as a senior. But he had to settle for an 8-0 win in the semifinals over Oregon State's John Dustin. Several times, Hodge had legal pinning holds on Dustin, but the referee made him break the hold when Dustin screamed in agony. Hodge ended the season with his third NCAA title and closed out at 16-0, with 15 pins. Dustin went on to become a high-ranking official with the AAU and ran the wrestling venue at the 2000 Olympic Games in Sydney. Decades later, Dustin recalled the match with Hodge.

"I didn't want to complain," he said with a faint smile, "but Hodge was breaking me up. He was so strong that every time he grabbed you, he hurt you. I was a pretty strong fellow too, but Hodge was simply in a different class from everyone else when it came to strength."

His legendary strength was the subject of stories from coast to coast. Dan claimed he was born with double tendons in his fingers, giving him a raw snapping power that normal men can only dream of. "It's a gift from God," declared the Sooner legend, on a number of occasions.

"Dan Hodge was as strong as nine acres of garlic," said Grady Peninger, a fellow Oklahoma matman who coached Michigan State University to the NCAA team title in 1967. "The tales about him crushing apples with his hands and bending the handles of a pair of pliers are certainly not over-exaggerated. Pound for pound, he is the strongest wrestler I have ever witnessed."

After completing his collegiate career with a 46-0 record and 36 pins (for a pinning percentage of .736), Hodge decided to try the other popular combative sport, boxing. He entered the Kansas Golden Gloves tournament in the heavyweight division and scored three quick wins, two by knockout. Suddenly, he was on his way to boxing fame, as well. After a long string of victories, he

Dan Hodge

entered the National Golden Gloves tournament, the nation's pre-eminent amateur boxing event in New York City. He powered his way to the finals. There, in Madison Square Garden, he ran into the defending national champion, Fred Hood, a seasoned boxer who was twenty pounds heavier than Hodge.

Fighting before a huge crowd in the storied arena, Hodge was knocked down in the first round. Leaping to his feet, Hodge tore after the champion. He knocked Hood down near the end of the first round and twice more in the second. Hood gained his feet the second time, but was wobbly and hurt. The referee stopped the fight and Dan Hodge was suddenly a national champion in both boxing and wrestling

"I remember being a bit dazed by the knockdown and thinking, 'I'd better get going. This guy is trying to hurt me!'" Hodge recalled decades later. "I jumped up and just went in swinging and suddenly it was over!"

As an amateur boxer, Hodge was 22-0, with 17 knockouts – the only athlete to ever win national titles in both boxing and wrestling. Feeling he was just coming into his athletic prime, he contemplated trying to make the 1960 United States Olympic team in three sports – freestyle wrestling, Greco-Roman wrestling and boxing. But the urgency of earning a living for his family (he and his wife, Dolores, his high school sweetheart, already had three children) took priority. When professional boxing promoters came calling, he listened to their talk of large payoffs.

He turned professional and drew tremendous media attention. He posed for photos with such legendary ring champions as Jack Dempsey, Rocky Marciano and Sugar Ray Robinson. He was a huge attraction in cities like Wichita and Tulsa. He was a two-fisted slugger in the mold of Marciano, constantly boring in and willing to take a foe's best punch in order to get in his own.

Perhaps his best showing came on July 14, 1958, in Wichita. Hodge and Don Jaspar, a very muscular heavyweight, stood toe to toe slugging it out. Hodge showed his ability to take a punch when he got caught with some tremendous shots and never winced. Hodge knocked Jaspar down several times and stopped him in the third round when he landed a punch that sent Jaspar sprawling half out of the ring.

In 1959, Hodge owned an 8-1 record (he avenged his only loss in a rematch) and was being discussed as a possible contender for the world heavyweight championship held by Floyd Patterson (who had won a gold medal in the 1952 Olympics in Helsinki). First, though, Hodge was scheduled to meet Willie Pastrano, a slick boxer about his size who later became light heavyweight champion of the world. The bout was set for April 28, 1959, in Wichita. When Pastrano was injured in training, the promoters substituted Nino Valdez, a huge Cuban heavyweight with many years of experience. Valdez had been rated a top contender for Maricano's title for two years.

Hodge never took a backward step in the fight and battled gamely against the highly-ranked Cuban despite giving away considerable height, weight and experience. The bout was stopped in the eighth round due to cuts and Valdez was the winner, with Hodge still on his feet and still ready to tangle. But the fight left a very bitter taste in his mouth.

"They weren't paying me," he said decades later. "Lots of talk, but the money wasn't coming. I never did get paid for that fight. I didn't like the lying and the way I was being handled. LeRoy McGuirk had been after me for years to try professional wrestling, so I did."

McGuirk was NCAA champion for Oklahoma State at 155 pounds in 1931 and became very successful as a professional wrestler. After losing his eyesight, McGuirk turned to promoting and developed a stable of Oklahoma wrestlers. Like everyone else in Oklahoma, he had been following the career of Hodge.

The two ex-college stars made a strong team. As a household name in Oklahoma, Hodge was a natural attraction there and in neighboring states. Hodge traveled mostly in the southwest part of the United States, but he also made nearly twenty trips

Dan Hodge

to Japan, where he was a major star. Along the way, Dan trained under the direction of the legendary Ed "Strangler" Lewis and made friends with Lou Thesz, the greatest professional champion of the 1940s and '50s.

"They were both great wrestlers and true gentlemen," said Dan. "They were masters on the mat and I loved traveling with them and learning from them. They didn't come any better than Ed and Lou, on the mat or off."

Thesz was known as a "hooker," a true submission wrestler, and was world heavyweight champion for a total of 13 years, wrestling over 6,000 matches. Hodge was the world junior heavyweight champion (210 pounds and under) for nearly a decade, and the two stars engaged in several hour-long bouts before huge crowds. It was a natural matchup, pitting great champions against each other in bouts that were almost devoid of theatrics and roughhouse tactics.

"Whenever you went into the ring with Dan Hodge, you had to be in the best condition possible," said Thesz. "It was always a great match, non-stop action with no fooling around. He was always in tremendous physical shape and he could hurt you with his hands. Most of the pros were scared to death of him. In some areas, he had a hard time getting matches because of his reputation for wanting to really wrestle with no frills, and for his strength. No one that I'm aware of ever tested Dan in the ring. They knew better."

Jack Brisco, another former NCAA champion (191 pounds, 1965, Oklahoma State) who became NWA world champion, said Hodge had a reputation in the pros for "stretching" foes who wanted to try him. "Stretching" is a pro term for really putting the other man in pain and showing him who was boss. Very few dared to test Hodge, said Brisco in his autobiography, and those who did quickly learned a painful lesson.

Hodge wrestled as a professional for nearly twenty years, until his career was cut short by a near-fatal car accident on March 15, 1976. That night, traveling alone, he fell asleep at the wheel of his Volkswagen station wagon. The car careened off a bridge railing and flew into a ditch filled with water. Suffering a broken neck and several teeth broken off at the root, he managed to pull himself out through the shattered windshield, holding his head erect with his right hand.

"I heard a voice telling me to keep my head up," said Dan. "I knew I had to keep fighting to stay alive."

Dan spent months in recovery, but never wrestled seriously again. Instead, he became one of the amateur sport's greatest ambassadors. He was the subject of a book *Two Guys Named Dan* (about Hodge and Gable) in 1976, and starred in the video movie "One More Shot" in 1995, produced by Wayne Boyd, 123-pound NCAA champion from Temple University in 1969.

Jack Roller, an amateur wrestling promoter from Tulsa, named his huge Reno kids tournament after Hodge. And in 1995, W.I.N. magazine created the Dan Hodge Trophy – a large, handsome award given each year (in cooperation with the International Wrestling Institute and Museum) to the top collegiate wrestler in the United States. It has become known as "the Heisman trophy of wrestling." On April 15, 2002, Dan Hodge was on hand at the Iowa State athletic banquet in Ames, Iowa, to present the trophy to Cael Sanderson for the third straight time. When introduced, Hodge drew a long standing ovation from the appreciative crowd.

"He is one of the most overpowering wrestlers of all time, and a true gentleman," said Bobby Douglas, head coach of Iowa State. "It's a great honor to even be in his presence."

"From time to time, people ask me if I ever wrestled Dan Hodge, knowing we are both from Oklahoma," said Doug Blubaugh, 1960 Olympic champion who was known for his bruising style of wrestling. " I tell them no and that I'm glad I never had to. I was a little bit smaller than Dan and I never balked at wrestling bigger men. But I couldn't have wrestled with Hodge, no one could.

"Port Robertson told me that Hodge was the only man who ever came in his room that he couldn't handle. No one could, as far as that goes. Hodge

— Dan Hodge —

is certainly the strongest wrestler I have ever seen or known."

Wayne Baughman, winner of 16 national titles and well known as a powerful, never-say-die style of athlete, was unrestrained when talking about his admiration for Hodge.

"I only got to wrestle Hodge one time in a practice situation and not in a real competition, which I'm glad I didn't," said Baughman. "I'm absolutely convinced he would have pinned me. I think Danny was a better wrestler than people give him credit for. The common comment was that he was all power and didn't have any skills, really. His power was absolutely magnified by his position, by his leverage, by the way he applied the power, by the way he blocked you where you had no where to turn except to your back.

"When I was on top there was no way I was going to turn him and couldn't even break him down for a second. When he got on top of me was when the doors absolutely closed. There was nowhere that I could go except to my back.

"I believe he would have done that to about anybody you can name. I have not wrestled all those guys in their prime but I've wrestled quite a few. When I was wrestling Hodge I was much closer to my prime and nobody else could come close to him.

"Hodge, to me, is in a category all to himself. I don't think we've had anybody that could come close to him."

In the mid 1990s, the Ultimate Fighting Championships (UFC) craze swept through the marital arts world, combining combat sports like wrestling, boxing, karate, sombo and jui jitsu. The name of Dan Hodge continued to re-surface as UFC admirers began to study the history of combat sports. In 1998, the most popular boxing magazine, *The Ring*, ran a long article on Dan Hodge, calling him "the ultimate champion" because he was the only man to ever win national titles in both boxing and wrestling.

"There's always been an aura about Dan Hodge," said Kyle Klingman, associate director of the International Wrestling Institute and Museum in Newton, Iowa. "He is one of the biggest legends in the history of wrestling. Every time I see him at an event, it is an honor just to walk up to him and shake his hand."

Though his amateur career was relatively brief, Dan Hodge has left a legacy that will be remembered as long as Mankind's Oldest Sport endures.

Highlights – Dan Hodge was a three-time NCAA champion at the University of Oklahoma, and two-time Outstanding Wrestler. He posted a 46-0 record in college, with 36 falls. He made the 1952 and 1956 Olympic teams, earning the silver medal at 174 pounds in 1956, with a 5-1 record. He won three AAU national freestyle titles and one Greco-Roman national title. Hodge was 22-0 as an amateur boxer and won the National Golden Gloves heavyweight title in 1959. His overall wrestling record is unknown but is probably around 150-5.

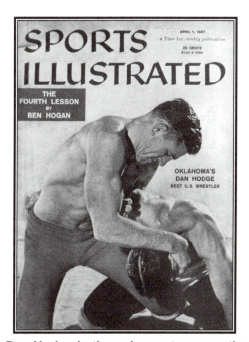

Dan Hodge is the only amateur wrestler ever to appear on the cover of *Sports Illustrated*. It was the April 1, 1957 issue.

Legends of the Mat – 55

Doug Blubaugh
The Epic Journey

"I'll never forget the first time I saw Doug Blubaugh wrestle," said Jim Duschen, with a touch of awe in his voice. "It was at a tournament at Iowa State Teachers College in 1958. Doug was so powerful and fierce looking. He couldn't see well without his glasses, and was squinting. He was chasing his opponent around the mat, trying to get his hands on him. He threw a whizzer on his foe and the other guy flew into the scoring table, and halfway into the stands. I had never seen anything like it."

Duschen went on to star for Iowa State University; he has rubbed shoulders with some of the greatest wrestlers in American history – men like the Peterson brothers, Chris Taylor and Dan Gable. But he has never forgotten the impact that Doug Blubaugh had on him when he was still a youngster.

Neither has another Iowa wrestler, one by the name of Dan Gable.

"I watched Blubaugh compete at that same tournament when I was just a kid," said Gable in 2002. "He picked up a guy and drove him into the stands! How often do you see something like that? I never forgot it."

It's the same impact that countless other young wrestlers have experienced and still vividly recall decades later. The fact is that Doug Blubaugh has left his mark all across the sport of amateur wrestling. As a collegiate wrestler, freestyle star, Olympic champion, great assistant coach at Michigan State and as a clinician, he has been a factor in the lives and careers of thousands of American wrestlers.

Doug's story began on a farm outside Ponca City, in northern Oklahoma. He never wrestled until ninth grade, and only got in three matches that season due to a severe case of asthma. The disease ran through the family to the extent that his mother would eventually die from it.

"We had canvas mats back then and the dust would fly when you hit the mat," Blubaugh recalled. "It was terrible for a kid with asthma. I could hardly breathe half the season."

He had an average season in tenth grade, then began to improve dramatically. His senior year, he was 21-0 and won the Oklahoma high school state title at 138 pounds. And he

Doug Blubaugh came off a farm near Ponca City, Oklahoma, to become one of the most celebrated wrestlers and coaches in American history.

rele...
wrestlin...
awesome s...
Olympics in Ro...
the gold medal in th...
weight division.

didn't have to look far to find two heroes in the sport of wrestling.

"My older brother, Jack, and Tommy Evans were my heroes," said Doug in 2004. "Jack never wrestled until he was a senior in high school, then placed third and fourth in the NCAA tournament for Oklahoma. He won the Pan-American Games at 125.5 pounds in 1955. In fact, we were the first brother team to ever win the Pan-American Games. (Doug followed suit in 1959). Jack was just tougher than nails. And Tommy Evans was the best wrestler I had ever seen at that point. They were my first heroes."

In Ponca City, Blubaugh also found an ideal teammate in Shelby Wilson. In 1960, they went to Rome together as members of the United States Olympic team. But in high school the two youngsters pushed one another to great heights. They were both driven by a fierce pride and unbelievable work ethic.

"I often got out of high school wrestling practice at dark and ran home; it was about five or six miles," said Blubaugh. "I did it every night. There wasn't any other way to get home. I didn't have a car; we had no money for one. Once in a while, someone would stop and give me a lift, but mostly I just ran. Shelby had the same work ethic I did. All we knew was to work as hard as we could, every minute of the day."

Running became an integral part of the Blubaugh training program. He ran everywhere, all the time.

"I ran to get rid of the asthma," he said, "and the more I ran the less it seemed to bother me. I would run to town and to school, then run home. No matter how far I ran, I always sprinted the last quarter of a mile or so to test my mental toughness."

When he was eighteen, there was a horse on the farm that wouldn't let anyone near it. Blubaugh decided he would run the horse down and tire him out so that he could ride him. It took a while to accomplish the task, but he was finally successful.

"I'd run up to him and he'd take off," said Blubaugh. "Then I'd run after him. He would run all over the place with me alongside him. It took

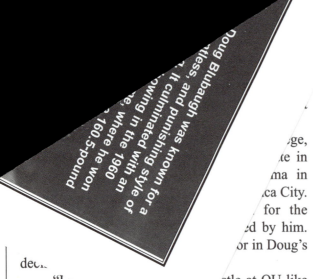

decided...

"I ... stle at OU like my brothers, Ja... Tommy Evans," said Doug. "I really ... Port Robertson. I knew he was interested in me. But my parents drove down to Norman and begged Coach Robertson not to recruit me.

"They said they needed me at the farm and if I went that far away I couldn't continue to do the farm work while I was in college. Port said he really wanted me, but that he would respect their wishes and would not recruit me any more. But he also told them if I came to him, he would give me a scholarship.

"I didn't know why he quit recruiting me until many years later, when my parents finally told me. So when Coach Griffith offered me a scholarship at A&M, I took it."

Blubaugh worked hard for his education. He often ran to school at the break of dawn and was cleaning latrines in the morning, before classes. After wrestling practice, he would usually drive home to Ponca City to work for several hours. Though schoolwork did not come easy for him, he graduated with a degree in agricultural science.

He also had to overcome a severe problem with his eyesight. He was legally blind but never considered the poor vision a handicap in wrestling.

"I made myself believe it was an advantage because I didn't look for things, I felt things," he maintained. "Sight can be deceiving but once I got hold of the other guy, I was okay."

To earn extra spending money, Blubaugh also shot rabbits on weekends when he came home from college. He would chase them down, shoot them, dress them and sell them, for thirty-five cents apiece.

"I was a good shot. Even though I couldn't see very well, I knew how to handle a gun and to shoot. The money I got from rabbits really came in handy at college. It allowed me to get a Coke and see a movie once in a while."

He was a three-time All-American for Oklahoma State, placing third in the NCAA Championships at 147 as a sophomore in 1955, taking second at 157 pounds as a junior and then winning the title at 157 pounds as a senior. He also captured national freestyle titles in 1957 and 1959, being named the Outstanding Wrestler the first time, when there were seven national champions in his weight class.

The Blubaugh legend really took hold in the 1960 Olympics. But first he had to make the Olympic team. In his path was another Oklahoma State former NCAA champion, the powerful Phil Kinyon. The two battled through a series of four scoreless draws in the finals before Blubaugh finally won a clear-cut victory.

In Rome, on the same United States Olympic team with a brash boxer from Louisville named Cassius Clay, Blubaugh wrestled six times, winning five matches by pin and one by decision. The biggest mach of his life came in the fifth round, against a legendary champion who had won the Olympic gold medal at 147.5 pounds four years earlier in Melbourne.

The Olympic experience is forever stamped upon Blubaugh's psyche. Forty-four years later, he could recall almost every moment.

"Hardly anybody knows it, but I weighed just 152 pounds, eight under the limit," he said. "I trained so hard that I was down to fighting weight for weeks before the competition. I didn't worry that I was so far under as I wrestled at a bodyweight where I felt great. When my bodyweight hit 152, it just stopped. I was at the limit of my weight. And I was in great shape, too.

"During the competition, I found a little cubby hole in the basilica and sat there by myself. I didn't watch other matches. I knew if I watched

Doug Blubaugh

the other guys on the team wrestle that I'd get too worn out from the emotion. I knew I couldn't help them at that point."

The combination of supreme physical conditioning and mental conditioning were the keys to his performance, he maintains. He had total confidence in his physical endurance and that gave him a mental confidence to compete at the highest level.

"I didn't know a whole lot of wrestling – but I knew I could go hard, very hard, for the entire twelve minutes," he said. "And then I knew I could come right back and go hard for another twelve minutes in the next match.

"I tell people yet today: 'If you're not good enough to outwrestle the other fellow then you have to be tough enough to outlast him.'"

Blubaugh was both tough enough and skilled enough to handle anything that came his way that summer of 1960 in Rome. He scored three straight falls, received a win by default, and then met the great Iranian wrestler, Emamali Habibi, a five-time world champion, in the fifth round. It was destined to become one of the most legendary matches in Olympic history.

"People kept coming up to me and said, 'Do you know who you have next?' I didn't know and I didn't want to know," recalled Blubaugh 45 years later. "You can't change what you do best in thirty minutes so I knew I just had to go out there and wrestle my match. As a matter of fact, I didn't know who Habibi was when I wrestled him, or for a long time after, actually."

Terry McCann believes Blubaugh had two other exceptional qualities that served him well in Rome – optimism and courage.

"You never saw anyone as optimistic as Doug," said McCann. "He never wavered, you never saw him concerned about anyone. He was one of the most fearless people I've ever known."

Blubaugh would need all his optimism and courage to survive the match with the Iranian star. Habibi took a quick lead on two explosive moves, getting back points along the way and forcing the Oklahoma farmer into a high bridge. But Blubaugh never lost his faith in himself and fought back. He escaped the danger, came to his feet and began stalking Habibi. A minute or so later, he threw the Iranian wrestler to his back and turned on the pressure in a style that Habibi had never experienced.

"I remember being thrown to my back, but I wasn't panicking at all," said Doug some four decades later. "I thought, 'How did I get in this position?' I even scratched my nose at one point and then fought off my back. Actually, he hit the same move on me twice. He tried it a third time; he came in high and low, one hand high the other low, and I caught him. I pancaked him right to his back.

"I had him in a vice-like grip. Every time he'd breathe, I'd tighten up on him. I squeezed so hard that he couldn't get his breath. He was there (in that position) for about a minute and a half. And then it was over."

The end came with a pin in three minutes and forty-three seconds. The match was divided into two distinct parts, said Blubaugh. "He beat the heck out of me for a minute and half and I beat the heck out of him for the next minute a half."

Of course, the second half is what counted. It sent Blubaugh into the sixth round with four pins and made him the overwhelming favorite for the gold medal. The dramatic photo of the kid from Ponca City pinning the great Habibi was made into a poster called "The Epic Struggle" in 1998 by Culture House, a company that markets the sport of wrestling. Over four thousand posters have been sold. In the photo, Blubaugh's right arm is wrapped tight around Habibi, and his face is buried in the Iranian's chest. Habibi's mouth is wide open and he is gasping for breath as stunned spectators watch.

"I was right there at matside and saw it all," said teammate Gray Simons. "It was a tremendous moment. Once Doug had him in that one-armed bear hug, it was all over."

Despite the sensational victory, the gold medal was far from clinched. In his next match, he faced Ismail Ogan of Turkey, who won the Olympic gold medal in 1964. The two had been in the sauna bath at the same time on several times

Doug Blubaugh

without being aware of who the other one was.

"I would go to the sauna, not to lose weight but just to relax," said Blubaugh. "I kept seeing this big, tough-looking guy in there. He had scars all over his face and looked huge. I knew he couldn't be in my weight class and I was glad to know that.

"But when I went out for the semifinals, after beating Habibi, there was this guy across the mat from me. I couldn't believe it! I couldn't see how he could make 160 pounds! And he was tough, tougher than nails."

Despite the apparent disparity in size, Blubaugh was ready to wrestle. In fact, had the officials been paying attention, the American would have pinned the Turk in just 53 seconds!

"When the official said 'Wrestle!' I charged straight into Ogan and caught him in a lace ride and ran him right off the mat," said Blubaugh. "I wheelbarreled him off the mat! The referee called it a fall, but most of the judges were still writing in their scorebooks. They didn't see it and didn't confirm the pin."

Blubaugh wound up with a 6-1 victory and found himself in the finals with Muhammad Bashir of Pakistan. He pinned him in less than a minute. With five pins and a lop-sided decision, Doug Blubaugh had won the Olympic gold medal. Ogan took the silver and Bashir the bronze, while Habibi finished fourth.

One person Blubaugh gives credit for helping him capture the gold medal is teammate Ed Dewitt, who finished fourth at 174 pounds. According to Blubaugh, the 1956 NCAA champion (at 167 pounds) from the University of Pittsburgh was also on track for the gold medal until suffering an injury.

"Ed should have won the Olympics," said Blubaugh. "He beat the Russian, but got his ribs hurt bad and wasn't the same after that. We trained together at West Point and had some terrific workouts that really helped prepare me. I probably would not have won without him."

Blubaugh's Ponca City teammate also came back home with a gold medal. Shelby Wilson turned in the tournament of his life with five straight wins at 147.5 pounds. Back in the United States, the Oklahoma stars were invited to appear on the popular national television show "I've Got A Secret." The format of the show was to have the guest walk onto the set and whisper to host Garry Moore his secret. The secret was then flashed on the screen so that the audience at home knew it, but the panel of four experts (all well-known celebrities of the day) had to ask questions and guess what the secret was.

Their secret was that they both won gold medals in Rome and were from the same hometown, and that Wilson, a minister, performed the ceremonies at Doug's wedding.

"The panel guessed the wrestling part because of our cauliflower ears," said Doug. "But they didn't get the second part, of course."

After his Rome and television experiences, Blubaugh returned to the quiet life of a farmer in Oklahoma. When he was voted the top amateur wrestler in the entire world by FILA a month after the Olympics, his trophy arrived in the mail. He came in from the field to unwrap the box, and returned to the plow with no fanfare.

"That's just how it was back then," said Blubaugh, with a shrug of resignation. "You worked hard and wrestled hard but there wasn't much publicity or fanfare."

For the next forty-five years, Doug poured his heart and soul into the sport that had become his passion. He was an assistant coach at the University of Oklahoma, West Point and Michigan State and then head coach at Indiana University. He coached international teams and became one of the nation's most respected summer camp technicians. The epic journey is the story of a man's love affair with the sport of wrestling. It is also the story of wrestling in America through several generations of wrestlers.

Though he is known for being a fine technician, he is remembered mostly for his relentless pursuit of physical perfection on the mat. And for his incredible work ethic.

"I remember going to the Olympic training

Doug Blubaugh

camp after the team was selected in 1960," said Gray Simons. "I was in pretty darn good shape, as I had been working all summer, lifting and stacking blocks of concrete. But I hadn't been running much, and at camp the coaches had us running everywhere, all the time, while carrying little weights.

"I said to Blubaugh, 'What are they trying to do, work us to death?'

"He stared back at me, and said, 'Simons, they can't make it tough enough for me.'

"That tells you where that guy was coming from," said Simons with a chuckle. "Doug was unbelievable, the way he trained. And tough? He was so darn tough it was just unbelievable."

Wayne Baughman, winner of 16 national titles himself, echoed that viewpoint. Even though he outweighed Blubaugh by nearly twenty pounds, Baughman recalled the experiences of working out with Blubaugh when Doug was an assistant coach at the University of Oklahoma and Baughman was a young student.

"Without doubt, Doug is the most physical person I ever had the misfortune of working out with. Dan Hodge was physical, but he just methodically wadded you up and gave you the choice of going to your back or breaking. With Doug, you came out of every workout feeling like you'd just been hit by a truck. His head is as hard as a concrete block and he keeps it in your face constantly." *(10)*

Baughman said he often had trouble getting out of bed the morning after a workout with Blubaugh. He made all wrestlers pay a terrific price, and at the same time making them much tougher mentally, and physically. It was that sort of mentality that he brought with him into the room at Michigan State in 1966.

Shelby Wilson (left), Terry McCann (center) and Doug Blubaugh won gold medals in the Rome Olympics. Wilson and Blubaugh grew up together in Ponca City, Oklahoma.

"I really wanted him as my assistant coach," said Grady Peninger in 2002, reflecting back on their great relationship, which made the Spartans one of the finest wrestling teams in the nation for nearly a decade. During the seven years Peninger and Blubaugh led Michigan State, they placed in the top ten in the nation seven times and captured the NCAA championship in 1967. The Spartans were the first Big Ten school to win the NCAA team title, long before the University of Iowa took

Legends of the Mat – 61

Doug Blubaugh

control in the 1970s

During that span, the Spartans also won the Big Ten championship seven straight years, a record that stood until the great Iowa dynasty of the 1980s and '90s. Among the brightest stars for Michigan State was Dale Anderson, who won NCAA titles at 137 pounds in both 1967 and 1968. Anderson was captain of the 1967 team and became an attorney who later was deeply involved in the fight for Title 9 justice.

"Doug was the catalyst for those great Michigan State teams," said Anderson. "Grady was a superb coach, but I have always believed it was Doug that made us so darn tough. He was just so tough himself, both physically and mentally. The stories of him in the room and his work ethic are some of the best stories in wrestling history. He showed us what it meant to be a champion. Doug and Grady were a great team."

There was another quality about Blubaugh that Anderson found exceptional: his ability to work with anyone and let them really wrestle, even if it meant letting them score occasionally.

"Doug could beat the crap out of anybody in the room, but he could also let the wrestlers take him down from time to time," said Anderson. "It didn't bother him a bit. It wasn't about his ego, it was about him teaching. He truly knew how to coach, as well as wrestle."

Wanting a shot at running his own program, Blubaugh left Michigan State in 1972 to become head coach at Indiana University of the Big Ten. He coached there for twelve years, and during the summers ran one of the most successful wrestling camps in the nation. He was also active as an international freestyle coach, helping many Americans reach down inside themselves. In 1971, he was head coach for both the Pan-American Games and the World.

"He is one of the three coaches that left a big impact on me, during the time I was preparing for the Olympics," said Dan Gable. "Blubaugh showed me intensity, drive and focus. When he trained us, he ran us to the hilt. There was a work ethic there that was perfect for me. Maybe some of the other guys didn't like it, but I loved it. He played a big role in my career."

"Doug Blubaugh was just a tough, tough individual," said Port Robertson, who was head coach of the 1960 Olympic team, in one of his last interviews before passing away in 2004. "He was a special young man, one who knew how to pay the price and get the job done. He and Dan Hodge were two very, very special men, two of my favorites."

Blubaugh left college coaching for good in 1984 and has since traveled the nation, attending wrestling events at all levels. He loves to see young people wrestling, no matter where or what time of day. He believes devoutly in the lessons for life that wrestling provides.

In 2003, he and Emil Habibi met in Dallas in a meeting arranged by Habibi's son, who lives in the United States. It was an emotional meeting for the two foes from Rome.

"He came to the U.S. in 1961 for a tournament looking for me," said Doug with a chuckle. "He would go up to American wrestlers and say, 'Where Blubaugh? Why is he not here?' He couldn't understand why I wasn't wrestling anymore.

"I told him that in Iran, wrestling made him a national hero. He was getting paid $100,000 a year to wrestle back then by the government. He won the World twice more after I beat him in Rome. But I had to make a living. I was cutting wheat in Oklahoma, trying to keep alive. I had a family to support.

"The truth is, I just didn't have the money to train and you couldn't make any money as a wrestler back then. I never felt like I was poor but when you came right down to it, I guess we were.

"I trained hard until 1972," said Doug. "I would have loved to have competed for two more Olympics, 1964 and 1968. But I just couldn't afford to. That's all there was to it.

"I'm just an Oklahoma farm boy who loved to wrestle," added Doug in 2004, back farming near Perry, Oklahoma, the hometown of Dan Hodge. "I had tunnel vision. Anything that was bad for wrestling, I didn't do. Anything that was

Doug Blubaugh

good for it, I did. I guess I found my niche in life.

"Wrestling was a way of life for me and my brothers. We grew up on a farm and never complained about hard work. In fact, we looked forward to it. We'd work from sun up 'til sun down, then run for five or six miles, then wrestle.

"I wouldn't have won the Olympics if I hadn't been raised on a farm. I was running a hay baler when I was ten years old. It was a man's job and gave me strength and determination. I used to go to the fields and work three straight days, and never even come home. We'd sleep for fifteen minutes and then just keep going.

"I never lifted weights a day in my life. If OSU had a weight room when I was there, I never knew where it was. I got my strength over an entire day's work. I could walk the length of a football field on my hands. If you do that every day, it will help your strength....and your balance."

He was named the Outstanding Wrestler at practically every level he ever competed in – his senior year in high school, the AAU nationals, the Wilkes tournament (one of the oldest and toughest in the nation), while wrestling in the Army and at the Olympics Games. He was the unofficial O.W. at the Pan-American Games and finished in the top three of the voting for the Sullivan Award in 1957, an almost unheard of accomplishment for a wrestler back then. He was voted into the National Wrestling Hall of Fame in 1979 and is a member of the prestigious Helms Athletic Hall of Fame of Los Angeles, and several others.

For all of his life, Doug Blubaugh has been a devotee of the hard-work ethic, and a prime example of its success in the world of athletics. He has had two true loves: Farming and wrestling.

"Wrestling gets under your skin," he said with emotion. "It's the greatest sport there is. I can't imagine what my life would have been like without it. And farming gave me the background to succeed in it."

Doug Blubaugh is one of wrestling's greatest products. He proved that in 1960 in the shadow of the ancient coliseum in Rome, when he pinned the fabled Habibi and was named the world's best wrestler. He is truly one of the sport's finest examples of what hard work can do for any person willing to pay the price.

Highlights – Doug Blubaugh placed third, second and first in the NCAA while at Oklahoma State University, winning the 157-pound NCAA title in 1957. He had an overall college record of 37-3-1. He won a 1960 Olympic gold medal and was voted the outstanding wrestler in the world that year. He also won the Pan-American Games in 1959. Blubaugh won two national freestyle titles, and was O.W. in 1957. His estimated overall record is 414-17.

Terry McCann
Small Body, Huge Heart

There have been many superb competitors in the long history of amateur wrestling in America, but it's safe to say that Terry McCann ranks near the very top of the list in that category. Men who trained with him in the late 1950s and early 1960s stand in near awe of his mental toughness and his warrior spirit.

"Terry McCann was one of the best wrestlers I've ever known or seen," said an Olympic teammate, Doug Blubaugh. "Terry was the wrestler of the Fifties. He was beating everyone. He was as intense on a mat as anyone I ever saw."

"He was about as fierce a competitor as you would ever hope to see," said Joe Henson, a bronze medallist in the 1952 Olympics who went on to become one of America's highest rated FILA officials. "He was respected all around the world for his attitude and his competitive spirit."

Alan Rice, an Olympic wrestler and coach who is a few years older than McCann, could well recall Terry's fiery nature when he talked about him in 2006. McCann lived in Minneapolis for a period in the 1960s and the two men worked out often.

"I was bigger and older than Terry, but that didn't matter at all to him," said Rice. "We had some real battles, let me tell you. And you couldn't leave the room if you got the last takedown. He just wouldn't leave until he got the last one, and some times it got pretty competitive, even though we were great friends."

Terry McCann discovered wrestling at a tender age. He was the first of six children in the family that lived in a tough area of north Chicago, and was very small as a youth. When eleven years old, he weighed just fifty-five pounds and stood just over four foot six inches. When the neighborhood kids chose up sides for their impromptu sporting events, ranging from baseball to football games, he was usually among the last to be chosen due to his size.

But he soon found his niche. The local playground had a wrestling program and Terry took to it immediately. He knew it was the sport for him, and he loved to tangle with anyone anywhere near his size. He took up running and push-ups and

Terry McCann is generally regarded as one of the most aggressive wrestlers to ever step on the mat. He was a two-time NCAA champion at Iowa and 1960 Olympic gold medallist.

Terry McCann works over a Japanese wrestler in a tournament held in Tulsa in 1959.

became a fitness fanatic for his era.

It was also during this time period that he saw a picture in a magazine that had a tremendous impact on his life.

"I was at a candy store across the street one day and I saw a picture of this little guy, Allie Morrison, getting a gold medal in the Olympics, for wrestling," he said in a 2006 interview. "I was very impressed. I thought he was just a little guy and that if he could do something so special in sports, so could I. That was the start. I had a vision."

When he arrived at Schurz High School, he was determined to become the best wrestler possible. He traveled all over northern Illinois looking for workouts. He would go to the wrestling room at various high schools, and to area colleges to work out with anyone, at any time.

"We didn't have a very good coach in high school, so I went anywhere I could to get workouts and to learn," he said years later. "I was self-created, self made. I had to be. I was working out seven days a week back then. I couldn't get enough of it."

McCann won the city championship three times. His senior year he qualified for the Illinois State High School Tournament, one of the best such meets in the nation. After battling his way to the finals at his weight division, his entrance onto the mat was a memorable one, according to author Larry Fox.

"Terry McCann was quite a sight as he walked out to compete for the 1952 Illinois high school wrestling championships in the 112-pound division. Only five foot, four inches tall and trained down to bone and sinew, McCann was wearing scruffy sneakers and ragged wrestling togs with a huge rip up the inside of one leg.

"Tournament officials called the youngster from Chicago to one side. 'Come on, let us borrow a pair of tights for you,' they offered, embarrassed that such a ragged-looking youngster would represent their sport in the state finals.

"'Never mind,'" McCann replied. "'I've been wrestling in these clothes all year. I might as well finish up in them.'

"So he strode out on the mat, trying to hide the holes in his pants, and pinned his opponent in 57 seconds of the first round. It was the fastest pin ever achieved in the state high school finals. 'I

Terry McCann

guess I had to win in a hurry, before my pants ripped any worse,' the 17 year-old high school senior grinned." *(11)*

His wrestling hero was the great Bill Koll, the undefeated star of Iowa State Teachers College. When Terry discovered that Koll's coach, Dave McCuskey, had moved from the small teachers school to the University of Iowa (in 1951), McCann decided he wanted to wrestle at Iowa for McCuskey.

But he hadn't spent much time in the classroom in high school and his grades weren't good enough to enter the University of Iowa without being put on probation. McCann started school in Iowa City in the fall with the immediate goal of improving his scholastic record. He scored a B average his first year at the University and was soon on his way, both in the classroom and on the mat.

Freshmen weren't eligible back in 1953, but he made the varsity in his sophomore year. At the 1954 NCAA tournament at 115 pounds, he lost a very close semifinal match to Hugh Peery of Pittsburgh, who was going for his third straight title (his father, Rex, had won three titles for Oklahoma A&M, and his brother, Ed, would also win three titles for Pittsburgh, giving the Peerys a stunning total of nine NCAA championships in one family). Terry wound up third in the NCAAs in his first try.

Peery defeated his finals foe 9-2, but had all he could handle in his match with McCann, according to Harold Keith, writing in the 1955 Official NCAA Wrestling Guide: "The speedy little Panther (Peery) got terrific competition in the semifinals from Terrance McCann, tigerish Iowa wrestler. This was the meet's fastest bout. McCann's eternal aggressiveness earned him a 5-5 draw on the scoreboard but Perry's superiority in riding time gave him a 6-5 victory in the thrilling duel of fast-moving gnatweights."

The writer had noted the McCann style of wrestling twice in the short paragraph, citing his "tigerish" attitude and "eternal aggressiveness." It was a style he had adopted from his idol.

"Early in my Iowa career, Bill Koll came to one of our matches," said McCann. "I had kind of a Chicago style, bouncing up and down and floating around on the mat a little before shooting. Koll came up to me afterwards and said, 'What the heck was that all about? Quit dancing around out there. You go all out, every second you're on the mat. Straight ahead! Attack!'

"I changed my attitude at that point. I worked myself into a lather before a match, into a heightened level of intensity, just like Bill Koll used to. Koll was the guy who taught me that, and I wrestled that way from that point on. I also adopted his fireman's carry and duck under. Those were my favorite takedowns."

The following year as a junior, McCann captured his first Big Ten championship, at 115 pounds, and then won the NCAA championship at the same weight, beating David Bowlin of Oklahoma A&M in the finals. In his senior season, 1956, he repeated as both Big Ten and NCAA champion. McCann defeated another Pittsburgh wrestler, Bill Hulings, in the NCAA finals as the Hawkeyes finished in fourth place in the team race. Along the way, he continued to build on his reputation as one of the most fierce warriors to ever step on a mat.

"He was something else when the competitive juices got flowing," said Ken Leuer, an Iowa teammate who won the NCAA title at 191 pounds in 1956 and went on to become a major general in the United States Army. "I remember once when a wrestler from Purdue said he was going to beat Terry. Word got back to Terry that this fellow was saying stuff, and Terry worked himself into a frenzy.

"'I'm gonna break that guy's neck!' Terry said. Well, it was just a figure of speech, but Terry went out, took the guy right down into a pinning hold and they stopped the match. The other guy was hurt, and had to default. Turns out he had a broken neck."

Leuer recalled another time when the Hawkeyes were taking on Oklahoma State in the hometown of the Cowboys.

"Someone in the crowd there in Stillwater was giving Terry a hard time and he went right up into the stands after him," said Leuer. "This guy was a former national champion from OSU, and at

Terry McCann

Toastmasters. When the United States Wrestling Federation was formed in 1969, McCann played a key role.

Though he was very busy as president of the Toastmasters International and had moved to California, McCann continued to work as one of wrestling's foremost leaders in the 1980s and '90s. He spent four years as president of USA Wrestling and six years on the board of FILA, and was a highly-regarded member of the United States Olympic Committee for nearly a decade.

After leading the Toastmasters organization for 30 years, McCann retired to spend more time with his wife, seven children and seventeen grandchildren. He also continued surfing and kayaking in the Pacific Ocean, near his home in Dana Point, California.

In April of 2005, McCann suffered the biggest blow of his life. He was diagnosed as having mesothelioma cancer, a debilitating disease with no known cure. It's a disease that attacks the lungs and though he never drank or smoked and lived a very healthy lifestyle, it was brought on by exposure to asbestos during his days working in the Oklahoma oil business four decades earlier. He underwent chemotherapy treatments and faced long periods of time without leaving his home. Still, he managed to work out when his body would allow him to do so.

"It's ironic that the oil refinery business allowed me the opportunity to train for the Olympics and I felt that it was wonderful," said McCann. "Now it turns out that the very same job that gave me the opportunity to go for the gold medal has also given me cancer that will shorten my life. I was immersed in asbestos during those years and this is the result, forty years later."

On June 7, 2006, mesothelioma cancer ended the life of Terry McCann. Tributes poured in from across the wrestling world. Jim Scherr, CEO of the U.S. Olympic Committee, called him a mentor, and Werner Holzer, another Olympian who worked with Terry in the early years of building the United States Wrestling Federation, called him the best wrestler America has ever produced.

Russ Hellickson, a silver medal winner in both the 1976 Olympics and 1979 World Championships, was asked to give the eulogy. He enjoyed a long and successful coaching career, at both the University of Wisconsin and Ohio State University, and said he owed his entire international career to Terry McCann.

Hellickson never placed in the NCAA tournament in college, but still had tremendous raw skills. McCann and Holzer saw the potential, and wrote him a letter, inviting him to train at the Mayor Daley Club.

"He changed my life," said Hellickson, "and influenced it in many ways. The first time I met Terry, it was an immediate response on my part. I would have run through a wall for him. Terry taught me an underhook, and it became my signature move," one that helped Hellickson win 11 national titles and make two Olympic teams. "He laid the foundation and framework that allowed me to compete.

"He was the most intense and passionate person I had ever met. I learned so much from him, not just about wrestling but about family life. Nancy and I were a young married couple and we would go over to the McCanns once in a while for dinner. I would see this very driven man, who was building a successful career and coaching, and yet still had time to devote to his family. It left a huge impression on both Nancy and me.

"There simply could not have been a more positive role model than Terry McCann."

He had come a long way from the rough Chicago neighborhood where as a young boy he dreamed of becoming an Olympic champion. Wrestling was his passport to a college education, Olympic fame, the highest echelons of sports service, and to a fascinating career in business. He excelled at every level of activity he attempted.

Highlights – Terry McCann was a two-time NCAA champion at the University of Iowa and placed third once, with an overall college record of 36-3-1. He won three AAU national titles and was 6-0-1 against the touring Russians. He won the gold medal at the 1960 Olympic Games at 125.5 pounds. He had an estimated overall record of 87-4-1.

Gray Simons
Seven Times a Collegiate King

It's safe to say that the dream of every wrestler who enters the college ranks is to win a national championship. It may be in any one of the four major divisions, which includes the three NCAA divisions and the NAIA, but the goal is the same – to earn the right to be called "national collegiate champion."

In the long history of college wrestling, dating back to 1928 and the first NCAA championship in Ames, Iowa, one man stands above the pack. Of the tens of thousands of men who have wrestled in college, Gray Simons is alone at the top because he owns an incredible seven national college championships!

Coming from Norfolk, Virginia, one might have suspected that Gray Simons would do very well in college. After all, he wrestled for a true high school coaching legend, Billy Martin. It was Martin who made Granby High School the most-talked about prep program in the entire nation, capturing 22 Virginia team titles in 23 years as coach, and Simons was his star pupil. Gray won state as a sophomore but was upset in the finals as a junior. He was undefeated as a senior but was ruled out of the second half of his final season due to a rules change regarding freshmen eligibility.

Gray selected tiny Lock Haven State College in western Pennsylvania to do his collegiate wrestling. Lock Haven was a member of the National Association of Intercollegiate Athletics (NAIA). The organization began its national meet in 1958 and has been going strong ever since. But in the 1950s and '60s, NAIA champions also qualified to participate in the NCAA Division I national tournament, as did Division II champions.

Wrestling most of his freshman season at 123 pounds, Gray got off to a good start. He won seven of his first nine matches, but was unhappy about losing two – even though one was to a post-graduate and the other was by one point, 8-7, to Paul Powell of Pittsburgh, the 1958 NCAA champion at 123 pounds. Then something happened to the young man from Norfolk. He suddenly kicked into another gear… and the Gray Simons legend took off like a jet. He won 84 consecutive matches, one of the longest winning streaks

Gray Simons captured seven national titles in college. Wrestling for Lock Haven State, he won four NAIA titles and three NCAA titles, and was named O.W. six times.

Gray Simons made two Olympic teams but was caught between weights and had difficulty with the cutting. Here he turns a foe in the 1960 Games in Rome.

in college history.

Gray captured four NAIA titles, all at 115 pounds, and was voted the outstanding wrestler all four times! Then, moving on to the NCAA Division I tournament for three years (freshmen couldn't compete at the NCAAs his first season), he won three more national titles. And to top it off, he was voted the outstanding wrestler twice, in both 1961 and 1962!

His toughest match came in the finals his sophomore year. Facing tough Dick Wilson, the No. 1 seed and NCAA runnerup the year before for Toledo University, the Lock Haven sophomore had his hands full. They battled to a 3-3 tie in regulation, then fought to a 2-2 stalemate in overtime. Simons was given the title on a referee's decision.

He met Wilson in the finals again in 1961. Wilson had finished second twice and was determined to go out with a title; but Simons was in control most of the way, posting a 7-3 triumph and being voted the meet's outstanding wrestler.

Gray captured his third straight Division I title in 1962, defeating Mark McCracken of Oklahoma State in the finals, 7-2.

When his college career was finally over, Gray Simons owned seven national championships and six O.W. awards. It's a performance that made him a hero in the sport, and will most likely never be duplicated.

"That was my goal coming out of high school, to win three NCAA championships," said Gray in 2004. "I wasn't thinking about the Olympics, I was focusing on college wrestling."

Although he didn't wrestle a great deal of freestyle, he did win a national AAU freestyle championship at 125.5 pounds in 1964, placing ahead of NCAA champions Dave Auble, Massaki Hatta and Andy Fitch. He served at West Point for two years after graduation from Lock Haven, and was assistant wrestling coach there.

Simons won a gold medal at the World Military Games in 1963, and was in top form. He looked like he was in position to win a gold medal at the World Championships that year when his

Gray Simons

knee locked up on him, and he found himself in a Bulgarian hospital as the competition began.

He also was a member of two Olympic teams, in 1960 and 1964. But the weight classes didn't line up well for him; he was a bit too small for 125.5 pounds and 114.5 pounds was a tremendous cut for a man who had fought his final three years of college to make 115 pounds.

Simons finished fifth at 114.5 pounds in the 1960 Olympics in Rome, winning three matches and losing two. He defeated the reigning world champion from Russia, but lost close matches to Turkey and Japan. He was mat side when his teammate Doug Blubaugh pulled off a stunning pin of the great Iranian wrestler Emmil Habibi at 160.5 pounds, and thoroughly enjoyed being in Rome for the grandest of all athletic spectacles.

"I had just turned 21, and had never really traveled much before that," said Simons. "It was a wonderful experience."

Four years later, in Tokyo, he never lost a match but still didn't earn a medal. Under the black-mark system, he was eliminated in the fourth round, even though he defeated the bronze medallist from Bulgaria. He finished seventh, with a record of two wins and two ties.

"By then, it was really tough keeping my weight down to 114.5 pounds," he said. "I was growing and didn't have the opportunity to train as much as I wanted. You had to maintain the weight through the trials, the training camp, and then the Olympics. That was a long, long haul for me."

Wayne Baughman, who was a member of five Olympic teams and 13 World championship teams as either a wrestler or coach, felt there was another major reason why Simons never made it to the top of the world, like he had in college.

"I do believe Gray should have been a World or Olympic champion, but the thing that hurt him was the soft, slow European mats," said Baughman. "Gray and our other fast wrestlers were slowed down substantially when they would sink in the mats up to their ankles. There was no consistency or dependability on those mats and they really threw Gray's timing off. No one in the world could stay with him on American mats." *(12)*

Simons retired from competition in late 1964 and began a long and successful coaching career, in demand everywhere as a clinician. He returned to his alma mater and was head coach at Lock Haven from 1964 through 1970, fashioning a 59-10-1 dual meet record. Twice he led the team to the NAIA national title and was named NAIA Coach of the Year.

He spent five seasons as coach at Indiana State University (1970-'75), then was head coach at the University of Tennessee for 11 seasons. The Volunteers were 193-87-3 during his tenure and placed eighth in the NCAA tournament in 1985.

He took over at Old Dominion University in 1986, located in his hometown of Norfolk, Virginia. He retired at the end of the 2000 season; Gray Simons had completed 35 years in coaching with a combined record of 297 wins, 128 losses and five ties.

Those who saw Gray Simons compete in the 1960s insist he was as smooth as glass on the mat, and many rank him as one of the four or five finest pure wrestlers in collegiate history. In 2005, the International Wrestling Institute and Museum of Newton, Iowa, named him to its all-time college first team, at 115 pounds.

Baughman said Simons was "probably the smoothest and best all-around wrestler" he saw during his decades of competition and coaching. He also said Simons had the highest score on the strength test for the 1964 Olympic team.

"Gray is probably the best finesse wrestler I ever saw," said Doug Blubaugh, his Olympic teammate and gold medallist in 1960. "He had it all. He was good enough to be Olympic champion, for sure. Some times, things just don't go your way and the best man doesn't always win."

When asked to evaluate his own successes, Simons said he felt it was mostly attributable to position.

"Technically, I feel I was sound. I was also fast and had good set-ups. If people say I was smooth, then I guess that's because I always tried to have good position. That's what makes someone

Gray Simons

look smooth… being in good position so you can work your stuff.

"The thing about wrestling is everyone has a little bit of all the skills required – Dan Hodge had strength in huge doses, Gable had conditioning, others had quickness, and other had lots of technique, all to varying degrees. Cael Sanderson had terrific positioning, he just never seemed to be out of position. And if he is for a split second, he can recover. I think positioning was a key to my success, too."

A quiet, dignified man, Simons is still very highly regarded in pockets of wrestling culture all around the nation, and particularly so in the state of Pennsylvania.

"In the late 1950s and '60s, wrestling started to explode in Pennsylvania, and Gray was one of the main reasons why," said Norm Palovcsik, one of the nation's top wrestling historians. "When I was wrestling at Penn State, Gray was the coach at Lock Haven and had some great teams. He was very personable and exuded class.

"He was revered back then – and is still revered today by the whole state of Pennsylvania when it comes to wrestling. He impacted the sport very much."

As the years go by and men gather to discuss the best wrestlers in American history, the same handful of names always come up. Gray Simons is one of those names. One thing seems certain: no other wrestler will ever win seven national collegiate championships again. In that arena, Gray Simons stands alone at the top of the heap.

Highlights – Gray Simons won three NCAA titles and four NAIA titles, with a total of six outstanding wrestler awards. His total college record was 91-2, including 84 consecutive victories. He was national freestyle champion in 1964, and World Military Games champion in 1963. He was a member of 1960 and 1964 Olympic teams, placing fifth in 1960, and seventh in 1964 despite not losing a match (two victories, two ties). His total record is not known.

Bobby Douglas
Champion at All Levels

The sport of wrestling has enjoyed a reputation for opening the door for self-made men; the sport has shown time and again its ability to help young men develop the skills and the mental toughness required to succeed at life in a variety of pursuits, and on various levels.

And there is no finer example of such than the amazing career of Bobby Douglas. He came from the most humble of origins to become a world-class wrestler, making two Olympic teams and three World teams. Then he became one of the nation's top coaches, on both the collegiate and international level.

He is also the author of several books, an outstanding clinician, and one of the most respected persons in the highly competitive field of athletics. He was the subject of a long feature story in *Sports Illustrated*, one of a handful of wrestlers to be so honored, in which the writer traced his heritage all the way back to the Nubian tribe of ancient Africa.

Most of all, though, Bobby Douglas is a man who loves wrestling. Wrestling is to some a way of life; to Bobby Douglas, it is life.

Bobby was born into abject poverty in Bellaire, Ohio. He used wrestling as a means of elevating his situation, and eventually as a vehicle of escape from his restrictive circumstances. The sport gave him an identity and made him the man he has become.

"I was saved and formed by two men, my grandfather and my high school coach, and they did it with the wrestling," he told *Sports Illustrated* writer Kenny Moore in that March 9, 1990, article called "A Man of the Ash." *(13)*

Bobby's father worked in the mines and did some boxing on the side. Severely injured in a car accident, his mother used alcohol to subdue the pain. It was a tough ghetto life and when he was just three years old Bobby suffered the horrifying experience of seeing his mother beaten and raped. A few years later, he was sent to live with his grandparents in Blaine, Ohio, just across the river from West Virginia. His grandfather, a huge man at six foot five inches and

Bobby Douglas came from a poverty-stricken childhood to become one of the most accomplished figures in the history of American wrestling.

Bobby Douglas was known for his explosive wrestling performances. He won five national freestyle titles and a silver medal in the 1966 World Championships.

240 pounds, also was a mine worker… and a part-time wrestler.

His grandfather filled Bobby's head with stories of a mythical ancestor named Ash who wrestled in an African tribe named the Nuba. His grandfather also taught the young Douglas how to wrestle, and how to exercise in order to make himself strong and tough. They were lessons for a lifetime.

"There is kind of a cosmic connection between wrestling and life," Douglas is quoted as saying by writer David W. Zang. "You wrestle out of the womb, you struggle when you're dying. Every day is somewhat of a wrestling match, in one way or another." *(14)*

Attending Bridgeport High School, Douglas found his escape. The school enjoyed tremendous athletic success. Among its famous graduates are John Havlicek, a member of the Boston Celtics who wound up in the basketball hall of fame, and former major league baseball stars Joe and Phil Nierko.

Though small, Douglas was an all-state football player "who displayed blazing speed at tailback and 140 pounds of sheer dynamite as a hitter in the secondary," wrote David Blomquist in a local paper.

Douglas hit so hard on the football field that he was knocked out himself in several games. "He would try and break you in half," said one former player. "He was a hitter who never backed down from a helmet-to-helmet collision."

Douglas led his team to an 8-1-1 record his senior year, drawing rave reviews from Blomquist: "On the season, the 5-6 stick of dynamite would rush for over 1,000 yards and intercept six passes from his safety position,

— Bobby Douglas —

earning all-conference and all-state honors along the way."

His senior year, Bobby also captured the Ohio state high school wrestling title in the 112-pound class, becoming the first black state champion in Ohio history.

Douglas selected West Liberty State, a small college located in West Virginia, as the place where he would continue his education, both on and off the athletic field. He played football for two seasons, but his true love was wrestling.

In 1962, he won the national NAIA title at 130 pounds. He took second the next year, thereby qualifying for the NCAA championships at Kent State. There, he lost a close match in the finals to Oklahoma's two-time NCAA champion, senior Mickey Martin. But he caught the eye of Myron Roderick, head coach at Oklahoma State, and soon after transferred to the Stillwater campus with the long tradition of championships on the mat. There was no redshirt rule in the 1960s and he was forced to skip an entire season for transferring schools.

In his senior year, 1965, Douglas was cruising along undefeated and ranked No. 1 in the nation. He captured the Big Eight championship at 147 pounds with an easy win over Veryl Long of Iowa State, and was a huge favorite to win his first NCAA title, in the tournament at Laramie, Wyoming.

But while wrestling Dan Divito of Southern Illinois-Carbondale in an early round, Douglas slammed his head hard onto the floor off the mat and was knocked out. He was revived and managed to win the match but suffered a concussion and had to withdraw from the tournament. Iowa State's Long wound up as the nation's 147-pound NCAA champion, with Douglas sitting on the sidelines.

It was doubly painful for Bobby; not only was he denied his NCAA title but his lost points undoubtedly cost Oklahoma State a national team championship, as well. Iowa State won the tournament, its first ever, by a one-point margin, 87-86, over the Cowboys.

Turning to post-college wrestling, Douglas captured five freestyle championships and won a Greco-Roman title, as well. In 1964, he made the United States Olympic team and placed fourth in the Tokyo Olympics at 138.5 pounds. He posted a record of 4-1, losing only to the bronze medal winner from Russia.

He won a silver medal at the 1966 World Championships at 138.5 and was considered a top candidate for a gold medal in the 1968 Olympics. His teammates thought so much of him that he was voted captain of the team. But he was hit by a variety of distractions – ranging from an infant son who got deathly sick and was fighting for his life, to a possible boycott of the Games by black Americans, to an intense case of food poisoning. Then, Douglas suffered two injuries in his opening match with Iran, and was forced to withdraw. It was a devastating blow to the Ohio native who many thought was on track to a gold or silver medal.

"The loss of Bobby Douglas was a real tragedy," said Tommy Evans, freestyle coach. "He was our captain, our leader, hardest worker, most respected man, a heck of a fine gentleman and a real help to me."

Moving up to 149.5, Douglas was fourth in the 1969 World Championships and earned a bronze medal at the same weight in 1970. The following year, after he and Dan Gable fought neck and neck in grueling bouts to make the 1971 World team at 149.5 pounds, Douglas retired in the midst of the camp. Gable took the spot and breezed to a gold medal in Sofia, Bulgaria, giving much of the credit to Douglas for making him so tough and determined. Douglas had once handed Gable an 11-1 loss at the 1968 Olympic trials, when Gable was just 19 years old and Douglas was a seasoned veteran of 25, and it was a lesson the Iowan never forgot.

"Bobby had a ton of natural ability," said Doug Blubaugh, 1960 Olympic champion and a veteran coach of international teams. "He was very physical and very strong, with great quick-

Bobby Douglas made a smooth transition from competitor to coach and climbed to the top of his profession. His Arizona State Sun Devils won the NCAA team title in 1988. He was also head coach of the Iowa State Cyclones from 1992 through 2006.
(Photo courtesy of Iowa State University)

ness. He was one of this country's best wrestlers for nearly a decade."

Entering coaching, Douglas blazed an impressive trail. After several assistant jobs at top programs, he was head coach for one year at the University of California at Santa Barbara. Then, in 1974, he became head coach at Arizona State. In 1988, he reached a tremendous milestone when he led the Sun Devils to the NCAA team title, making them the first team west of the Rocky Mountains to ever win the nationals. ASU scored 93 points, leaving the Big Three in its wake Iowa with 85.5, Iowa State with 83.75 and Oklahoma State with 80.5.

The next two years, the Sun Devils placed second in the NCAA tournament.

During Douglas's 18 years at Arizona State, his teams won nearly 75 percent of their dual matches (225-77-6). For his efforts, Douglas was named national coach of the year in 1988 and conference coach of the year nine times. His ASU record included nine conference team titles, and ten finishes in the NCAA's top ten.

In 1992, Douglas was named to head one of the finest college programs in the United States, taking over the top spot at Iowa State University.

Along the way, Douglas has broken many a racial barrier in wrestling. He was the first

Legends of the Mat – 77

Bobby Douglas

African-American Ohio high school state champion; he was the first African-American to wrestle in the Olympic Games, and he was the first African-American to win a national team title as a wrestling coach. In 1987, he became the first African-American to be voted into the National Wrestling Hall of Fame.

Douglas is also one of the most successful and active freestyle coaches in the nation. He was head coach of the 1992 U.S. Olympic freestyle wrestling team that competed in Barcelona, Spain. The U.S. claimed six individual medals, led by gold medallists John Smith, Kevin Jackson and Bruce Baumgartner.

He has served as head coach of three United States teams at the World Championships. He led the 1989 and 1991 U.S. teams to second-place finishes at the World Championships behind the Soviet Union. In 1989, the U.S. had six medallists, including two champions: Smith and Kenny Monday. In 1991, the U.S. won six medals, including three champions: Zeke Jones, Smith and Jackson. In 2003, his U.S. team finished in second place at the World Championships in Madison Square Garden.

Douglas was a member of the coaching staff of the 1988, 1996 and 2004 U.S. Olympic teams. He coached the 1989 U.S. World Cup team as well as the 1991 Pan-American Games team. He has been an assistant coach on numerous other U.S. international teams.

For many years, he was a coach with the Sunkist Kids, one of the most successful wrestling clubs in the United States. He has helped coach numerous U.S. athletes to World and Olympic medals as part of the Sunkist Kids program.

In 2002, the Cyclones finished second in the NCAA and Douglas faced incredible pressures along the way. The team's star was Cael Sanderson, perhaps the greatest college wrestler of all time. As Cael was approaching his final 159-0 record, the pressures on Douglas intensified to an almost unbearable point. The media and the fans were relentless in their pursuit of Sanderson stories and memorabilia, and nearly every other coach was watching and analyzing his every move.

"No one will ever really know what went on behind the scenes," said Douglas as he sat at Dan Gable's table in Cedar Rapids, Iowa, on April 15, 2002, waiting for President George W. Bush to walk on stage twenty feet in front and address a crowd of 1,000 GOP faithful. "The pressure was unbelievable. I have never been so tired in my life. Just bone tired."

Yet the next night, Douglas seemed full of energy as he hosted the wrestling banquet in Ames. Before a full house, he and Cael Sanderson and other Cyclones talked about what wrestling has meant to their lives. And he received a standing ovation when he was named National Coach of the Year by Wrestling International Magazine (WIN).

On March 29, 2006, his long and illustrious coaching career came to an end when he stepped aside at Iowa State after 14 years and a 198-75-3 record. Taking his place as head coach of the Cyclones was his most famous pupil, Cael Sanderson.

The honors continue to pile up for this son of Bridgeport, Ohio. He has been inducted into five halls of fame and has authored five books. He has been involved with nearly every Olympic Games since 1964. Besides being a world-class athlete and coach, he is a recognized author, clinician and historian.

He stands uniquely alone as a man who not only proves that wrestling is a cultural icon worth praising, he is proof in the flesh that wrestling is far more than a sport in which men test one another's skills and resolve.

Sanderson once called him "the Bruce Lee of wrestling, especially takedowns, a master without peers." But nothing about Bobby Douglas should surprise anyone who knows him. From incredibly humble beginnings, he has become an all-around leader in Mankind's Oldest Sport. His mother, grandfather and a man

— Bobby Douglas —

named Ash would be very proud to see all that he has accomplished in the world of wrestling. He has helped to make it a brotherhood and stands tall as one of its greatest legends.

"Wrestling is my best friend," he said in his 2005 book, *The Last Takedown*. Bobby Douglas has also been a very good friend of wrestling!

Highlights – Bobby Douglas won six national titles after college, including five in freestyle and one in Greco-Roman. He placed second in the World Championships in 1966, third in 1970 and fourth in 1969. He made the 1964 and 1968 Olympic teams, placing fourth in 1964. In college, Douglas won the NAIA national title as a sophomore in 1962 at West Liberty State College and was NCAA runner-up in 1963. His overall record from college through the World Championships was 303-17-7.

Rick Sanders
A Maverick Who Excelled

Rick Sanders put Portland State on the wrestling map with his amazing career. He was also one of the most exciting wrestlers to ever step on the mat.

Just about everyone who ever saw Rick Sanders wrestle has a story to tell about him. Some of the stories are about his extraordinary talent and skills, others are about his off-the-wall lifestyle and his free spirit. But just about everyone who saw him admits the same thing: Rick Sanders was one of the greatest American wrestlers to ever step on a mat.

He was raised in Portland, Oregon, just like Robin Reed nearly four decades earlier. Sanders won three states titles in high school and fashioned a record of 80-1 along the way. In 1964, the summer after his final year of high school, he gave notice to the wrestling community that he would be someone special. He battled his way through the Olympic trials in the freestyle division, losing in the 114.5-pound finals to Gray Simons. He was invited to the final training camp in New York to work out with the finest freestyle wrestlers in the nation.

He enrolled that fall at Portland State College in his hometown and quickly established himself as one of the greatest collegiate wrestlers of all time, winning national titles on three different collegiate levels. He captured the NAIA national championship at 115 pounds in 1965 and was named O.W. A year later, Portland State moved to Division II of the NCAA and he finished third in those nationals at 123 pounds in 1966. Two weeks later, he exploded onto the national scene in Ames, Iowa.

At the Division I tournament, he dropped down to 115 pounds and roared through the weight class. He ran over two early-round foes, and then pinned the defending NCAA champion, Tadaaki Hatta of Oklahoma State, in the semifinals. In the championship match, he whipped the No. 2 seed, Ernie Gillum of Iowa State, 9-2.

The following season, he scored a rare double, winning the Division I and Division II crowns, both at 115 pounds. He was also named the outstanding wrestler of both divisions, and appeared a shoo-in to win his third straight NCAA Division I

Legends of the Mat – 80

In one of the classic matchups in American history, Rick Sanders (left) edges Don Behm to make the 1972 Olympic team at 125.5 pounds. Both were silver medallists in the Olympic Games. *(Photo by John Hoke, courtesy of Amateur Wrestling News)*

title the following year. At the 1968 tournament held at Penn State University, he breezed into the finals at 123 pounds, facing Dwayne Keller, a sophomore from Oklahoma State. Sanders scored the opening takedown but wound up losing, 4-2. Sanders and the huge crowd were stunned.

Losing in the finals at 115 pounds that same year was Sergio Gonzalez of UCLA. The two wrestlers were destined to become close friends and be teammates on the 1972 Olympic team.

"I was really down in the dumps after the NCAA finals and remember walking by Rick's room at the hotel where we were staying," said Gonzalez in 2006. "I heard laughter from inside the room and looked in. Rick was sitting on the bed having a beer and there were lots of other people in there, all having a good time. I remember thinking that he sure wasn't taking it very hard, losing his last match in college.

"Later, I heard from Rick that he hurt his neck in the match and lost all his strength in his arm. But he never used that as an excuse, it's just something that came out when we were talking a couple of years later."

Rick Sanders

Sanders finished his collegiate career with 103 wins and just two losses, one of the best records ever compiled. In addition, he compiled a dual meet record of 63-0, with 46 pins. His combined record for high school and college was an astounding 183-3.

But he was already thinking more about freestyle than folkstyle. Most observers felt he was better at freestyle and he had gone a long way to prove them correct. As a freshman in college in 1965, he won his first national freestyle title (125.5) and made the World Team (114.5), but failed to place.

After college, however, Sanders really hit his stride. Employing a wide-open, aggressive and unorthodox style, he became one of the most talked-about wrestlers to ever compete in America. He would crouch low and nearly glide across the mat in pursuit of a foe; when someone shot in for a single leg, he would hop around on one leg showing no concern at all, trying for heel picks or anything else that came to mind. Once when a Soviet Union wrestler shot in for a powerful double leg takedown and lifted Sanders onto his shoulder, looking for a place to deposit him, Sanders calmly crawled down the Soviet's back, grabbed his ankle and eventually wound up with the takedown, confusing his adversary and delighting the partisan crowd.

His trademark was his ability to shock everyone, from coaches to foes to the fans, with unorthodox training and unorthodox moves on the mat. He loved to find himself in a predicament and then work his way out of it.

"Surprise delighted Sanders," wrote David W. Zang. "He learned not to just squirm out of trouble, but to turn it into stunning reversals of fortune. He concocted imaginative, unprovable theories. Don Behm, later one of Sanders's fiercest rivals but closest friends, remembers in particular Sanders' "contraction and expansion theory," a belief that his hips worked in tandem through a countervailing tendency to shrink and enlarge." *(15)*

Sanders won a bronze medal in the World Championships in 1966 at 114.5, and moved up to a silver medal in 1967, the highest placing for the American team. In 1969, competing in Mar del Plata, Argentina, he became the first American wrestler to ever win a gold medal in the World Championships. Competing at 114.5 pounds, he pinned his first four foes and scored a 7-4 triumph over Mohammad Ghrbani of Iran in the finals. Fred Fozzard, also of Oregon, earned the second gold medal later in the same tournament, at 180.5.

He also made two Olympic teams, winning silver medals in both 1968 and 1972. He posted records of 5-1 in Mexico City (1968) and 6-1 in Munich (1972), losing close matches to a Japanese wrestler both times. Of his combined eleven Olympic wins, nine of them came by fall. He won a gold medal at the Pan-American Games of 1967.

Through all his success, Sanders was considered a maverick of the first order… an athlete who always seemed on or near the edge. He wore his hair long before it was fashionable, and sported a beard. He liked to pose for photos with beads around his neck. Stories of his escapades are legendary. He was accused of smoking marijuana, hitchhiking naked down an interstate highway, having sex in rubber sweat suits and various other stunts. He once boarded a 747 jet and proceeded to run up and down the aisle in his sweat clothes, trying to cut weight.

But there was also another side to Sanders. He loved to talk wrestling and often gave free clinics for youth, anywhere he could find them assembled. Wrestling was his life. It was, his older sister explained once, "in his soul." He recognized that he was marching to the beat of a different drummer than the rest, and reveled in it.

"Sure, our lifestyles are different, and so are our wrestling styles," he said about comparisons between himself and Dan Gable at the

Rick Sanders

Munich Olympics. "Most Americans don't have style. Me, I'm a cosmopolite. I can wrestle like a Japanese, a Rumanian, or a Russian. I used to work hard all the time. But as you get older, you don't work as hard." *(16)*

"He was a very entertaining and talented wrestler, maybe the best pure wrestler that America has ever had," said Doug Blubaugh, 1960 Olympic champion and a man who coached Sanders several times in major tournaments. "But his attitude and work ethic wouldn't allow him to reach his full potential."

"As a wrestler, his greatest asset was his flexibility," said Bill Farrell, who coached him at the World Championships in 1969 and at the Munich Olympics. "He could do crotch lifts, step-overs, low singles, everything. He had great natural ability.

"You didn't really coach Sanders, you just tried not to hurt him. With most great wrestlers you don't change their styles or anything like that, you just try not to get in their way. Everybody liked Rick, but he was hard to control. You had to watch him all the time. He was a terrific guy, wrestling was his whole life."

Farrell also felt that Sanders was a team player and very unselfish in his approach to the sport. In 1970, he and Behm engaged in a legendary tryout to make the World team at 125.5 pounds. Just the year before, Sanders had won the World at 114.5 and Behm had placed second at 125.5.

"Sanders won the 125.5-pound spot in a very tough wrestle-off with Behm," said Farrell. "But Rick was convinced the team would be better with him at 114.5 and Don at 125.5, so he gave up the 125.5-pound spot and tried extremely hard to make 114.5. He couldn't and had to forfeit his spot on the team."

Gonzalez remembers Sanders as a fair-minded individual who was willing to hand out praise whenever he felt it was earned. The two wrestlers had battled tooth and nail in the finals of the 1968 Olympic trials. Early on, Gonzalez scored a takedown that took Sanders to his back. Gonzalez wound up losing 7-5 but he felt he had scored a pin earlier on. He then lost the second match and Sanders was on the Olympic team, while Gonzalez was on his way back to California.

"Before I left camp, I ran into Rick," said Gonzalez. "He shook my hand and said, 'You know, if that was an international match I could have been called for being pinned.' I was really impressed that he would say that."

Sanders' last great claim to fame came in Munich, in the 1972 Olympics. Wrestling at 125.5 pounds, he scored three relatively easy victories, but then lost 4-2 to Japan's Hideaki Yanagida. He won his last three matches to close out 6-1 and claim a silver medal. In the final medal match, Sanders was leading Hungary's Laszlo Klinga 16-5 when he pinned him.

Afterwards, Sanders approached Gable, who had won the gold medal at 149.5 without surrendering a single point. He told Gable that he was going to come to Iowa and train with him to learn how to beat the Japanese. But he never made it.

Sanders had trouble with the Japanese and their quickness. He could handle the Soviets with little problem, but Japanese wrestlers were troublesome. On the other hand, Gable had pinned the great Japanese wrestler, Kikuo Wada, in the 1971 World tournament and shut him out 6-0 in the Olympics.

"Right after the medal ceremonies, he came up to me and said, 'Well, Gable, I guess I'm going to have to start doing what you do,'" said Dan in 2005. "I said, 'Good, great. The Petersons (Ben and John) and I are going on a run tomorrow morning. Go with us.'

"Sanders was surprised that we were going running the day after the wrestling had ended, but he said, 'Okay, come get me at my room in the morning.'"

When Gable and the two Petersons showed up at Sanders' room bright and early, they had to pound on the door to get him up. A sleepy Sanders peered out at them and said, "I'll start first thing tomorrow."

"That's the last time I ever saw him," said Gable.

Gonzalez, who was on the Olympic team at 105.5, also saw Sanders that day. The two had become very close friends. They worked out together often, Sanders always trying creative moves and then stopping to explain to Sergio what he was doing.

"We had both talked about hitchhiking around Europe after the Games, but we were going separate ways," said Sergio. "I knocked on his door and he opened it, naked as could be. We talked for a couple of minutes then hugged goodbye, saying we'd hook up back in the States."

Sergio paused in the re-telling of the story, then sighed.

"Walking away, I had this strange feeling... a premonition that I would never see Rick again."

The next day, Sanders and a friend, Helen Antionette Torre, a student at San Francisco State College, left Munich to go site seeing. They were hitchhiking through Yugoslavia on their way to Greece when tragedy struck. They caught a ride with a local man. The car he was driving collided head-on with a bus, and all three were killed instantly. The accident occurred about six miles north of Skolpje, in southern Yugoslavia. The date was October 20, 1972. Rick Sanders was 27 years old.

Ron and Donna Pineda went to the train station with Sanders and Torre and saw them off. Torre was the fiancé of Buck Deadrich, the 220-pounder on the Greco-Roman team and Sanders and Deadrich were best friends. They were all going to meet up in Greece later.

"I had known Rick for years," said Pineda in 2005. "We were probably the last Americans to see them. When the news got back that Rick had been killed, it was devastating."

Wrestlers and wrestling fans across the nation were struck hard by the news that the carefree Rick Sanders was gone.

"I liked him and respected him a lot," said Gable, "even though our styles of training were about as different as they could be. He was fun to be around and brought a lot of excitement to the sport."

After his death, writer Leo Davis expressed his viewpoint in the Portland newspaper: "Much of the non-wrestling world misunderstood Rick Sanders and never knew what it missed. A pity.

"He was a sensitive man, not unaware of his image. But to his everlasting credit, Rick refused to back away from principal." He said that Sanders wore a beard mainly because he hated to shave, and carved beads to keep his hands busy so he wouldn't smoke.

"He was a peaceful warrior," said Gonzalez. "He was a free spirit who lived life to the fullest. He lived in the now. He was living life now, for today. He promoted peace wherever he went, promoting harmony with his fellow man. We both wore our hair long at the time, like Deadrich and several others did, living a bit outside the box. But Rick was always approachable by young athletes; he liked being a mentor and talking about wrestling whenever he got the chance.

"People still ask me if Rick was really so wild and crazy. I say, he wasn't that crazy. He did what a lot of others were doing but he didn't try to hide it. He just wanted to let other wrestlers know they could be different, outside the norm in some ways – and still be respectable and a good athlete.

"He was a guy who had a deep passion for the sport, just like Dave Schultz had."

"The death of Rick Sanders leaves me with an empty feeling," wrote Don Behm. "Everything Rick had came through wrestling and the sport of wrestling cannot replace him."

Inducted into the National Wrestling Hall of Fame in 1987, his bio there reads thusly:

Rick Sanders

"His career was like a meteor – a streak of brilliance and then, tragically, he was gone. But for a dozen years, Rick Sanders was the golden boy of wrestling, our first World champion, and one who would leave an indelible mark on our sport. He is one we will never forget."

Highlights – Rick Sanders was 103-2 in college and won five national collegiate titles on three levels. He also won five national freestyle titles. He was on two Olympic teams, earning silver medals both times. He was on four World teams and won a gold, silver and bronze medal. He also won a gold medal in the 1967 Pan-American Games. His overall record is unknown.

Rick Sanders (fourth from left, front row) talks to Sergio Gonzalez (second from left) at the conclusion of the 1972 Olympic Games in Munich. Rick was to die a few days later. Also in the photo are (front row from left) Don Behm, alternate at 125.5; Gonzalez, 105.5; Jimmy Carr, 114.5; Sanders, silver medallist at 125.5; Gene Davis, 136.5; Dan Gable, gold medallist at 149.5; Wayne Wells, gold medallist at 163; (back row from left) head coach Bill Farrell; unidentified; John Peterson, silver medallist at 180.5; Ben Peterson, gold medallist at 198; Henk Schenk, 220; Chris Taylor bronze medallist at heavyweight; assistant coach, Jim Peckham, and assistant coach Bill Weick.

Wayne Baughman
Owner of 16 National Titles

When Wayne Baughman began wrestling as a sophomore at John Marshall High School in Oklahoma City, Oklahoma, the prospects of a legendary career in the sport looked bleak. There was no way of predicting that one of the most distinguished careers in amateur wrestling was on the horizon.

The year was 1956 and Baughman had just been kicked off the basketball team for fighting. The basketball coach told him that if he wanted to fight he should go out for wrestling. Wayne agreed, but the head wrestling coach, Virgil Milliron, didn't want trouble on his team.

Baughman was finally allowed to join the wrestling team on the condition that he wouldn't cause any trouble. Milliron told Baughman he didn't think he would last long in the wrestling room, and after the first several weeks of practice Baughman wanted to quit. But the desire to prove his new coach wrong motivated him to keep going.

Although his first year on the team wasn't successful in terms of record, Coach Milliron developed in Baughman an attitude toward wrestling that he carried with him throughout his entire wrestling career. It became the cornerstone of Baughman's philosophy toward the sport.

Wayne Baughman has distinguished himself as one of the leading figures in U.S. wrestling annals. After winning sixteen national titles as a competitor, he became a top international and collegiate coach.
(Photo courtesy of Wayne Baughman)

"I was taught that you should go out to pin your opponent or defeat him as soundly as possible but to never humiliate or unnecessarily intimidate your opponent – to respect your opponent and not do anything to embarrass him," said Baughman. "I learned that respect could be earned even in defeat or lost in victory if one did not demonstrate respect for his opponent.

"We had a philosophy in both competition and in the workout room. Coach Milliron told us that that attitude would make us better, and our opponent better, too. Confidence, pride, respect – anything less than that – than a total commitment – is not fair to either oneself or his opponent. It's a lesson I have never forgotten."

After placing third his senior year at the state tourna-

Wayne Baughman sends a foe flying through the air during the 1966 Interservice Wrestling Championships. Baughman won titles on every level available, including collegiate, freestyle, Greco-Roman and sombo. *(Photo courtesy of Wayne Baughman)*

ment, Baughman weighed his options for the future. He was offered partial scholarships to Oklahoma State and to the University of Oklahoma, and chose the latter for two simple reasons: Head coach Port Robertson and assistant coach Tommy Evans.

The University of Oklahoma was near Wayne's hometown, and the tough and aggressive style that Robertson and Evans brought to the wrestling room was a much better fit for him than Myron Roderick's skilled and technical approach at Oklahoma State.

NCAA rules at the time prohibited freshmen from competing so Baughman had to hone and develop his skills in the Sooner practice room. A key component to Baughman's success in wrestling was having good workout partners who could push him in practice. During his first year at Oklahoma, Baughman took his share of punishment from the best wrestlers in the country every day in the Sooner wrestling room.

A short list of training partners he faced that

Wayne Baughman

year in practice includes Dale Lewis, NCAA champion at heavyweight, George Goodner, NCAA champion at 191 pounds, Dave Campbell, NCAA runner-up at 177 pounds, and Sid Terry, NCAA runner-up at 157 pounds. For the young freshman, it was the training environment he needed to become a champion.

"I think the workout room is critical," said Baughman. "I got more experience in one year than most guys get in two or three. How hard your workout partners push you is what helps individuals win championships. You can certainly hone and fine-tune it in competition but you'll never get the amount of competition or competitive mat time from real competition that you can get in the practice room. It's the old cliché; you're going to wrestle like you practice every day in the room.

"If you put some guys that have some talent in a room with a Tom or Terry Brands and people like that, you're either going to get tough and get tougher or you're going to die, quit, and then leave. Oklahoma and Iowa State in my era was similar to Iowa under Gable."

The beatings Baughman took as a freshman prepared him for the years ahead. As a sophomore, Baughman made the Sooner wrestling team at 167 pounds, but he had to cut a tremendous amount of weight to do so. During his first semester on varsity, Baughman won all his matches on a west coast swing but paid the price physically in the process.

Over the Christmas holiday Baughman got as heavy as 195 pounds. He was nearly six foot two inches tall and still lean at 195, so he decided that his days of sucking weight were over. It was time to quit the team and walk away from wrestling undefeated. However, head coach Port Robertson had different ideas.

Robertson told him to get down to 177 pounds and try out there. The problem was that Dave Campbell, the 177-pound NCAA runner-up, was standing in his way. In their two-match series, Baughman proved to be the better man though, winning both matches handily.

At the NCAA championships in 1961, it was Baughman who entered the tournament as the Oklahoma's representative at 177 pounds. Baughman was seeded third; he won his first three matches and gained the finals, where he lost 9-5 to Oklahoma State's Bob Johnson. It was a remarkable accomplishment for a 20-year-old college student who had just taken third at the state tournament just two years before.

As a junior, he moved up to 191 pounds and won the NCAA tournament as the number two seed over Oklahoma State's fourth seeded Joe James. Based on appearance alone, James was quite possibly the most physically-imposing wrestler to ever step on a college wrestling mat. His impressive physique has become part of college wrestling lore. James won an NCAA title of his own at heavyweight two years later, in 1964.

Baughman's 2-1 win over James gave him his first national title, and allowed him to close out the 1962 season with a record of 18-3.

However, it was the disappointing finish to his senior year that would be the turning point in Baughman's career. Entering the 1963 NCAA tournament undefeated and seeded first, the Sooner star cruised to the 191-pound finals without a close match.

Facing Jack Barden of Michigan for his second NCAA title, Baughman dropped a tough 4-2 decision, losing his last match as a collegian. Yet it was that one loss that sparked a decade-long career in wrestling the likes of which very few wrestlers have ever matched.

Disappointed with how his college career had ended, Baughman entered the 1963 National AAU tournament in both Greco-Roman and freestyle as a way of redeeming himself. Inexperienced in the international style of wrestling, Baughman took first place in the Greco-Roman division (defeating 1960 Olympian Russ Camilleri on a weigh-in) and second in the freestyle competition.

From that point on, Baughman accomplished almost everything the sport has to offer. Over the course of the next ten years he made three Greco-Roman Olympic teams, eight World teams (including a rare freestyle/Greco-Roman double in 1965),

Wayne Baughman

and won 16 national titles. In 25 national tournaments, he never placed lower than third. He is also the only person who has won national championships in the four recognized wrestling styles (collegiate, freestyle, Greco-Roman, and sombo).

He won a gold medal in freestyle at the 1967 Pan-American Games, and placed fifth in Greco-Roman at the Olympics in Mexico City in 1968. But he was just one move away from winning an Olympic silver medal. While wrestling the defending champion from the Soviet Union, Baughman led late in the match, 3-0. The match was close to being over; eight and one half minutes had expired with only 30 seconds left to go. Baughman was almost home free, but was pinned for the first time since high school.

"I was ahead and I lost respect for my opponent," said Baughman. "He had quit, I really felt that. And that's why I lost respect. Then I relaxed on the side of the mat when he threw a sloppy move. Instead of stepping off that mat, which was acceptable under those rules, I stayed in there and fought the move. It was a mental breakdown that cost me.

"Losing respect for an opponent, relaxing on the mat edge toward the end of a period, not using the rules in one's favor – the little things we often underestimate – are the areas which frequently make a big difference."

The 1972 Olympic Games in Munich was the last wrestling competition Baughman participated in and he failed to win a medal. But in 1973, he added yet another feat to his already impressive resume. Trying his hand at sombo (a jacket form of wrestling similar to judo, made popular in the old Soviet Union), Baughman made the U.S. team that year and placed fifth at the World Championships. This gave Baughman the distinction of being one of only two U.S. wrestlers to have placed in a World or Olympic Championship in the three international styles of freestyle, Greco-Roman and sombo (Greg Gibson being the other).

Years later, Baughman attributed much of his success to what he called "negative reinforcement."

"I think most people who excel, particularly in wrestling, are often reacting to a negative personality trait," he said. "In my own particular case, I had a lot of resentment, honestly. I didn't particularly like myself or anyone else. I wanted to get an education to prove to all the people at my high school that I wasn't the bum that they thought I was. That was my major motivation."

Not only did Baughman excel at wrestling and nearly everything else he tried, but he became a superb role model for others and, eventually, a coach of tremendous impact. Five-time world medalist Larry Kristoff calls him one of the classiest guys he's ever met and wrestling icon Dan Gable calls Baughman "one tough dude".

"He probably doesn't know how much I watched him," said Gable. "Because of where I was at in my career, I was looking for wrestlers with a similar mindset. When I was at some of these camps where Baughman was involved, one way or the other I was scouting him out because he was somebody I was drawn to.

"I just think of a guy who strapped a pistol on his side and walked to the top of the highest mountain in Colorado. I'll never forget back in '68 at a training camp, for some reason he had a pistol strapped to his side and he hiked up that mountain. That was one of the workouts we had to do one day and he went through that workout pretty easy."

John Peterson, a gold medallist at the 1976 Olympics, calls Baughman a man of great integrity. Peterson speaks with near reverence about the time Baughman stood up to the AAU when the "committee" questioned how well John and his brother Ben would do at the Olympics in 1972. (Ben and John eventually won a gold and silver medal respectively).

Baughman has also shown incredible resolve outside of wrestling. His list of undertakings in other sports is mind-boggling. He's twice finished the Leadville Trail 100, a gruelling, 100-mile foot race at an average elevation of over 10,000 feet. His meager training schedule consisted of the same 4.7-mile route six times a week (an average of under 30 miles a week) while most runners were

Wayne Baughman

putting in 100-mile weeks with a 30-mile long run. Weighing 195 pounds, he was the heaviest competitor to finish the race at the time.

The former wrestler also completed several triathlons (including the Hawaii Ironman), finished the Pikes Peak marathon, and hiked all 54 of the 14,000-foot peaks in Colorado. He entered a winner-take-all Toughman contest in Pueblo, Colorado, for a chance at $1,000 and he thought it might be interesting to give rodeo a try (both bull and bareback). His other athletic endeavors include short stints in swimming, fencing, handball, volleyball, rowing, canoeing, shooting, luge, badminton, racquetball, tennis, golf, and a slew of other sports.

Despite all of his accomplishments in wrestling, it is the praise of his peers that speaks loudest for Baughman

"There's tough wrestling specific and then there is just tough," said J Robinson, an Olympian and NCAA championship coach at Minnesota. "When your life spills over into other things you do, I think it gives you a different kind of toughness because you're not just one dimensional in wrestling. Baughman is just tough. He just is. He's a warrior. That's the way I would sum him up.

"If I was a Roman soldier fighting in a line, I would want Wayne Baughman right next to me on my right hand side. He'd be there for the duration hacking and slashing his way through. That's the kind of guy you want. He's dependable, he's loyal, and he's a great person.

"I think Baughman sums it all up. He was a great motivator, he was a great competitor and he had durability which most people don't. He won some ungodly number of national titles. He was on multiple World and Olympic teams and he was an Olympic coach.

"He epitomized a guy that stayed in the sport and does everything there is to do. When you look at his durability and what he did it's pretty amazing.

"I think he would tell you he wasn't the greatest technician or the greatest actual wrestler but he was tough, he was physically and mentally tough. One of the attributes of wrestling is you can go a long way if you have those two attributes, which Wayne does."

One of the great stories that both Robinson and Baughman like to tell is when they were at the International Military Games in Turkey in 1972. Robinson had reached the finals and was wrestling a Turk with a Turkish referee. In that match, Robinson was involved in what Baughman considers one of the worst "hose-jobs" he's ever seen.

The match ended with Robinson losing after several "questionable" calls, numerous fake injury timeouts by the Turk, and some clock management at the scorer's table. When the Turk was awarded the victory, Baughman protested the match and got into a shoving match with the official, which led to a personal escort out of the stadium with an automatic weapon placed in his stomach.

When Robinson showed his displeasure with the decision, both Baughman and Robinson were met with a volley of bottles and other projectiles being launched in their direction. To Robinson, it was a moment that defined who Wayne Baughman was as a person.

"I mean he was always there," said Robinson. "Wayne Baughman – and there aren't a lot of people you can say this about – if you needed someone to stand behind you, I would have no doubt Wayne Baughman would be standing behind me the whole time, giving me everything he could give. I don't think there is any bigger compliment you could give a person, is to always know that he would be there for you."

In 1973, the former three-time Olympian was there to help other wrestlers pursue success at international competitions. From 1973 through 1975, Baughman was the head coach for the United States at the freestyle World Championships and in 1976 he was appointed the head coach of the freestyle Olympic team. The ten member freestyle wrestling team turned in a solid performance under Baughman's guidance at the Montreal Olympics. The final medal count for the Americans was three silvers, two bronzes, and one gold.

Wayne Baughman

Baughman served his first term as head wrestling coach at the Air Force Academy from 1975 through 1984 while on active duty in the Air Force. In 1988 he came back as a civilian and coached through the 2006 season. On July 31, 2006, Baughman officially retired as the Falcons' head wrestling coach, ending his 27-year career with 17 winning seasons and a 183-134-5 dual meet record.

The 2006 NCAA wrestling tournament marked the 50-year anniversary of Wayne Baughman's start in wrestling. Appropriately, the NCAA tournament was held in Oklahoma City, the same city where he began his wrestling career as a sophomore at John Marshall High School in 1956. It was a fitting ending to a legendary career.

Highlights – Wayne Baughman was a three-time All-American at the University of Oklahoma and won the NCAA title in 1962. His college record was 53-7. He won a total of 16 national titles, including five in freestyle, nine in Greco-Roman and one in sombo and the NCAA. He was a member of three Olympic and eight World teams. His overall record is unknown.

Dan Gable
Obsession and Domination

Dan Gable won 181 consecutive matches during his high school and college career and won the 1972 Olympics without surrendering a single point in six matches.

In 1972, when Gary Kurdelmeier publicly announced that Dan Gable would become his assistant coach at the University of Iowa, he made a startling behind-the-scenes statement to close friends.

"When his career is over, Dan Gable will be better known for his coaching than for his wrestling," said Kurdelmeier.

Hardly anyone believed Kurdelmeier. After all, Gable was just coming off the most sensational wrestling career in American history. After winning 181 consecutive matches over seven years in high school and college, he had suffered a loss in the finals of the NCAA tournament as a senior.

But he had rebounded with a vengeance. He won the World Championships in 1971 in Sofia, Bulgaria, without a close match. Then he won the Olympic gold medal at 149.5 pounds in Munich without surrendering a single point in six matches, despite an injured left knee and a gashed eyebrow that required seven stitches. At age 23, he was an absolute legend as a wrestler. How, people asked, could he possibly do more as a coach than as an athlete?

The years may have proven Kurdelmeier correct. As amazing as was Gable's career on the mat, his accomplishments as a coach are even more incredible. When he retired from coaching after leading his Iowa Hawkeyes to the 1997 NCAA championship, here's what the record book had to say about Dan Gable, the coach:

- 15 NCAA team titles in 21 seasons;
- 21 Big Ten titles in 21 seasons;
- An overall coaching mark of 355-21-5;
- A Big Ten coaching record of 131-2-1;
- A Carver-Hawkeye Arena record of 98-1;
- A total of 106 Big Ten champions, more than the rest of the league combined;
- A total of 152 All-Americans;
- A total of 45 NCAA individual championships;
- Nine former wrestlers on Olympic teams, including four gold medals.

Gable's march toward immortality began in Waterloo, Iowa, a town of 80,000 known for being the hometown of the largest John Deere tractor plant in the world, and for being a breeding ground for tough wrestlers. Long before Gable arrived on the scene,

Wearing a bandage around his head after suffering a split eyebrow, Gable overpowered six straight foes in the Munich Olympics.

Waterloo was cranking out top-flight wrestlers and champions, including Lowell Lange, who won three NCAA titles for tiny Cornell College in the 1947-50 era.

He was born on October 25, 1948, to Mack and Katie Gable. He was interested in all sports at an early age; he was a YMCA state champion in swimming, the quarterback on his junior high football team and a skilled baseball player. But moving into high school, he decided to devote all his time and energies toward one sport, wrestling.

With legendary coach Bob Siddens serving as his mentor, he posted a 64-0 record during his three-year career at West Waterloo High School, winning state titles at 95 pounds, 103 pounds and 112 pounds. The Gable legend kicked into high gear when he entered the 1966 Midlands Tournament in Evanston, Illinois, as a pure freshman at Iowa State University.

Back then, the Midlands was considered to be the toughest mat meet in America, because it allowed the best collegians and post-graduates, too. No one expected Gable to place very high in the tournament. But he made it to the semifinals, and then defeated Michigan State senior Don Behm, already a NCAA runnerup, 9-5. In the finals, he faced former NCAA champion Massaki Hatta, a two-time Midlands champion and a seasoned veteran.

Gable won the match 8-2, and was named the Outstanding Wrestler. All of a sudden, the Gable name was known in wrestling circles all over the nation.

He went 15-0 as a pure freshman but freshmen weren't eligible for the NCAAs in 1967. Gable was on a tear by the time his sophomore season started. Dave McGuire of Oklahoma was the defending NCAA champion at 130, and Gable beat him twice, by scores of 8-2 and 4-1, the latter in the 1968 NCAA finals. Earlier, he defeated another NCAA champion, Dale Anderson of Michigan State, in the finals of the Midlands at 137, in an overtime match.

His junior season was phenomenal. He posted a 31-0 record, including 29 pins. He won his second NCAA title, pinning all five foes. He was named the 1969 NCAA tournament's outstanding wrestler and *Sports Illustrated* printed a long article on him, dubbing him "Super Wrestler." Others called him The Machine and he entered his senior season with the tag "unbeatable" attached.

Continuing his pinning ways into his senior season, Gable recorded a total of 24 consecutive pins, breaking Dan Hodge's record of 22 in a row. Lehigh's Herb Campbell managed to survive in a 23-3 battering, and Gable rattled off eight more pins in a row, giving him 33 pins in 34 matches. Near the end of the season, he surprised wrestling fans by going up a weight (from 142 pounds to 150) to challenge defending NCAA champion Mike Grant on his home turf, in Oklahoma, defeating him 9-4.

Gable pinned his first five foes at the 1970 NCAA meet, giving him a total of 60 pins in 65 matches as a junior and senior, and 13 pins in 16 NCAA matches. But on the other side of the bracket was a surprising and audacious sophomore from the University of Washington. Larry Owings had announced to the press that he was coming to Evanston to defeat Dan Gable and he, too, had five pins heading into the finals.

The tension was thick as sold-out McGaw Hall witnessed history on March 28. With television cameras from ABC and scores of reporters from all over the nation on hand, Owings took a quick 7-2 lead on the Iowa State superstar. Gable fought back for a thin 9-8 edge, but Owings took him down in a great flurry and even gained crucial back points. Owings wound up with a shocking 13-11 victory – the biggest upset in wrestling history.

Gable received a long and emotional standing ovation as he stood on the second-place platform for the first time in his seven-year wrestling career. Shortly after, he re-dedicated himself, training harder than ever before. At the famous Tbilisi Tournament in Russia, he made one Soviet star quit in pure exhaustion and was voted the meet's outstanding wrestler. He won the World gold medal in 1971, scoring two lop-sided decisions and four pins.

His victories over Soviet Union wrestlers demoralized them to the point that the Soviet coaches declared their No. 1 goal in 1972 was to find a wrestler who could beat Gable in Munich.

Entering the Olympic regional trials in Iowa City, Gable outscored his six foes 121-0 before pinning all six. At the final trials in Anoka, Minnesota, he won six more matches, giving up a single point to Owings in a 7-1 victory. In his final effort to make the Olympic team, Gable defeated Lloyd Keaser 22-0 and 11-0. Just one year later, Keaser won the World championship.

Despite an injured left knee, Gable was the overwhelming favorite to win the gold medal at 149.5 pounds in Munich. In the opening round, however, a head butt by the Yugoslavia wrestler, Safer Sali, split his eyebrow and blood poured down his face. Facing an injury disqualification, coaches Bill Farrell and Bill Weick worked feverishly to stop the flow of blood. They finally wrapped his head and sent him back out. He then pined Sali.

Dean Rockwell, coach of the 1964 Olympic Greco-Roman team, was on hand for the match and it left a lasting impression on him.

"Most people don't realize what was going on back then," said Rockwell many years later. "I think they were trying to injure Dan and get him out of the Olympics. But they simply couldn't stop him. Nothing was going to deter him at that point, not even a bad injury like that. He had a great heart."

When it was all over, Gable had won six matches without surrendering a single point. His teammates, defying Olympic protocol, picked him up and carried him off the mat.

His trail to the Olympic gold medal had been incredible. In his last twenty-one matches, against the finest wrestlers in the United States and the

Dan Gable shows the same intensity as a coach that he did as a wrestler. Gable led his Hawkeyes to twenty-one straight Big Ten titles and fifteen NCAA titles during his twenty-one years as head coach. *(Photo courtesy of University of Iowa)*

World, he had surrendered just one point!

Returning to a hero's welcome in America, Gable was invited to appear on several national TV shows, and accepted the offer from Kurdelmeier to coach at the University of Iowa. Dr. Harold Nichols, the head coach at Iowa State University, tried desperately at the last moment to create a spot for Gable on the ISU staff, but it was too late.

Iowa City quickly became a Mecca for wrestlers. They began pouring in from all around the nation, and from foreign countries, to be around Gable. Day after day, the Hawkeye wrestling room would find a new visitor or two from somewhere.

Even his old foes from the Soviet Union were amazed by Gable, according to a very popular Soviet training book, *Wrestling Is A Man's Game*.

"Gable astounded us with his inexhaustible energy and at the same time with his perfect technique. We were used to recognizing a great master by his filigree technique, precision and expediency of action. Gable refuted all these notions. Out on the mat he cascaded on an opponent, a mass of pushes and pulls. Beginning one element, he would drop it unfinished and launch another one, then a third and so on... then a tirednesss would envelop his opponent as if a shroud. That's when Gable would get up steam. Without giving his opponent a minute's respite, he would wear him out and finally win." *(17)*

Gable was a driven athlete – to the point of obsession, say those how knew him best. He was already highly-motivated when his older sister, Diane, was brutally murdered in 1964, after Dan's sophomore year in high school. Rather than allow his parents to sell the house to escape the trauma, he moved into his sister's room. He began training with a fanatical edge, often working out late at night, and two or three times a day. He pushed training companions to the breaking point, then left them gasping in exhaustion as he searched for a fresh partner. His workouts became legendary in sports circles across the nation, transcending the sport itself.

"I think courage has many faces," wrote famous sportscaster Frank Gifford in his book *Courage*. "Dan Gable's single-minded assault on a dream set as a teenager is, to me, heroic. To dedicate one's mind, body and heart to an almost unreachable goal every day of every year from adolescence through high school, college and two years further requires an extraordinary intensity of purpose and discipline." *(18)*

It was a combination of the Gable work ethic, dedication and determination that astounded people.

"Anyone who has never been on the mat with Dan just doesn't know what he was like," said

Dan Gable

Jim Duschen, a very powerful 220-pounder who was captain of the Iowa State team when Gable was a sophomore and made the 1973 World team. "You could not tire him out. I saw him go through three or four men in a workout, good wrestlers, and simply just wear them to a frazzle.

"He was extremely tough at Iowa State. He would work out with guys like Dave Martin (NCAA champion at 158), Chuck Jean (two-time NCAA champion at 177) and Jason Smith (two-time NCAA champion at 167) and dominate them. He would beat up on All-Americans several weights above him day after day.

"He was in a class by himself, both mentally and physically. He could probably get himself up mentally better than anyone ever has. It's the same ability that he passed on to his Iowa teams for about twenty-five years."

Both Peterson brothers were gold medallists at higher weight classes (Ben at 198 pounds in 1972 and John at 180.5 pounds in 1976) and candidly admit they could not defeat the much lighter Gable.

"I wrestled him probably about three hundred times in practice, and I think I might have gone even with him once," said John with a smile.

For years as coach, Gable was the terror of the Iowa workout room, able to defeat any Hawkeye champion, regardless of weight or age.

"I've wrestled a total of 27 world or Olympic medal winners in my life, and beaten 24 of them," said Randy Lewis, 1984 Olympic champion. "I've always thought I had a chance to beat anyone who was close to my weight... except Gable. I knew every time I wrestled him that I could never beat him, at any stage of our careers. Nothing I tried worked on him. He is tremendously strong and actually gets stronger as the match goes on. And he is never out of position. He is the best there ever was, in my estimation."

Rockwell, who passed away in 2005 at age 93, was an encyclopedia of knowledge who had attended eleven Olympics and many world championships. He felt Gable was the best American wrestler of all time.

"He hit a peak in 1972 that I've never seen, before or since," said Rockwell. "I think he's the best wrestler America has ever produced."

Retiring from competition at the age of 23, Gable became perhaps the most successful coach in any sport in NCAA history. In 21 seasons at the University of Iowa, he won 15 NCAA team titles, 21 Big Ten team titles, and posted a dual meet record of 355 wins, 21 loses and five ties. His record against other Big Ten teams was 131 wins and just two losses, with one tie! In 14 seasons at Carver-Hawkeye Arena, his record was an astounding 98-1.

His wrestlers won a total of 45 individual NCAA titles and were All-Americans 152 times. Incredibly, he led his wrestlers to 106 individual Big Ten titles – more than the other ten teams combined! He sent nine of his athletes to the Olympic Games and six earned medals, including four gold medals.

Gable's single-minded approach to the sport attracted attention in circles far outside wrestling. No other person has brought so much attention to the sport. Four books have been written about him, and several video documentaries have chronicled his rise to fame. In 1999, he was voted the No. 1 athlete in Iowa history by *Sports Illustrated*, ahead of legendary Hall of Fame baseball star Bob Feller and Heisman Trophy-winning football legend Nile Kinnick.

Tom Cruise, the top movie star of the 1990s, said Gable was a hero when Cruise was wrestling in high school in New Jersey. Actors like Tom Selleck and Kirk Douglas have praised him, and best-selling author John Irving is one of his most devoted fans. Former wrestling coach Dennis Hastert, Speaker of the House in the United States Congress, is also a big fan.

His accomplishments even caught the eye of President George W. Bush, who in 2002 named Gable to the President's Council on Physical Fitness. In the fall of 2003, he was invited by Donald Rumsfeld, Secretary of Defense and a former wrestler, to speak to military leaders at the Pentagon.

— Dan Gable —

Through it all, Gable has lived a modest but very comfortable existence. He and his wife, Kathy, raised four daughters on their acreage north of Iowa City. For years, Gable traveled the nation, extolling the virtues of the sport that made him famous. And then, the wrestling world was shocked by the announcement that he was returning to coaching. In the spring of 2006, Tom Brands was named Iowa head coach and he asked Gable to be one of his assistants. Gable agreed to do so, hoping to serve as a mentor to one of his most famous pupils.

At the same time, it was announced that the International Wrestling Institute and Museum in Newton, Iowa, was moving to Gable's hometown of Waterloo and would be renamed the Dan Gable International Wrestling Institute and Museum. For a man who has dedicated nearly his entire life to the sport, it was a fitting tribute.

"Wrestling is important to America," Dan Gable is fond of saying, "because it teaches the very same values– hard work, dedication, goal-setting, determination – that made America great."

They are also the same values that made Dan Gable a legend for all time.

Highlights – Dan Gable was 64-0 in high school, and 118-1 at Iowa State University for a combined record of 182-1 in high school and college. He had a 29-1-1 record in international competition. He holds the NCAA record of 24 consecutive pins. Gable was 31-0 at the Midlands, with six straight titles and was named O.W. five times. He won two NCAA titles and three national freestyle titles. He was a Pan-American Games champion, Tbilisi champion, World champion and Olympic champion. His overall record from high school through his last match was 305-7-2.

Chris Taylor
The Gentle Giant

At 445 pounds, Chris Taylor was the largest athlete to ever compete in the NCAA tournament. He was undefeated his two years at Iowa State University.

It was in March of 1972 that the largest wrestler ever to appear at the NCAA tournament made his auspicious debut. Iowa State University's Chris Taylor, weighing in at 445 pounds, won five matches and the first of his two titles at the University of Maryland. During his two-year career at Iowa State, Taylor became one of the most-talked about wrestlers of all time and drew huge crowds wherever the Cyclones appeared. But by 2006, the man who was called "The Gentle Giant" was largely forgotten by all but the most dedicated fans.

He came into the world in Dowagiac, Michigan, on June 13, 1950, the first of three children born to Vera and James Taylor. He weighed just seven pounds and four ounces, hardly what one would expect from a fellow who would become known as a giant. But then he began to grow. At age five he weighed 75 pounds and he had a heart that was double the size of an average child his age. Playing on the freshman football team, he checked in at between 250 and 300 pounds. By his senior year, he stood six foot five and weighed over 380 pounds.

As a high school student, few knew about him outside his hometown area, despite his immense size. He wrestled very little as a sophomore but won the state heavyweight title as a junior while weighing 360 pounds. His senior year he lost in the finals in overtime to Ben Lewis, a tough wrestler he had defeated 6-5 in the state meet the year before. Taylor finished his final season with a 33-1 record.

He entered Muskegon Community College in the fall of 1969 and weighed close to 400 pounds that season. He captured the junior college national title at the end of the season. In the final match, he edged the defending national champion, Harry Geris of Joliet Junior College, 3-2. Taylor compiled a record of 31-3 in all matches that season.

College recruiters and fans began to take notice when he appeared in the Midlands tourney in 1968 and 1969, finishing fourth both times. "How did the Giant do?" was heard constantly around the arena as people began to be fascinated by his size and appearance.

Chris Taylor

Oklahoma State, Arizona, Arizona State and the University of Oklahoma all were very interested in him. So was Iowa State University, which had won its first NCAA team title in 1965 and was making a name for itself with head coach Dr. Harold Nichols and assistant Les Anderson leading the way.

But the key to Taylor's choice may have been former two-time 177-pound NCAA champion Tom Peckham, who was still working out in the Cyclone room, and freshman heavyweight Ed Huffman. Taylor had seen the 205-pound Peckham win the Midlands at heavyweight in 1969, when Chris placed fourth. And Huffman had given Chris a tough match in that same tournament before losing to him. Taylor knew that finding suitable workout partners would be the key to his advancement in college, and ISU had three of the best possible in Peckham, Huffman and powerful Jim Duschen, a two-time Big Eight champion at 191 pounds who was still training in Ames for the 1972 Olympics.

Taylor made a big splash in his first few weeks on the ISU campus. The Des Moines Register, Iowa's largest newspaper, ran a story about him being weighed on a livestock scale at the meat lab because no other scale on campus could handle him. He tipped the scales at 416 pounds, and told a reporter that it was bit more than he wanted to weigh while competing.

The tough workouts in the Cyclone room with Peckham, Duschen and Huffman were just what Taylor needed to take a giant step forward. After Nichols had a special uniform and robe made to fit him, he was ready to be unleashed on the nation's collegiate wrestling fans.

"I wrestled him every night for two years," recalled Huffman a decade later. "We became inseparable. I got up over 300 pounds, too. I'll tell you this – Chris was great but I never saw him beat Peckham in the room. Not once. That Peckham was one tough guy, the toughest man I've ever known."

Those workouts are what took Taylor to the next level. He was 39-0-1 his first season, with 26 pins. His only blemish came when Bill Struve of Oklahoma, some 200 pounds lighter, wrestled him to a 1-1 tie in a dual meet. In the 1972 NCAA tournament, Taylor scored two pins and three decisions. His toughest match came in a 2-0 win over Mike McCready of Northern Iowa in the third round. He then defeated old rival Harry Geris, now of Oklahoma State, 6-2, and posted a 6-1 decision over defending NCAA champion Greg Wojciechowski of Toledo in the finals. The Cyclones ran away with the team title by a 103-72.5 margin over runner-up Michigan State.

Between his junior and senior years at Iowa State, Taylor made the 1972 Olympic team in both freestyle and Greco-Roman. As the largest Olympian ever, he became a media sensation and a fan attraction of the first rank at home and abroad. He was such a hit in Munich that he had to sneak out of the Olympic Village at night to do any sightseeing.

Dan Gable, who won a gold medal at 149.5 pounds in Munich, recalled one moment during the Olympics when spectators in a Munich tavern spotted Taylor and swarmed him.

"They just wouldn't let him leave," said Gable. "Everyone had to have a picture taken with him, or an autograph. Even the other athletes wouldn't leave him alone. People just tried to get around him. It was amazing to watch. I think he was the most popular athlete in the entire Olympic Village."

Taylor drew nine-time World champion Alexander Medved in the first round of the freestyle competition, and lost a highly-disputed 3-2 decision. While most observers felt Medved back-pedaled the entire match and should have been called for passivity, he was clever enough to score a back-trip takedown in the closing minute for the margin of victory. The official who called the match was criticized in many quarters for not calling the Soviet for passivity and was even barred from working any other matches during the Games.

However, Taylor rallied with four straight matches after that setback and came away with a bronze medal.

He also competed in Greco-Roman competition at the Olympics, and one result is the most famous photo in wrestling history. He was gripped

Jim Waschek of Iowa was six foot, three inches tall but looked much smaller when facing the Gentle Giant.

Chris Taylor

around the waist and thrown in a belly-to-belly suplay by West Germany's Wilfred Dietrich, who is sporting a wide grin in the photo. The spectacular (and gutsy) move wound up with Taylor being pinned. A former world champion in both freestyle wrestling and judo, Dietrich was 1960 Olympic champion, as well. Ironically, Chris had met Dietrich in the freestyle competition a few days earlier and defeated him by decision.

Several days before the wrestling event began, the West German walked up to Taylor in the Olympic village and began talking with him in a very animated style. At one point, he tried to bear hug Taylor. According to several witnesses, including Gable, they felt Dietrich was measuring Taylor's girth to see if he could get his arms around him and lock his hands in back.

Following the Olympics, Taylor returned to Ames for his senior year. The Gentle Giant, as he was known, was now one of the biggest attractions in wrestling history. He drew huge crowds wherever the Cyclones went for the 1972-73 season, and was a big hit around Ames, as well.

"Before he became famous, girls always treated him sort of badly," said Huffman. "He had warts around his neck and he was conscious of them. He tried to cover them up. I think he had a lot of emotions inside that he bottled up. He always felt like the underdog, because of his size.

"But as his fame grew, he could have had lots of dates, if he wanted them. But he and Lynne were pretty thick by then."

He had met Lynne Hart at Muskegon Community College, where she was a basketball player. She followed him to Ames and they became a steady pair during his first year there. They eventually married on September 8, 1973.

A Cyclone trip out East during Chris's senior season was a real eye-opener for his coach, concerning the fame of his super heavyweight.

"When we were in Washington D.C. I was impressed with how many people came up to him," said Nichols. "Everywhere we went, all the tourists were taking pictures of Chris. When we were in the Capitol Rotunda, a large crowd gathered around Chris and just stared at him. He was as big an attraction as the Capitol and the Lincoln Memorial."

Later that season, a sportswriter from Seattle, Washington, was equally impressed.

"When Chris Taylor competes at a regular dual meet nowadays it some times takes him 45 minutes to leave the arena," wrote the reporter in 1973. "It's the kids; they swarm around him, shoving pencils and paper toward his huge frame, touching, gawking."

Even Red Smith, the legendary veteran sports writer for the New York Times, a man who had covered such sporting icons as Jack Dempsey and Babe Ruth in his long career, was moved to write about the ISU phenomenon.

"Chris Taylor rivals Disneyland as an attraction," wrote Smith in his nationally-syndicated column, "and the Iowa State team breaks attendance records wherever it goes. Taylor is a king-size kewpie with red hair, blue eyes and a smile that is just plain sweet. He is an athlete, almost assuredly the best athlete of his size – or the biggest good athlete – in recorded history.

"Goliath stood nine feet six inches, about three feet taller than Chris, but his won-lost record was 0-1."

Taylor went 48-0 as a senior, scoring 44 pins along the way, still the NCAA record for most falls in a season. But he had a few close matches. Oregon State's Jim Hagen, a gusty 200-pounder, held Taylor to a 3-0 decision. The following week, with 8,000 fans in Hilton Coliseum, ISU's new arena, Taylor was almost pinned! Bill Kalbrenner, a tough 235-pound sophomore from the University of Oklahoma, took Taylor down to his back and nearly had a fall. Trailing 5-0, and with the fans going wild, Taylor fought back and scored a pin at the 2:29 mark.

The Gentle Giant closed out his collegiate career by pinning his way through the NCAA tournament in 1973, just the fourth wrestler to accomplish the feat since World War II. The big guy flattened five foes in an aggregate time of 13 minutes and 52 seconds. The 200-pound Hagen, who had gone the distance earlier in a dual meet, was the last man to face Taylor on a collegiate mat.

Taylor was tipping the scales at around 445

— Chris Taylor —

pounds by then. Huffman estimates he went over the 500-pound mark during the next couple of years, when he was wrestling as a professional.

During his two-year career with the Cyclones, Taylor posted a record of 87-0-1. His 70 falls in 88 matches translates into a stunning 80 percent pinning mark. Dan Hodge (1955-1957), University of Oklahoma) and Dan Gable (1968-70, Iowa State) are close behind with career pinning percentages of 73 percent, Hodge in a three-year career and Gable over four years, though freshman were restricted then in what they could enter.

The Gentle Giant also made a ton of fans around the country with his pleasing personality and his incredible patience with autograph seekers. It was common for Taylor to stay around for an hour after meets to talk with fans and sign items for them.

"He was so big, outstanding, noticeable and personable to everyone," said Nichols. "He loved kids and they would stand in line waiting to get his autograph for as long as it took. During the meets, people would stay to the every end just to see him wrestle. It didn't even matter which team was ahead, they just wanted to see Chris.

"He was a wonderful ambassador for Iowa State University and the entire sport of wrestling."

At the end of his college career, the Big Eight Conference selected him Athlete of the Year for 1973. Taylor made big news the following spring when he declared he would go out for football at Iowa State. He had played throughout high school and enjoyed the sport. Chris reported for ISU's practice on the opening day but two days later the dream died when the football staff simply could not find equipment big enough to accommodate him.

How large was Taylor at the time he was wrestling in the NCAA tournament in 1973?

"When his car went down the road it actually tilted," Gable said. "His hands were so huge, it was like shaking hands with a pillow."

When measured for his Olympic clothing in 1972, Chris wore a size 58 long jacket and a size 15EEE shoe. Other measurements included a 22-inch neck, 52-inch waist and a 60-inch chest.

Some more facts about Chris Taylor:

- He was the largest athlete ever to compete in the Big Eight Conference;
- He was the largest athlete ever to compete in the Division I NCAA tournament;
- He is the largest athlete ever to compete in the Olympic Games;
- He was heavier than five Olga Korbuts, the pixyish Soviet Union gymnast who was a sensation in the 1972 Olympics and weighed 87 pounds;
- He weighed as much as three Dan Gables when Gable won the gold medal at 149.5 pounds in 1972;
- He was twice as heavy as Muhammad Ali, former world heavyweight boxing champion, at his peak;
- At 450 pounds, he was more than 150 pounds larger than the average lineman in the NFL today.

While Taylor was the biggest man to ever wrestle in the NCAA tournament, there were several almost as large. Tab Thacker won the NCAA title for North Carolina State in 1984 and Mitch Shelton placed third for Oklahoma State in 1983. Both were at the 400-pound mark.

Jimmy Jackson won three straight NCAA titles for Oklahoma State, in the years 1976-78. He weighed around 330 pounds when he was competing as a Cowboy.

Today, Taylor, Thacker, Shelton, and Jackson would not be able to compete in the NCAA tournament, or any NCAA dual meet, for that matter. In 1986, the NCAA set a limit on weight at 275 pounds, largely for safety reasons.

Nearly thirty years after his last amateur match, it's interesting to contemplate his position among the all-time great heavyweights. Interestingly, he never could defeat the taller, much trimmer big men from the Soviet Union. He was 0-7 against three Soviet heavyweights during his career.

Among Americans, both Bruce Baumgartner and Larry Kristoff would certainly be rated ahead of him on the international level, but he may have been the top college heavyweight ever. It is hard to imagine any college heavyweight – with the possi-

Chris Taylor

ble exceptions of Carlton Haselrig, three-time NCAA champion from Pitt-Johnstown, Lou Banach, two-time NCAA champion from Iowa, and Steven Neal, two-time NCAA champion from Cal-Bakersfield – having much chance against him. Haselrig weighed around 245 and was such a good athlete that he played several years in the NFL. Banach weighed in the 215-pound range but defeated much larger foes, while Neal weighed around 260 and won a World title before becoming an NFL regular.

One of the best evaluations comes from Jim Duschen, an extremely powerful wrestler who competed successfully at both 191 and heavyweight and has seen almost every top heavyweight of the past 35 years.

"He was as strong as anyone I've ever known," said Duschen. "Once he pressed 135 pounds overhead a couple of times with one hand. It was very hard to use strength against him because he just shut your strength down whenever he wanted.

"Chris seemed to hold back a lot in practice and in some matches, maybe because he was concerned about hurting someone. But when he went all out he was almost unstoppable. There have been a few other massive heavyweights, a few guys who weighed around 400 pounds. But the thing that set Chris apart was that he could really move on his feet."

"He used his hips well, for both movement and good position, and that's one of the major keys to wrestling," said Gable. "He was also light on his feet, which was amazing, considering his weight. Once, on a trip to the Soviet Union, everyone else was warming up and Chris was just standing there, with all the Soviets watching him. All of a sudden, he did a front somersault – and the place went up for grabs. They just kept cheering him."

There is also another factor to be considered.

"Most people were afraid of him, and that was a big advantage," said Gable.

Chris wrestled as a professional for several years after college, working out of the AWA stable of former college and pro star Verne Gagne in Minneapolis. But he never really caught on, due in part to his fear of hurting smaller men, and the demanding travel. It was a grueling schedule of one-night stands and long car rides through the night and he gave it up after just a few years.

"He had great fan appeal but I think the actual ring work and the travel was a lot tougher than he thought it was going to be," said Gagne many years later. "Chris was really a very nice guy and the pro wrestling world can be pretty tough on nice guys."

Taylor was living in the tiny town of Story City – just a few miles from Ames, where he had earned such great fame a few short years earlier – and making a few public appearances when his great body gave out. He died on June 30, 1979, from complications arising from his weight and phlebitis. Chris was just seven days past his 29th birthday.

"I noticed his body was starting to sag some at the end," said Gable. "He had probably put his body through a total life at the age of 29."

Today, he is seldom mentioned in discussions of the greatest wrestlers of all time, even though he had a superb two-year career at the Division I level. But he is certainly remembered as the largest wrestler in collegiate history, and as an athlete who drew a tremendous amount of attention to the sport in his brief career. For those who saw him and knew him in the early 1970s, he left an unforgettable impression and will always be remembered as "The Gentle Giant."

Highlights – Chris Taylor was junior college national champion and runnerup at Muskegon Community College, with a 56-4 record. He was two-time NCAA champion at Iowa State University with a record of 87-0-1, for a combined college record of 143-5-1. He won a bronze medal in freestyle at the 1972 Olympics with a 4-1 record but was 0-2 in Greco-Roman. He did not compete in any freestyle national tournaments, but won three Midlands titles. His overall record is estimated at 172-9-1.

John and Ben Peterson
In the Footsteps of Jacob

Ben Peterson, never a state champion in high school, won two NCAA titles for Iowa State University. He also was a three-time Olympian.

When the 1972 Olympic freestyle trials concluded in Anoka, Minnesota, there were more than a few wrestling experts who were shocked by the results at 180.5 pounds and 198 pounds. In fact, these experts were ready to concede that America had little, if any, chance to even place in the top six at those two weights at the 1972 Olympics in Munich, let alone win a medal.

All wrestling fans the world over were just as shocked as the action unfolded in Munich. The entrants in those two classes, John and Ben Peterson, began scoring points in bunches, and winning matches consistently. When the wrestling was finished in Munich and the mats were cleared once and for all, the brothers had fashioned a combined record of eleven wins and just one defeat, with one tie! John stepped onto the awards platform to accept the silver medal at 180.5 pounds, and Ben stood on the platform hours later to accept the gold medal at 198 pounds!

The Munich story was just the start of a long and successful international career by the two men who are as well known in wrestling circles for their commitment to the Bible and to Jesus Christ as they are for any accomplishments on the mat.

For while John and Ben have been among the nation's finest wrestlers for years, they have traveled the globe spreading the Gospel in any way they could. They have taken risks that would make ordinary men shrink in fear, and have faced the wrath of Soviet officials. And yet, they have marched steadily forward, unbowed and unrelenting in their efforts to spread the word of God.

The Hebrew patriarch Jacob is known primarily in wrestling circles for wrestling the angel of the Lord as described in Genesis. But the Peterson boys are known primarily in wrestling circles for their Olympic achievements – and for their devotion to the Holy Bible.

The two boys grew up in a Christian home in tiny Comstock, Wisconsin. Their father was a dairy

John Peterson came from Stout State to become a two-time Olympian. He won a silver medal in 1972 and then captured a gold medal in 1976.

farmer, but when the farm blew down one night, he gave up that career and operated a feed mill the rest of his career. All members of the Peterson family fully understood the value of hard work, discipline and commitment and gave those characteristics the utmost respect; but they honored the Bible above all else.

Phil and Tom, the eldest of the brothers, played football in high school. Phil went into basketball but Tom, not wanting to follow his older brother into everything, decided to try wrestling. Their parents were concerned about the decision, fearing it was like the television variety. A few weeks into the season of his junior year, Phil switched to wrestling, and the sport of Jacob soon became prevalent in the Peterson home.

"Tom would come home and teach us moves all the time," recalled John with a smile. "We all wrestled at home on the floor, in every room but the living room, for years. That's how Ben and I got into the sport."

John and Ben had high hopes in high school, but both came up short of their ultimate goal, which was to become a state champion. John didn't even make it to the state tournament as a senior, while Ben placed second the next year.

"I had my heart set on being a state champion," said John. "I was devastated when I didn't even get to state."

The pivotal moment in their wrestling careers came when Ben, just a high school senior, was spotted at the 1968 Olympic trials by Dr. Harold Nichols, the long-time head coach at Iowa State University. Though Ben lost every match in the tournament, Nichols was impressed by the young wrestler's drive and determination. Ben fought hard every inch of the way, asking no quarter and giving none. Nichols offered him a partial scholarship to Iowa State, which was one of the top three programs in the nation at the time.

John was in his second year at Stout State College in Wisconsin when Ben arrived on the ISU campus in the fall of 1968. Ben was hit hard by culture shock. The Cyclones not only had a reputation for wrestling aggressively on the mat, but for playing hard off the mat, as well. Sitting in his dorm room late at night during his freshman year, Ben was often invited to partake in various forms of entertainment. He steadfastly refused. He was at college, he told those who asked, to get an education and to wrestle, not to party.

Freshmen were not eligible for varsity competition in Ben's freshman year, but he worked incredibly hard, often staying late after regular practice to learn all he could. Among the stars in the room were Dan Gable and Tom Peckham, two of the toughest men to ever step foot on a mat. Gable was in the midst of his long winning streak, and Peckham had graduated and was working in the area, and still found time to come into the room. A very physical and punishing wrestler, Peckham was a two-time NCAA champion at 177 pounds and was so rugged that he once won the

John and Ben Peterson

Midlands at heavyweight, with a young 420-pound Chris Taylor in the same class!

Two other imposing wrestlers in the room were Chuck Jean, who was to win the NCAA title that year at 177 pounds, and Jim Duschen, a former two-time Big Eight champion at 191 pounds. Despite his eagerness and determination, Ben often felt that he was out of place.

"They were all very physical wrestlers who kept excellent position," said Ben, reflecting back on the formative years. "They would just pound on you. I was too stubborn to give into them, but I wasn't sure I could ever get to that level. I certainly had no idea at that point that I would be as successful as I later became.

"Those were some workouts. Actually, it was just a matter of survival at that point."

Few believed he had what it took to be a success at the college level, but Nichols and assistant coach Les Anderson, who had been a two-time NCAA champion for the Cyclones a decade earlier, recognized the potential that was lurking beneath the surface.

"Ben was not a diamond in the rough," assistant coach Les Anderson said years later. "He was more like a piece of coal. But when polished, he turned into a fine diamond."

One of the keys to Ben's success in college was his devotion to weight training. He was determined to build himself into a top-flight wrestler and had learned from Phil the benefits of dedicated weight training. A three-year starter on the University of Wisconsin football team, Phil had been a devout weight trainer during the summers back home in Comstock, inviting John and Ben to join in the workouts.

Kim Wood, who served as the weight training coach for the Cincinnati Bengals of the NFL for over two decades, knew Phil well.

"We played together at the University of Wisconsin and I'll tell you, Phil was a very, very dedicated and tough athlete," said Wood. "We all had great respect for him. I think Phil Peterson passed a lot of that toughness and dedication on to his younger brothers."

Ben would need all of the Peterson grit to make the ISU team.

"Chuck Jean was at 177 pounds and I couldn't beat him going into my sophomore year," said Ben. "In fact, he whipped the tar out of me. I figured if I wanted to make the team I had to go up to 190 pounds. I became a relentless weightlifter for many years. I built myself into a 190-pounder in college, and then after college the freestyle weight class was 198 pounds, and I had to lift my way into that class, too."

Ben wrestled a few pick-up matches as a freshman, but was relatively unknown when the 1970 season began. He surprised a few people by making the team at 190 pounds. Then he surprised more fans by winning match after match. He won the Big Eight Championships and wound up fourth in the NCAAs. It was a very impressive beginning for the young Christian from Wisconsin. But at least one former Cyclone was not surprised.

"I was a senior when Ben arrived as a pure freshman," said Duschen, who was captain of the 1969 team and finished fifth in the NCAA tournament. "I was more mature physically than Ben was at that point, so I didn't have a lot of trouble with him in practice that year. But every time I came into the room, he was there and ready to go. He had a great attitude and a tremendous work ethic. I figured right there that he was going to be pretty darn good. Of course, I can't say I predicted he was going to be as great as he eventually became, but I knew he was going to do very well in college."

His junior season as a Cyclone, Ben showed dramatic improvement. He finished second in the tough Midlands tourney and defeated the defending NCAA champion, Geoff Baum of Oklahoma State, in a dual meet. He won his second Big Eight crown at 190 pounds, with Baum dropping to 177 pounds. Ben then won the NCAA championship as the Cyclones finished second as a team.

His senior season was even better. Serving as a captain, Ben took a leadership role with his quiet, unassuming manner. He stamped himself as one of the finest wrestlers in Cyclone history by winning

John Peterson shows the intensity that marked his career as he attempts to throw a foe during the 1976 Olympic Trials.
(Photo courtesy of John Peterson and Athletes in Action)

his third Big Eight title and his second NCAA crown. As a team, Iowa State finished first – with Carl Adams (158) and the Gentle Giant, Chris Taylor (heavyweight) winning titles, and four other Cyclones placing. Much of the credit for the team's success was given by head coach Dr. Harold Nichols to Ben's quiet but extremely effective style of leadership.

"I can remember that Chris Taylor didn't like to run, and when practice got under way, he announced he wasn't going to run any sprints," said Ben with a grin decades later. "I said to him, 'You're part of this team. The team is running, and you're going to run, too.'"

The Gentle Giant wound up running sprints with everyone else.

When his folkstyle career ended in the spring of 1972, Ben quickly turned his attention to freestyle, devoting to it the same intensity that had made him a huge success as a collegian. Ben made his mark quickly with a series of victories, but still lost 9-0 to former Oklahoma State star Bill Harlow in the USAW senior freestyle nationals in the spring of 1972. The loss made him work out all the harder and all the longer; he also had the perfect role model and the perfect workout partner to help him improve by leaps and bounds.

A year older than Ben, John placed fifth in the NAIA nationals in 1971. That summer, he was anticipating being drafted by the Army. He began practicing with Ben and Dan Gable. It was another key event in the lives of the Peterson brothers. Working with and against Gable, determined to keep pace with his phenomenal training methods, lifted them to new heights in a short amount of time.

"Ben got invited to train at the 1971 Pan-American Games camp," recalled John. "Doug Blubaugh was the coach, and Ben asked him if I could come along. Doug said, 'Sure; if he's as hard a worker as you are, he's welcome.'

"That was a big turning point in my career,"

John and Ben Peterson

said John. "That training camp showed me a whole different way of wrestling."

"Ben told me he wanted his brother in camp for a training partner," recalled Blubaugh. "I said if John was anything like Ben, he was more than welcome in the camp. Obviously, it turned out great for everyone involved. The Petersons are two of the hardest workers I've ever seen in wrestling."

Soon, John was putting in just as much time on the mat, and in running and lifting weights, as was Ben. And he began to improve by leaps and bounds.

With Gable preparing for the 1971 World Games trials, John began to ponder entering the tryouts, as well. But he was weighing around 175 pounds and didn't know if he could make the cut to 163. When Gable told him to forget 163 and wrestle at 180.5, John thought he was too light for the heavier class. But he decided to concentrate all his energies on technique training and power training, and not on cutting weight.

At the World pre-camp tournament, he failed to qualify in freestyle. Undaunted, he entered the Greco-Roman side of the competition.

"There were only two entries at 220 pounds," he chuckled years later. "I placed second, weighing about 183, and that allowed me to go to the final trials in freestyle. Back in those days, you could more easily switch from one style to another. And I wound up making the freestyle team.

"People called it a fluke, but I called it God's divine providence," said John, recalling his decision to enter the Greco competition at the last second.

He didn't place in the 1971 World Championships in Sofia, Bulgaria, but he gained invaluable experience, and confidence. He continued to train in Ames with Gable, Ben and anyone else who ventured into the workout room. By the time the Olympic trials began in 1972, John Peterson was a solid threat at 180.5. He won the final trials in impressive fashion, as did Ben at 198. Still, there was not much optimism in U.S. wrestling circles about the Peterson boys – until the wrestling began.

John won five matches and lost only to the Soviet Union's Levan Tediashvili, acknowledged as one of the greatest wrestlers in history. Ben drew with the Soviet Union's Gennadi Strakhov, but won his other five matches. When Ben and Strakhov finished in a tie for first place, the gold medal was awarded to the wrestler with the most pins – and the young man from Comstock, Wisconsin, won by a 3-2 margin. One of those pins was a real shocker; in his finals match, Ben pinned Roussi Petrov, the defending world champion from Bulgaria.

The Petersons had accomplished the unthinkable. They returned home with a gold and silver medal between them.

"I admit I didn't think at the outset that they would do as well as they did," said Bill Farrell, coach of the 1972 freestyle team, thirty years later. "They really came out of obscurity in the trials. But they were such incredibly hard workers. Of course, Gable had the biggest influence on them. They followed his work example and he also helped them improve skill wise. Gable turned them from 'good' wrestlers into 'very good' wrestlers.

"By the time they got to Munich, what they accomplished did not surprise me," Farrell added. "The only thing I could do for them at that point was to try to build their confidence. My biggest contribution was that, and strategy.

"They had great conditioning. They could go for twenty or thirty minutes at top speed. They improved so fast that it was unbelievable. They got better every day in the training camp; by the time they got to the Olympics, they were getting better every match!"

Farrell also gives credit to assistant coaches Bill Weick and Jim Peckham for their tremendous improvements, but added again: "Gable was really the key." That and their total preparation.

Building on the success of Munich, the Petersons continued to improve and to compete at the very highest level for nearly a decade. Ironically, it was another foray into the world of Greco-Roman that John feels was the key to his

Ben Peterson (front) works for an escape during the Midlands Championships at Northwestern. Ben won six Midlands titles to go along with his seven national freestyle championships. Ben's foe is Mark Johnson, former Michigan All-American and 1980 Olympian.

eventual gold medal success. In 1974, John passed up the World freestyle tryouts and went to the Greco-Roman camp instead.

"It was one of the best things I ever did," he confided. "Working out with Dan Chandler and others was great. I don't think I would have won the Olympics in 1976 without that upper-body experience. I don't think I would have beaten (Istvan) Kovacs of Hungary if I hadn't had the Greco experience, because he was a big thrower. I couldn't throw much, but at least I learned how to cope with throwers."

Like Ben, John was also a devout weight trainer. He lifted tremendously hard for the length of his freestyle career, building strength in the key positions that allowed him to compete successfully against the powerful Soviets.

John was sensational at the Olympic Games in Montreal in 1976, winning six straight matches. Along the way, he steam-rolled two World champions back to back: first he hammered the Soviet Union's 1974 World champion Viktor Novajilov 20-4 and then he beat 1975 World champion Adolph Seger of West Germany 14-4. His final victory, 13-5 over Mehmet Uzun of Turkey, gave him the gold medal.

Ben also won six matches and captured a silver medal to go with his gold medal from 1972.

John and Ben Peterson

Ben and John Peterson were featured in the popular card set "Sportscasters," showing them lifting weights together prior to the Munich Olympics. The 1977 card is a collectors item for fans of sports memorabilia.

Ironically, his only loss in seven matches was by a 11-6 score to Levan Tediashvili, the same Soviet wrestler who had denied John a gold medal four years earlier!

In 1980, Ben Peterson became one of just four American wrestlers to earn a spot on three Olympic teams, but was denied a shot at another medal when President Jimmy Carter boycotted the Moscow Games.

Ben also earned gold medals from the 1975 Pan-American Games and the 1980 World Cup, and earned medals in three World meets. John wound up his fabulous career with medals from two World championships, and gold medals from three World Cups in addition to his Olympic medals.

In analyzing the Petersons' remarkable careers, both Farrell and Gable quickly point to their work ethic – and to a force outside of wrestling.

"What made them so successful? They were extremely hard workers. But I feel it was their strong beliefs that set them apart; faith is a big part of it," said Gable. "They have such a strong basis for life, all revolving around their faith in God. They applied those same principles of strong belief and commitment to everything they did, including the sport of wrestling. It goes from one to the other."

With their competition days behind them, the Petersons devoted their time to spreading the word about their two passions – the Bible and wrestling. Their Camp of Champs is one of the most popular in the nation year after year, and campers learn as

John and Ben Peterson

much about the Christian faith and lifestyle as they do the sport of Jacob.

John has been employed by Athletes in Action since 1977 and travels the world spreading the teachings of Jesus Christ. He has visited the former Soviet Union at least thirty times, and becomes excited just talking about his ministry there.

"I can't imagine I'm still involved in wrestling after all these years," said John in 2004, "but it opens doors everywhere. There are places in Russia where wrestling is king – and it gives me the opportunity to talk about Jesus."

Ben taught and coached at Maranatha Bible College in Watertown, Wisconsin, for many years and continues coaching there today. He gave up teaching in 1998 to concentrate on public speaking and his camps.

Their impact on the sport of wrestling has been immense, both on and off the mat.

"I like to think one of the things Ben and I did for wrestling is show that you can stick around for a long time, if you train hard and take care of yourself," said John.

Between them they made five Olympic teams and eight World teams. For nearly three decades, they have exerted an extremely positive influence on the entire sport of wrestling, and on the lives of thousands of wrestlers around the world. That includes their former Olympic teammate, Dan Gable.

"I go to their camp every year, because it's good for me," Gable said on a radio talk show in 2002. "Some times I may get on the wrong track, or forget what is really important in life, and that's one of the reasons I like to get up to their camp, to get back on track myself."

The Petersons have indeed come a long, long way from the days of wrestling on the kitchen floor in their farmhouse in Comstock, Wisconsin, dreaming of state titles. Now their commitment to Jesus Christ, to wrestling and to the values that make a great wrestler serve as an inspiration to thousands of young wrestlers all around the world.

Highlights – Ben Peterson was a two-time NCAA champion and fourth place finisher at the NCAA tournament while at Iowa State, and won three Big Eight championships. His college record was 74-4. He won seven national freestyle titles and six Midlands titles. Ben was 1972 Olympic champion and 1976 Olympic silver medallist. He made the 1980 Olympic team to become a rare three-time Olympian. He also won the 1980 World Cup and the 1975 Pan-American Games and was second in the 1973 Worlds. His total record is unknown.

Highlights – John Peterson placed fifth in the NAIA nationals for Stout State, Wisconsin. He won a gold medal in the 1976 Olympics and a silver medal in 1972. He made four World teams, winning one silver medal and one bronze medal. He also won the World Cup three times. John captured three national freestyle titles, and won the Midlands five times. His total record is unknown.

Wade Schalles
Mr. Excitement

Wade Schalles helped make Clarion State a national power when he exploded on the scene in the 1970s. Schalles was one of the most dynamic pinners in the history of the sport. *(Photo courtesy of Clarion University)*

As a senior at Hollidaysburg Area High School, Wade Schalles battled his way to the finals of the 1969 Pennsylvania state championship at 154 pounds, where he found himself face to face with John Chatman, who already owned two state titles and was going for his third. In one of the most exciting matches in the history of the state tournament, Schalles battled back from a 4-0 deficit and scored a stunning pin. He won the Outstanding Wrestler award – the first of many over the next decade – and finished 23-0 for the season, with 21 pins!

Pennsylvania prep wrestling fans in attendance that night were treated to the birth of a legend. Over the next decade, Wade Schalles would show crowds from coast to coast and around the world how exciting the sport of wrestling could really be. By the time he was ready to hang up his headgear for the last time, in 1980, he would be called by *Sports Illustrated* "the most exciting wrestler ever" and would hold pinning records that are hard to believe.

Just three years after winning the state high school tournament, he exploded on the national scene in the same stunning fashion. He won the Division II national title at 150 pounds and then moved onto the 1972 NCAA Division I championships in College Park, Maryland. In the finals at 150 pounds, the lanky sophomore from Clarion State College pinned Michigan star Jarrett Hubbard and became the talk of the tournament.

The Golden Eagle star was the first sophomore voted Outstanding Wrestler at the Division I NCAA meet since Tommy Evans in 1952. The next season, he moved up to 158 pounds and won his second Division II title. At the Division I meet in Seattle, Washington, he pinned four of his five opponents en route to his second championship, beating Mike Jones of Oregon State in the finals.

He made big news during his senior year when Clarion traveled to face archrival Lock Haven State and he was pitted against Al Frickel, the all-time pin leader for Lock Haven.

"It was Clarion's greatest pinner against Lock Haven's greatest pinner," said Norm Palovcsik, a state champion himself and one of the nation's top wrestling historians. "The fans couldn't wait for the match. But before the meet even began, Wade marked an X on the spot where he said he

Known for his unorthodox moves, Wade Schalles was an expert at reaching back and hooking foes.
(Photo courtesy of Steve Brown)

would pin Frickel.

"And he pinned Frickel on that very spot, after putting him on his back and dragging him over to it. Bob Bubb (Clarion coach) was furious with Wade, but it helped create the Schalles legend."

So did another dual meet match up later that season. Wade was on track for a third NCAA title in 1974 when he was ruled ineligible due to a couple of matches he had wrestled as a freshman. It was a devastating setback to Schalles, Clarion State College and to thousands of wrestling fans across the nation. But he made an incredible statement in has last official college match, in a dual meet with Clarion's archrival, Bloomsburg State.

Schalles shocked nearly everyone by jumping up two weight classes to tackle Bloomsburg's top star, the powerful Floyd "Shorty" Hitchcock. In a wild flurry in the third period, before a packed house of screaming fans, Schalles took Hitchcock to his back and pinned him. Little more than a month later, Hitchcock not only won the NCAA Division I tittle at 177 pounds, he was voted the Outstanding Wrestler, as well. But many fans felt the nation's truly outstanding college wrestler was sitting in the stands, unfairly denied an opportunity to compete because of some ficklc rule.

Two words that became synonymous with the name Schalles were "pinning" and "excitement." Many wrestling buffs consider him the most exciting wrestler ever, and the most dangerous wrestler to ever step on a mat

"There are three men who epitomize Pennsylvania wrestling – Mike Caruso, Stan Dziedzic and Wade Schalles," said John Purnell, owner of Brute wrestling products and a longtime observer of the Pennsylvania wrestling scene. "Wade's style of wrestling and ability to pin no matter what the score was brought excitement to our state and the entire sport. He was captivating to watch. He is a true and enduring legend in the sport."

"Wade developed a gutsy, unorthodox, no-one-can-coach style that was fun to watch," said Palovcsik. "He was a showman, and the mat was his stage. His legend continued to grow because he could talk the talk and walk the walk."

But there was more to it, said Palovcsik.

Wade Schalles

"He also had the greatest hips you're ever going to find," he said. "In the down position, he could get away with no hand control, stand up and reach back, and then throw his opponent straight to his back. He was as close to a Rick Sanders as anyone you're ever going to see."

His Clarion State record was 156-5-2, with a stunning 106 pins – the most in Division I history. By the time he had wrapped up his collegiate career, he was recognized alongside Bill Koll, Dan Hodge and Dan Gable as one of the greatest pinners in college history.

Always eager to take on new challenges, Schalles tried his hand at various styles of wrestling and eventually won national titles in folkstyle, freestyle, sombo (Russian judo) and in judo. In 1975, he won the national sombo title at 180 pounds by defeating legendary judo star and fourth-degree black belt Hayward Nishioka via submission in a wild finals match.

Nishioka scored first with a dramatic body scissors and arm lock that had Wade in serious trouble. With the crowd shouting in excitement, Schalles reversed the situation and caught Nishioka in the same punishing move. Moments later, the judo star submitted!

He continued to rack up wrestling titles the length of the globe. Competing at the highly-regarded Tbilisi Tournament in Russia in 1976, he came away with the 163-pound title after pinning all six foes – including three former world champions!

"At Tbilisi, I hit them with my backyard junk," said Schalles many years later, with a big grin. "They had never seen wrestling like mine before. I think it was a shock to their systems."

In the 1976 Olympic trials, he was deadlocked in a fierce battle with long-time rival Stan Dziedzic for the 163-pound berth. In the ranking trials, Schalles emerged No. 1 ahead of Lee Kemp and Dziedzic. But in the final trials in Brockport, New York, Dziedzic beat Kemp two straight to earn the right to challenge Schalles for the spot.

Coach Jim Peckham was putting the team through grueling workouts and Schalles was paired up with warriors like Gable, the Petersons and Dave Schultz, still in high school.

"I was physically stronger than I had ever been, in the best shape of my life and mentally at the zenith of strength," said Schalles. "As a result, for my first match with Stan I never felt more confident, or ready. In the past it seemed, not always supported by fact, that the first three-minutes of any of our nine-minute matches were mine and the last three were his. What scoring took place in the middle usually decided the outcome."

While executing a takedown, Schalles drove his head into the mat. After an injury timeout and seeing double, Schalles knew he was in trouble: "As the match continued the gym began to spin and breathing became difficult. I sensed that if I bent over to protect my legs there was a real possibility that I would fall over. Something was definitely wrong but just the same I had to go on."

Finally with less than a minute remaining, and the score knotted at 3-3, he passed out and was disqualified for not moving. He woke up in a hospital. His dream of Olympic glory had ended and Dziedzic went to Montreal, earning a bronze medal.

Against American wrestlers who owned World titles at 163 pounds, Schalles owned an edge on all but Dziedzic. He was 2-0 against Dave Schultz and 3-0 against Lee Kemp. Against Dziedzic, who was World champion in 1977, he had a losing record.

"Stan knew how to wrestle him and keep control of the match," said Palovcsik. "That was the key when you were wrestling Wade, to try and slow him down."

"Stan had a style that was very difficult for me," admitted Schalles. "I liked to go out and shoot the works. He played more of a chess match. I didn't match up well with that kind of a style, I guess."

Despite the intense rivalry, Schalles admired his longtime foe, an admiration that grew with the passing of the years.

"Something I never told Stan, even to this day, I guess it's the competitor in me, or maybe it's what makes all great athletes great, is the fact I was his biggest fan. Just as I was many things he wasn't, he was many things I wasn't. I actually marveled at his consistency, focus and knowledge of the game.

"During those years, there was no one who

Wade Schalles

knew more wrestling than Stan or me. Others knew as much, but no one knew more. Tactics, technique, strategy, the approach to competition, we had it all. And he drove me crazy trying to find a crack in his armor," said Schalles.

"However in the end, we became the first two Pennsylvanians to ever be inducted into the National Wrestling Hall of Fame. Most likely, just as steel sharpens steel, we either carried, pushed, prodded or chased one another there."

Schalles was inducted in 1991, and Dziedzic in 1996.

His unorthodox, go-for-broke style of wrestling may have seemed a form of gambling to many, but Schalles actually had an extremely keen awareness of mat position that he carried with him at all times. He had an uncanny sense of not only where he was on a mat at any given time, but how to put his opponent into the danger zone at any second of any match.

Although he missed out on his dream of Olympic gold, in 1977 Schalles earned a gold medal at the highly-competitive World University Games in Sofia, Bulgaria, pinning every single foe he faced. By the time he bowed out of active competition in 1980, Schalles had become a true wrestling legend. He was listed in the Guinness Book of World Records for owning the American record for most wins (937) and most pins (659). His incredible record included wins over 10 World champions (six by pin) and 35 victories (15 by pin) over various U.S. national champions. Included among his victims were 16 Division I NCAA champions.

He retired from the mat in the early 1980s, but Schalles was far from finished with the sport. Earning advanced degrees from Arizona State and South Dakota State, he became head wrestling coach at Clemson University, as well as assistant professor and department chairman. He also coached at Old Dominion.

As one of the nation's leading officials, he worked many of the top dual meets around the nation and the NCAA tournament. He was in demand as one of the sport's most popular clinicians and as a public speaker for a wide variety of events from coast to coast.

He also authored two books, and produced a series of top videos. He became a columnist for W.I.N. magazine. He is a member of several halls of fame. He has been honored as athlete of the year, coach of the year and wrestling writer of the year. For eight years, between 1998 and 2005, Schalles was a top executive at AAU headquarters in Orlando, Florida, then left to start his own business. His Star Awards program breaks traditional boundaries by being the first wrestling program to offer belts for achievement, just like the martial arts have for centuries.

"It's interesting to note that all throughout my career losing never entered my mind but the thought of not winning, not feeling the thrill of achievement, that scared me more than anything and has always been one of life's great motivators," he said in 2006.

As the owner of numerous national titles, Schalles stands tall as one of the sport's biggest names of all time. But perhaps the highest tribute came from a story on him that appeared in *Sports Illustrated* magazine. In that issue, he was called "the most exciting wrestler to ever step on a wrestling mat."

It was a statement that means a great deal to Wade: "Wrestling is not just about winning, it's also about entertainment, and I always wanted to entertain the fans," he said. "Wrestling needs to entertain its fans, just like every other top sport, if it hopes to survive and grow in the years ahead."

Legions of wrestling fans would certainly agree that Wade Schalles could talk the talk, and he could walk the walk.

Highlights – Wade Schalles posted a 156-5-2 record at Clarion State College (now Clarion University), with 106 pins. He won a total of four national collegiate titles (two in Division II and two in Division I) and 937 matches and 659 pins during his long college and post-college career, both listed in the Guinness Book of World Records. He won two NCAA titles and a total of 15 national titles in all forms of wrestling. He also won gold medals at the famed Tbilisi Tournament and the World University Games.

Lee Kemp
As Good As It Gets

Lee Kemp won three NCAA titles for the University of Wisconsin, and three World titles for the United States of America.

Basketball's loss will forever be wrestling's gain when it comes to one Lee Roy Kemp. It was in eighth grade in Chardon, Ohio, when Kemp was cut from the junior high basketball program. Nursing his crushed feelings soon after the painful move, he wandered down a long hallway, and found himself peering into the wrestling room. He paused and took a long, hard look.

"They seemed to be having lots of fun, so I decided to give it a try," said Kemp, many years later.

It was a wonderful choice, both for Kemp and the entire sport of wrestling. In all of recorded American wrestling history, few athletes have been as successful as Kemp and he has realized tremendous success off the mat, as well. Handsome, articulate and soft-spoken, he has become a very successful businessman as owner of Lee Kemp Ford Motors in Forest Hills, Minnesota. He stands tall as one of the sport's finest ambassadors.

Despite the late start, Kemp learned quickly and soon discovered that he had the perfect blend of physical and mental tools necessary for the sport of wrestling. He won two state championships in high school and then showed his tremendous potential the summer after his senior year (1974) by winning the prestigious USA Wrestling Junior Nationals in Iowa City. In a matchup of men destined to become three-time NCAA champions, he defeated another very talented prep star, Mark Churella of Michigan, in the finals at 154 pounds.

Coaches Duane Kleven and Russ Hellickson recognized the enormous talent that Kemp possessed and offered him a scholarship to the University of Wisconsin. It didn't take long for their faith in the Ohio matman to pay off.

Kemp not only made the team as a legitimate freshman in 1975 but he soon began an intense rivalry with a great Iowa wrestler, Chuck Yagla. The two met in the finals of the Northern Open in Kemp's first season and the Badger won in overtime. A month later, Yagla scored a 4-0 victory in the dual meet and then defeated Kemp again in the Big Ten finals by the same score.

But in the NCAA finals, it was a different story. The two "never-say-die" warriors battled to a 4-4 tie in regulation time, then traded stalling points and wound up in a

Lee Kemp (right) utilized tremendous athletic skills and self-discipline to create one of the greatest wrestling machines in American history.

1-1 tie in overtime. The Hawkeye was awarded the victory on a split referee's decision – giving Yagla his first of two NCAA titles and denying Kemp the honor of making history. As the future unfolded on Lee Kemp's career, it was that very narrow loss that kept him from becoming the first four-time NCAA champion in collegiate history.

Over the next three years, Kemp moved up to 158 pounds and was unstoppable. In the Northern Open of his sophomore year, he shocked the nation's wrestling fans by posting a 7-6 triumph over Dan Gable in the 158-pound finals. Though he had been out of competition for three years and was the assistant coach at Iowa, Gable was toying with the idea of a comeback. Hampered with a neck injury, Gable was hardly the same wrestler who had breezed through the Olympics in 1972 without a point being scored on him but the match served notice that Kemp was on track for greatness.

In the East-West All-Star Classic, the Badger star avenged his loss to Yagla with a 10-3 victory. He finished the season unbeaten with a 39-0 record and capped it off with a 4-0 triumph over Tom Brown of the University of Washington in the NCAA finals.

In 1977, Kemp claimed his second title by beating Iowa State's Kelly Ward in the finals, 9-5, as the Badgers placed sixth. In 1978, as a senior, he won his third title as the team was second in the Big Ten and fourth in the NCAAs. Once again, he faced Ward in the finals, winning this time by a 10-8 margin.

Kemp bowed out with a career college record of 143-6-1, for a winning percentage of .957. Five of the six losses came during his true freshman year and he was 110-1-1 his final three seasons. He won three NCAA titles at 158 pounds, won 96 consecutive matches and went 109 straight matches without a loss, the only blemish coming in a tie with Ward in another East-West All-Star meet.

In addition, he led a resurgence at the University of Wisconsin. With Kemp in the lineup and setting the standard, the Badgers took fourth in the nation in 1978, the best finish in Wisconsin history.

"Lee Kemp is the reason that Wisconsin wrestling emerged," said Joe Kaster, publisher of The Crossface, the state's wrestling newspaper, and a longtime coach and referee. "George Martin (the University of Wisconsin coach for 32 years, ending in 1970) did wonders to help spread high school wrestling in Wisconsin, but really didn't do that much to promote college wrestling.

"Lee Kemp put Wisconsin on the wrestling map. People just couldn't get enough of him. He's without question the biggest name in Wisconsin wrestling history. He's our Dan Gable."

Kemp was also a keen student of the sport, always eager to seek out advice wherever he could find it. During his junior year, he heard that Gable was giving a clinic near his hometown in Ohio. Kemp drove down from Madison, Wisconsin, and spent four hours with Gable. It was an experience that Kemp relished.

"He taught his session and when it was over I walked up to him and asked him to work out and we worked out for probably two hours," said Kemp years later. "We were going at each other hard; you know how he was, he just never stopped. I was trying to learn from him and the best way to learn it was to do it. That's an example of how unselfish he was with his time." *(19)*

Kemp was also known for a work ethic that was second to none, and for pushing himself to his limits in practice sessions. He was a weight trainer who believed in punishing workout sessions, and was also very strict with his diet. As a result, his body often looked like it was chiseled from granite by the time he walked onto a mat.

"From 1976 through 1980, Lee was probably the best workout partner I could have had," said Russ Hellickson, assistant coach at Wisconsin at the time and a world-class wrestler himself, at 220 pounds. "Even though I had a big weight advantage, he was so powerful that he was a great workout partner. Lee was the same a half hour into the workout as he was when it started. He had great endurance and positioning to go with his strength.

"He was very dedicated and disciplined. He controlled his diet, his sleep, his training, and everything around him. He never lost control. He was very focused on what it took to be the best."

As remarkable as the college career had been, there was even more ahead. Lee made a very quick and smooth transition to the international freestyle form of wrestling. Immediately after his final year of college, he earned the 163-pound spot on the 1978 World team and flew off to Mexico City for the World Games.

Facing an extremely tough draw, he defeated the eventual silver medal winner from Iran in his

Lee Kemp

very first match, 9-4, and the Russian bronze medallist in his second match, 7-4. He fought his way to the finals and then defeated Bulgaria's Alexander Nanev 7-4 to win the gold medal. Not only was he the only American to capture a title that year, but at 21 years and eight months, he became the youngest World champion in U.S. history!

"Kemp became the seventh U.S. wrestler to capture a World Title, winning the 163-pound class the hard way," reported *Amateur Wrestling News* as it was announcing Kemp its Man of the Year for 1978, "by meeting and defeating all five of the other placewinners in his class during the four days of competition."

In 1979, he captured the World Championships in San Diego – and again was the only American to win the gold, even though six others earned medals. Kemp didn't have a close match and defeated Martin Knosp of West Germany in the finals, 6-2. Yagla had made the American team at 149.5 and recalled the workouts the two former competitors engaged in at the camp.

"I think I had a 3-2 edge on Lee in college wrestling, but I never beat him in five or six tries at freestyle," said Yagla in 2005. "He was very, very good on defense; he was very quick, had great position and was so strong. The three times I beat him in college, I was able to wear him down some and get him to shoot from his knees, then counter and go behind.

"But later on, he was just too good and too strong. We worked out at the 1979 World camp a lot and he was very, very tough. He was almost impossible to score on. He was probably the strongest man, pound for pound, that I ever wrestled in competition."

Nearly everyone in the wrestling community, at home and abroad, expected Kemp to win the Olympics at 163 pounds in 1980. He made the American team with a pair of wins over Dave Schultz, 5-4 and 7-4, but that was as far as he got. President Jimmy Carter declared that America would boycott the Moscow Games as a way of protesting the Soviet Union's invasion of Afghanistan. Suddenly, Kemp and 19 other United States wrestlers were on the sidelines, along with the entire American Olympic team.

Kemp earned a spot on the 1981 World team, marking the fourth straight year he had been America's best hope at 163 pounds. Competing in Skoplje, Yugoslavia, he won his first four matches, then suffered his only loss ever in four World Championships. In a very controversial match, he dropped a 1-0 decision to West Germany's Knosp, and finished with the bronze medal.

With Dave Schultz arriving on the scene, the competition to make the World team at 163 pounds was growing increasingly fierce. Kemp defeated Schultz for the 163-pound spot in 1982, so Dave bumped up to 180.5 pounds. Competing as teammates in Edmonton, Canada, Kemp was back on top, winning the gold medal for the third time. After two lopsided wins, he avenged his loss the previous year to Knosp with a 2-1 decision, then won three more matches by scores of 1-0, 3-2 and 3-0. Meanwhile, Schultz earned the bronze medal in the next class up.

But Kemp had not seen the last of Schultz. While Lee took a long break from the sport, bypassing the World team trials in 1983, Schultz was honing his game. Dropping back down to his natural competition weight of 163 pounds, Schultz made the 1983 World team – and came back from Kiev, Russia, with the gold medal.

Schultz and Kemp engaged in a fierce battle for the 163-pound position on the 1984 Olympic team. The wrestling world was treated to the spectacle of two world champions fighting for one highly-coveted spot. Schultz finally emerged on top and went on to claim the gold medal in Los Angeles.

"Maybe Lee had just stayed around a little bit too long, because of the pain of missing the 1980 Olympic year," said one longtime observer of the sport. "He might have felt he needed that Olympic gold to close out his career the way he wanted."

After defeating a Cuban in a dual meet in Madison in 1984, Lee Kemp retired from amateur

Lee Kemp

wrestling with a record of 59-8 in international competition. He had added three World titles, seven national freestyle titles, five World Cup gold medals and two Pan-American Games championships to his three NCAA titles. It was one of the most impressive resumes in the history of American wrestling!

But he had one last fling with the sport that he had grown to love so much. In 1985, he wrestled in the Professional Freestyle Wrestling Association and captured the middleweight world championship. Shortly after, he left wrestling for good.

He had traveled the globe and competed against the very best the world had to offer. He had grown as an athlete and as a person.

Lee earned a master's degree in business administration and considered coaching. But he turned instead to the business world and worked for two years in New York City for the Clairol Company. He left Clairol to enter the Ford Motor Ownership program, and in 1991 opened the Lee Kemp Ford Dealership in Lake Forest, Minnesota. He felt that wrestling had prepared him well for success in the business world.

"Being an athlete helps you to be competitive and I've chosen one of the most competitive careers there is," he said in 2004. "The sport of wrestling is very competitive and so is owning your own business.

"My business started with 14 employees and now we have 45. There are a lot of responsibilities and we have five departments and all need to be profitable in order to be successful. As an athlete, you're under pressure to compete well and you want to win. Now, as a business owner, wanting to win is about profit, not about medals. It's about making your money than you're spending and pleasing your customers."

In 1998, Kemp was one of five men featured on a poster called "America Needs Wrestling." Nearly 10,000 of them have been distributed to wrestling coaches and supporters all across the nation as a means of marketing the values of the sport. A total of 40 names are listed on the borders, ranging from Abraham Lincoln to Tom Cruise, all with wrestling backgrounds.

The five wrestlers pictured are Dan Gable, actor Billy Baldwin, writer John Irving, politician Dennis Hastert, Speaker of the House of the United States Congress, and Kemp, a respected business leader. Here's what Lee wrote for the poster:

"Wrestling has positively impacted my life in many ways, but perhaps the one singular thing that I gained from wrestling that stands out the most is – wrestling provided me the opportunity to learn mental toughness! A person's mental toughness is what allows them to demand of themselves anything and everything necessary to achieve the desired goal, or basically speaking, people that are mentally tough get the job done!"

In the history books, Lee Kemp stands tall as one of the sport's biggest legends. Until Pat Smith won his fourth NCAA title in 1994, Kemp came the closest of any wrestler to being the sport's first-four time NCAA champion, losing out only by a split referee's decision as a pure freshman to another great wrestler.

"He was incredibly strong and solid, never out of position," said Randy Lewis, 1984 Olympic champion. "He never made a mistake. He went five years with only one loss at the highest levels of international competition, and that one loss wasn't really a fair deal. He is without question one of the greatest wrestlers in not only American history, but in the World, as well."

It is a claim that no one can argue with. But Kemp, known for his quiet manner and modesty, keeps a low profile in the wrestling world until he is sought out from time to time by journalists who want to know more about his amazing career.

"A humble man, Kemp believes strongly in his Christian values and now preaches more about life than he does wrestling," wrote Matt Krumrie. "His two sons have shown an in interest in wrestling, but Kemp hopes they go into the sport for the right reasons. 'Wrestling builds character, lifelong skills and that is the biggest reason I hope they are involved with the sport,'" he told

Lee Kemp

Krumrie. *(20)*

Hellickson and Joe Kaster are also as impressed with Kemp's character as they were with his wrestling ability.

"Lee was always a gentleman, so much class and so polite. I don't think I ever saw him mad or upset all the years I was around him. He was in control of his emotions," said Hellickson.

"He never lost his humility, even after winning the World title three times. Some times people change when they reach tremendous success, but not Lee. He is surprisingly good in small groups; he can interact with anybody."

"He's so soft spoken, that it's hard to believe he was such a brute on the mat," said Kaster. "He looked like he was chiseled out of stone, and yet he's such a classy man, a real gentleman."

In an interview with Kyle Klingman in 2004, Kemp assessed various elements of his career, and some of the foreign wrestlers he respected.

"The Soviets were always hard," he said. "I'd say one of the toughest guys I had to wrestler was the West German Knosp. I guess it would be similar to the feeling guys have when they wrestle Cael Sanderson. Just because he was so tactical. Just the anxiety of having to wrestle a guy who is going to be moving so much, trying to shoot at your ankles and doing all of those unorthodox types of holds and that's the way Martin Knosp was." *(21)*

Some wrestling fans were critical of Kemp's close scores through the years. He was known for low-scoring matches and using what could be described as a "control style" of wrestling. But Hellickson offered an explanation for that, as well.

"Lee didn't dominate like a Dan Gable, that's true," he said. "But I don't think Lee liked to beat people up on the mat. It just wasn't who he was. He just wanted to go out, do his very best, and win."

In more ways than one, Lee Kemp found his true sporting identity that very day he was cut from the basketball team in Chardon, Ohio.

Highlights – Lee Kemp was a three-time NCAA champion at Wisconsin with a 143-6-1 overall record. He also won seven national freestyle championships for a total of ten national titles. He was a three-time World champion and a bronze medallist. A member of the 1980 Olympic team, which boycotted the Moscow Games, he was considered the favorite for a gold medal at 163 pounds. He won five World Cup titles and two gold medals at the Pan-American games. His international record was 59-8. His overall record is estimated at 425-35-7.

Bruce Baumgartner
King of the Big Men

When chronicling the amazing career of super heavyweight Bruce Baumgartner, one needs to get out a large pad of paper to write down all the championships and awards that he has earned on a wrestling mat. The fact of the matter is that he has won more national titles than any other wrestler in American history, and far more World/Olympic medals.

Baumgartner got his first taste of wrestling as a student in junior high at Haledon, New Jersey. He liked the sport and found success. At Manchester Regional High School, he placed third in the New Jersey state high school championships as a senior in 1977, and also placed in the state track meet in the shot put. That summer, he won the Junior Nationals in Iowa City, but college coaches still weren't beating down his door. When it came time to settle on a college, he picked Indiana State University in Terre Haute, Indiana, a college made famous by a basketball player named Larry Bird, who had transferred in from Indiana University.

For a heavyweight, Baumgartner was fast and mobile and he hit his stride during his second season in college. He was 22-8 as a freshman, then posted a 26-3 record his following season, making it all the way to the NCAA finals of 1980 before losing to an Oregon State buzzsaw named Howard Harris.

Baumgartner rebounded with a terrific junior season. He won the Midlands championships by pinning Iowa's Lou Banach in the finals, but Lou returned the insult three months later at the 1981 NCAA Championships held at Princeton University. In one of the most exciting heavyweight bouts ever, Banach caught Baumgartner in a near-side cradle in the third period and pinned him. It was the only disappointment in a tremendous season as Baumgartner finished 42-1.

His senior year Bruce wasn't about to be denied. Wrestling in Hilton Coliseum on the Iowa State University campus, Baumgartner won the school's first-ever Division I NCAA wrestling championship by defeating Oklahoma's huge and powerful Steve "Dr. Death" in the finals, 4-2. It was the climax to a perfect 44-0 season for Baumgartner, but not all of his achievements came on a wrestling mat.

Bruce Baumgartner was a three-time All-American and NCAA champion for Indiana State. And then his career really took off! He became America's all-time leader in national titles (18) and medals won in Olympic/World competition (13).

Bruce Baumgartner displays his tremendous power as he whizzers an opponent off his feet en route to one of his thirteen Olympic/World medals. *(Photo courtesy of Steve Brown)*

He graduated with honors, earning a degree in industrial arts education, and was a 1982 NCAA Top Five winner, an award given for success in athletics, academics and leadership.

In 1980, while still in college, Baumgartner had won the AAU national freestyle championship. The following year, however, he was beaten twice in the same tourney, and failed to place in the top six. Ron Carlisle, who finished second, and Dan Cook, who finished fifth, were the men who handed him the losses in the 1981 tournament.

They would be the last two Americans to beat Bruce Baumgartner for sixteen consecutive years! In a streak that would extend to over 200 matches, Baumgartner defeated every single American he faced. By the time he retired from wrestling in 1997, he had won a staggering total of eighteen national titles – more than any other wrestler in American history. Included in that incredible string were fifteen USA Wrestling freestyle titles, two AAU national freestyle titles, and one NCAA title.

He also made history at the annual Midlands tournament, one of the nation's most competitive meets. There, Bruce set records for most championships (eight) and consecutive victories (40), though both marks were eventually broken by Joe Williams of Iowa.

Legends of the Mat – 123

Bruce Baumgartner

As impressive as those accomplishments were, his greatest achievements were reserved for the international scene. Between the years of 1984 and 1997, Bruce set the world on its cauliflower ear. Before he hit the scene, a United States heavyweight had not won a gold medal in the Olympics or World Championships since Harry Steel back in 1924.

To start it off, Baumgartner placed third at the World Championships in 1983. Then, at the 1984 Olympics in Los Angeles, he ended an American drought of sixty years when he captured the gold medal. He warmed up for Los Angeles by going 9-0 in a tour of the Soviet Union, then won all three Olympic matches going away. He defeated Bob Molle of Canada in the finals, 10-2. Molle had placed fifth in the world the year before.

Baumgartner startled members of the press corps when he told them he had never played an organized game of football, stating that he much preferred the "do it yourself" aspect of wrestling. Then he further shocked them when asked if he would do a beer commercial.

"It would be fraudulent to do a beer commercial because I don't drink beer," he said quietly. "I just drink juice and water… and milk. I could do a milk commercial."

From 1984 on, there was practically no stopping the 270-pounder from New Jersey. Baumgartner was world champion in the years 1986, 1993 and 1995, and won another Olympic gold medal in 1992 – for a grand total of five gold medals at the highest level possible.

He also won a silver medal in the 1988 Olympics and a bronze in 1996 – making him only the sixth athlete in American history in any sport to medal in four different Olympics. In addition, his total of 13 medals in either World or Olympic competition is the most of any wrestler in history, matched only by the great Alexander Karelin in the 2000 Olympics.

The trophy case in Baumgartner's house in Edinboro, Pennsylvania, should be bursting at the seams, for his total medal count far exceeds those from the Olympics and Worlds. He was a seven-time World Cup champion, and a three-time Pan-American Games champion. With 18 national titles and 13 World/Olympic medals, he is alone at the top of the U.S. record books.

There were several reasons for his success, according to Greg Strobel, who served as National Teams Coach at USA Wrestling during much of Baumgartner's career, and was himself a two-time NCAA champion (190 pounds, Oregon State).

"First of all, he was brutally strong," said Strobel. "I remember once overseas we were all in a gym and guys were climbing ropes to the top. I had never seen anyone that size climb a rope without using his legs, but Bruce did. He sat on the floor and then just pulled himself up, hand over hand, all the way to the top. It was amazing.

"When he pulled in on a leg or on a gut wrench, he was king," said Strobel with a chuckle. "He was gifted, strength wise, and worked to improve it.

"He also did all the technique work the lighter weights did. He did a lot of drilling, putting in the extra time. It didn't come easy for Bruce, and maybe that's why he was somewhat of a late bloomer in college. But he worked very hard at his technique, lots of drilling. And that helped him stay in the sport for a long time. When you get older and slow down a bit, great technique can be a huge factor in keeping you in the game.

"Thirdly, he never took anything for granted. Just because he had won a certain title, he didn't think it was automatic he would win it again. Each time, it was new and fresh, wanting to win the title like it was the first time. He had self-doubts, like most athletes do. He would get to thinking, 'I'm not sure I can beat this guy.'

"We call it 'chasing the demons!' Everyone goes through it, to some degree. So, as coaches, we would devise a game plan and Bruce would stick to it. He would call up (Dan) Gable all the time and ask questions. Gable really helped him in those areas.

"Bruce was very coachable and always willing to reach out and listen to others," Strobel concluded.

Baumgartner brought a lot to the table in terms of genetic gifts and determination, but he also

America's finest heavyweight of all time, Bruce Baumgartner lifts Tom Erikson off the mat en route to a big throw during the 1996 Olympic Trials. *(Photo courtesy of Steve Brown)*

— Bruce Baumgartner —

brought the desire to work hard to improve. And a passion for the sport that few others could match. Those qualities allowed him to excel over a longer period of time than any other American ever has.

"Bruce Baumgartner loved wrestling," said Gary Abbott, director of media relations for USA Wrestling. "That is why he was able to dominate the sport for almost two decades and become an international wrestling hero.

"Easily, the most common question that he was asked by the media in his last two Olympic cycles was why did he remain in wrestling so long. The answer was always the same. It was that he still enjoyed the sport and would continue to wrestle as long as it was fun for him. Bruce enjoyed the hard work and sacrifice that it took to be a champion, and he enjoyed the challenge of facing the world's best at his game."

One of his greatest accomplishments came in 1992 when, at the age of 33, he dominated the Olympics. He tore through the heavyweight class, outscoring his six foes by a 35-1 margin and pinning one man in a mere 11 seconds!

"People do not give Bruce enough credit for his amazing performance at the 1992 Olympics in Barcelona," said Abbott. "Without doubt, he had the most dominant performance of all the U.S. wrestling champions, and perhaps the best performance of any of the U.S. gold medallists in any sport at the 1992 Games.

"His last-second win over Russia's David Gobedjishvili in the early rounds was inspiring, and nobody else even was close to challenging him the rest of the way."

Baumgartner claimed almost as many honors off the mat as he did on the mat. He was USA Wrestling Man of the Year in 1992 and was twice a runner-up for USOC Athlete of the Year. In 1995, he became the second wrestler to ever win the James E. Sullivan Award, handed out annually since 1933 by the AAU to the top amateur athlete in the nation.

In 1996, he was selected in a vote of the United States team to be the athlete carrying the American flag during opening ceremonies of the Olympic Games in Atlanta. It was a huge honor that was seen by an estimated 3.5 billion people on television screens around the globe.

With all the hype and attention on him from the opening ceremonies, and a bit past his prime, Baumgartner suffered a 6-1 setback in the second round to Andrey Shumilin of Russia. But he battled back with three straight wins, putting himself in a position to go out with a medal. With the world watching, he was pitted against Shumilin, the same man who had defeated him earlier. This time, in an incredibly hard-fought match, Bruce was the victor 1-1 in overtime.

"His last Olympic match was one of the greatest memories I have in 20 years as a wrestling journalist," said Abbott. "The strength that he needed to pull in the leg and score the winning takedown over Shumilin of Russia in the bronze-medal match was unbelievable. Bruce Baumgartner was so strong mentally that he just took that match away from Shumilin to win his fourth Olympic medal."

Baumgartner began his coaching career as a graduate assistant coach at Oklahoma State while earning his master's degree, and then accepted a full-time assistant coach position at Edinboro University in Pennsylvania. He served in that capacity under Mike DeAnna for six years, and then was head coach for another seven seasons. His finest year as coach came in the 1996-1997 season when his team posted a 14-0 dual meet record and placed sixth in the NCAA tourney, the best finish ever for the Fighting Scots.

He gave up coaching for a great career advancement opportunity in 1998. He was named athletic director at Edinboro University and continues to be in demand nationally as a wrestling clinician and motivational speaker.

Baumgartner has been very active in other fronts, as well. He served on the board of USA Wrestling, the sport's national governing body, for several years as an athlete representative. In August of 1998, he was elected to serve as president of the Group A Olympic team member.

Off the mat, the honors began to pile up. In 1999, he received the FILA Gold Star, the top

— Bruce Baumgartner —

honor in international wrestling. He was voted into the National Wrestling Hall of Fame in 2002, and one year later he was voted into the inaugural class of the FILA International Wrestling Hall of Fame. He was one of just two Americans to be so honored, the other being John Smith.

In a 1994 article in W.I.N. magazine, Baumgartner gave this assessment regarding his wrestling accomplishments: "I have enough size and strength that other heavyweights find it difficult to push me around.

"I am not the biggest wrestler, I am not the strongest wrestler, I am not the quickest, I don't have the best conditioning or the best technique. But I'm good enough in all those areas that if you take all those features and put them together, then I'm able to do good."

The Baumgartner impact on wrestling has been huge, from ocean to ocean, and overseas as well. It's amazing that he won a total of 18 national titles, and 13 world-level medals. But perhaps the most amazing fact of all is that he entered every major tournament in America and went over 17 years without losing. It's an achievement that may never be surpassed.

Highlights – Bruce Baumgartner was a three-time All-American at Indiana State University and NCAA champion in 1982, posting a record of 134-12 in college. Overall, he won a total of 18 national titles, and was undefeated in an estimated 200-plus matches against Americans, from 1982 through 1996. He won two Olympic gold medals, a silver and bronze. He also won three World gold medals, as well as seven other medals. He won seven World Cups and three Pan-American Games titles. Baumgartner was Midlands champion eight times. His total record is unknown.

Ed and Lou Banach
Never-Say-Quit Battlers

It's safe to say that few wrestling fans of the 1980s were disappointed whenever one of the Banach twins stepped onto the mat to compete. The fans always knew they were going to get an all-out effort, from start to finish. From the day the Banachs walked into the University of Iowa wrestling room in the fall of 1978 right up through their final matches in the 1984 Olympics, it was 100 percent commitment and constant action.

Ed and Lou were part of a large family that was split apart when the twins were two years old. Their parents, Warclaw and Genevieve Banach, had immigrated to the United States after World War II, and settled on a farm in New Jersey. The couple had a total of 14 children, five girls and nine boys. A series of unfortunate circumstances, including the burning down of the farmhouse, caused the family to break apart. Three boys – Steve, Ed and Lou – wound up being raised by Alan and Stephanie Tooley, in Port Jervis, New York.

In high school, the three Banach boys carved out a reputation in football and wrestling. Ed placed in the New York state meet three times, winning the 167-pound title as a senior. Lou, on the other hand, won state as a junior and was third as a senior.. Steve placed third in the 167-pound weight class at the state tournament his senior year.

"All three of us were wrestling at the same time on the three mats during the semifinal round," said Ed. " Steve kept looking over at Lou and me to see how we were doing while he was wrestling. Mark Faller, our coach, thought that it cost him his match."

Recruited by many of the nation's best wrestling schools, the twins settled on Iowa primarily in order to wrestle for Dan Gable. They red-shirted their first year, and it turned out to be a rocky road for both. Lou wasn't sure he wanted to pay the price that college wrestling demanded, while Ed told teammates he came to Iowa to win four NCAA titles, and yet he was constantly being handled in the room, often by men who weighed considerably less.

But Ed had one quality that always carried him through – a spirit that never buckled, that never threw

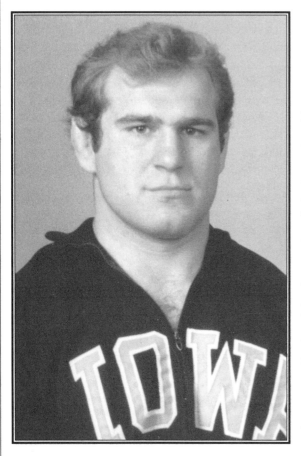

Ed Banach was a four-time NCAA finalist and three-time NCAA champion for the University of Iowa. He and his twin brother, Lou, electrified college crowds across the nation with their aggressive style of wrestling, and then both won gold medals at the 1984 Olympics.

Lou Banach was one of the most exciting heavyweight wrestlers of all time. Outweighed in nearly every match, he still managed to win two NCAA titles and place third another time. He also won a gold medal in the 220-pound class in the 1984 Olympics.

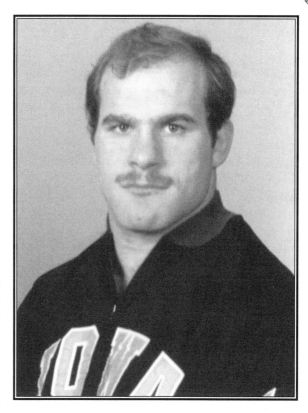

in the towel. He kept an optimistic, upbeat outlook and was one of the hardest workers to ever come through the doors of the Iowa practice room. He was willing to pay a tremendous price to become the wrestler he wanted to become.

"Dan and J Robinson had tried to teach Ed technique, but it was a slow and arduous undertaking," said Lou. "Ed's style was not one of finesse but of rock-hard, jolting, never-say-die wrestling. A foe, to have any chance of beating him, had to build a huge early lead and then try to withstand the battering that was sure to follow in the closing minutes. Ed was a machine from the same mold as Gable himself and was capable of intimidating an opponent before the match ever began." *(22)*

Ed exploded on the national scene his redshirt freshman year. He won the tough Midlands, then claimed the Big Ten crown. At the 1980 NCAA Championships in Corvallis, Oregon, he won the 177-pound NCAA title, defeating All-American Dave Allen of Iowa State in the finals, 16-5. He had arrived as a legitimate collegiate star.

Lou, meanwhile, suffered through an up-and-down season that culminated with him leaving the team. He and Ed had scored dramatic pins in a spectacular come-from-behind Hawkeye dual meet victory over archrival Iowa State, but after that high spot Lou hit the wall. He decided wrestling wasn't what he wanted and boarded a bus, headed for Texas. But by the time he reached Oklahoma City, he decided to return to Iowa City and tell Gable that he would continue wrestling, but only if he could be at heavyweight. He was sick of cutting weight to make 190 pounds.

Gable agreed and Lou eventually found new life in collegiate wrestling. As a sophomore, weighing a muscular 215 pounds, he finished second in the prestigious Midlands. To reach the finals, he defeated 1978 NCAA heavyweight runnerup, John Sefter of Princeton, and two-time Olympian Russ Hellickson. He took an early 4-0 lead on Indiana State's Bruce Baumgartner, NCAA runnerup the year before, then was pinned while trying to turn Baumgartner to his back.

Undaunted, he ran through the rest of the season with little trouble. He gained the NCAA finals, beating the talented Dan Severn, of Arizona State, along the way, 20-10. In one of the most exciting finals ever seen at heavyweight, Lou gained revenge by pinning Baumgartner.

At one point, the two heavyweight stars engaged in a stunning flurry of activity that caused ABC announcer Ken Kraft to say it was the type of action that fans usually see from lightweights. At

Ed and Lou Banach

the start of the third period, Lou remained very aggressive despite a comfortable 8-3 lead. He locked in a near-side cradle and took the much larger Baumgartner to his back for a dramatic pin.

Lou's win was the second title for a Banach that night, as Ed had claimed No. 2 earlier in the evening by pinning Charlie Heller of Clarion in the finals at 177 pounds. The finals were carried live on ABC Television to a national audience, and the dynamic twins from Port Jervis, New York, had become the talk of the wrestling world for their aggressive, crowd-pleasing style.

If the 1981 season was sensational for the Hawkeye stars, their junior year was a letdown. Ed's goal was to become the first four-time NCAA champion ever, and he started the season off in high style. In the finals of the Midlands, he faced Oklahoma's Mark Schultz, who had moved up to 177 after winning the NCAA title at 167 pounds the previous year. In a great match, Ed prevailed, 5-4.

The two warriors met again in the dual meet at the University of Oklahoma, with Schultz posting a 9-8 victory in another terrific bout. The stage was set for one of the most-anticipated NCAA showdowns ever. Both warriors made it to the 177-pound finals and the huge crowd was buzzing with excitement.

Banach took a quick 4-0 lead. But Schultz battled back for a 10-8 lead entering the final period. With the two champions battling chest to chest, a wild flurry began, with Ed winding up on bottom. He fought valiantly to avoid a pin, and lost 16-8. His dream of four NCAA titles was over.

Lou had been battling a severe shoulder injury all season long and entered the NCAA tournament weighing just 206 pounds. After a first-round win, he scored one of the most sensational victories in NCAA history when he pinned 410-pound Tab Thacker of North Carolina State in the quarterfinals. The two were battling on their feet when Lou slipped in a lace leg and drove Thacker straight to his back.

Despite the sensational victory, Lou's shoulder problems persisted and he lost in the semis to Steve Williams of Oklahoma, 7-4. He wound up third, defeating Iowa State's Wayne Cole in a wild match, 11-10.

The Banachs entered their final season without NCAA titles to defend. Ed, unable to make 177 any longer, opted for 190 pounds and lost three times to Iowa State's rugged All-American Mike Mann. In a dual meet, Lou lost by pin to Oklahoma State's 400-pound Mitch Shelton. By the time of the 1983 NCAA tournament, neither was favored to win a title.

But the fighting spirit that the twins were known for came to the forefront once again. Gable had devised an incredibly demanding workout program for Ed after his last loss to Mann and the two, coach and pupil, met at 4 a.m. every morning for a private practice, before the two regular practices later in the day. Trained to a razor's edge both mentally and physically, Ed scored the only takedown in the finals and defeated Mann, 4-3. He had his third NCAA title.

Lou had to change his strategy against Shelton. In the dual, he had plowed right into the giant Cowboy and tried to throw him to his back. As he fought to lift Shelton, his legs buckled and Lou fell to his own back, trapped. In the nationals, he met Shelton in the semifinal round and was outweighed by nearly 200 pounds. Lou tugged and pulled on the Cowboy star, moving laterally and tiring him out. Lou scored a reversal and riding time against an escape for a 3-1 victory. In the finals, he pinned Cole of Iowa State to claim his second title. He had posted a record of 15-1 in three NCAA tournaments at heavyweight, despite being outweighed in every match but one! Ed was 19-1 in his four NCAA tournaments.

With a collegiate record of 141-9-1, Ed stands fourth on the all-time Iowa career victory list. He still holds the career record at Iowa for most pins in a career, with 73, and his 22 pins in the 1982-83 season has him tied for second (with John Bowlsby) for most pins in a single season. Lou had a career mark of 90-14-2 and is 10th on the all-time pin list with 40.

Topping off his tremendous collegiate career,

In the 1984 Olympics, Ed Banach ran over five foes and captured the 198-pound gold medal without a close match. He then retired to move into coaching. *(Photo courtesy of Steve Brown)*

Ed was named Big Ten Male Athlete of the Year for 1983, drawing more votes than football and basketball players in one of the nation's most respected athletic conferences. Lou became an author his senior year, writing a book entitled *The New Breed: Living Iowa Wrestling*, with Mike Chapman, a longtime sports journalist. In the book, Lou explained the long road he had taken in collegiate wrestling and how it had changed his life.

"Maybe I was that new breed of athlete that Eddie was… I cared for wrestling, academics and social growth equally. But the biggest lesson of all was that I learned – and I mean learned, sometimes the hard way – to listen to my coach. Maybe Dan, the other coaches and some of the wrestlers thought at times that I was given preferential treatment, but I don't view it that way at all. I was given individual treatment and a dose of understanding. Dan adapted to my style and I adapted to his, and we met halfway.

"He accepted me as an individual, someone who simply could not live wrestling day in and day out." *(23)*

With their college careers over, both Banachs turned their focus on the international style of wrestling, aiming specifically at the 1984 Olympics. Neither had trained much in freestyle – in fact, Ed and Lou entered just one national freestyle senior tournament in their entire career.

"The demands on your time as both a wrestler and student were just too much," explained Ed years later. "Both Lou and I wanted to make sure we did well in school. Having the NCAA tournament in March and the freestyle tournaments just a month later was too much. I did

Ed and Lou Banach

it my first year, but after that I just wasn't interested."

But the dream of an Olympic title was enough to get them into the freestyle mode for at least a year. They had nearly eight months after their last collegiate tournament to get ready for the biggest wrestling event in the world, held every four years.

In the Olympic qualifier tournament held in Iowa City, Ed roared through the pack at 198 pounds with seven straight victories, most by lopsided scores. He defeated Mitch Hull 6-2 in the last bout to make the team. Along the way, he also defeated Steve Fraser, who would go on to win a gold medal in the Greco-Roman style in Los Angeles.

Standing in Lou's path were two tremendously talented athletes, Dan Severn and Greg Gibson. Both would go on to considerable fame, Severn as the Ultimate Fighting Champion and a holder of several black belts, and Gibson as one of the most versatile wrestlers in U.S. history.

Having won a silver medal in the World Championships just the year prior at 220, Gibson was the favorite to make the team. He and Lou squared off in the semifinal round. At one point in the match, Lou shot in deep for a high-crotch takedown. Gibson blocked him and sprawled all across Lou's back, catching Banach in a deep squat, with his knees almost touching the mat. Slowly, Banach rose up straight, Gibson still draped over his back, and then slammed Gibson to the mat for the takedown. It was an awesome display of hip and thigh power, as well as balance and determination.

Sitting mat side was Mike McCready, a heavyweight who would eventually own 15 national titles, on various levels. He shook his head in amazement at the performance.

"I didn't see that move," he said softly. "It's physically impossible to do what Lou Banach just did."

Lou then defeated Severn in the finals, 6-1, to join his brother on the Olympic freestyle team.

Even though the Soviet Union boycotted the 1984 Olympics, in retaliation for the U.S. boycotting the 1980 Games in Moscow, there was plenty of tough competition waiting for the wrestlers in Los Angeles. Turkey, Japan, Romania and West Germany were among the world powers on hand, but when the Americans marched into the Anaheim Convention Center, they were ready. They captured nine gold medals in the 20 weight classes, and two of them were won by the Banach twins.

Lou had four pins, all in the first period, and added an 11-1 win over Wayne Brightwell of Canada. His pins came in the times of 1:14 (Turkey), 1:45 (Senegal), 1:56 (Japan) and 1:02 (Syria).

"Maybe there is a better man somewhere in the world, there always is a better man somewhere," said the philosophical ex-Hawkeye after his final match. "But today, everything clicked for me. I showed I could make the transition (from college style to the international style). Now, I can go out a champion."

Ed's path to the gold medal was not quite as smooth, but just as satisfying. While Lou gave up one point in his five matches, Ed gave up seven. He opened the freestyle competition with a 15-2 romp over Edward Lins of Australia and never looked back. He reeled off wins of 11-0 (Turkey), 11-2 (Canada), 48 seconds (Pakistan) and 15-3 (Japan). Among his victim's were a 1982 World silver medal winner, Clark Davis of Canada, and a 1983 World fourth place winner, Akira Ohta of Japan.

While Lou hung up his wrestling shoes for good after the 1984 Olympics, Ed competed in one last event. He was enticed into entering a newly-formed league called the Professional Freestyle Wrestling Association and won the cruiserweight world title with a victory over Charlie Gadsen. It was his final match.

"Ed and Lou were two of the best competitors I have ever seen in all my years with wrestling," said Mark Johnson, the coach who rebuilt the program at the University of Illinois. Johnson was an assistant at Iowa during the Banach years and worked out with them on numer-

Lou Banach celebrates after pinning Bruce Baumgartner to win his first NCAA crown in Princeton, New Jersey, in 1981. Lou finished third the next year and won his second title in 1983 by pinning Wayne Cole, Iowa State, in the finals.

Ed and Lou Banach

ous occasions.

"The better the competition, the better they wrestled. They did it with technique, power and mental toughness that only the very elite athletes possess. But as tough as they were, they were complete gentlemen off the mat. They are a credit to the entire sport."

For years, the twins admired their older brother, Steve, and saw him as a role model. He wrestled at Clemson for two years, then transferred to Iowa in 1981 and wrestled in and out of the lineup at 190 pounds. Though he wasn't as successful in the wrestling world, both Eddie and Lou consider him the toughest man they know.

After graduating from Iowa in 1983, Steve was commissioned as an officer in the United States Army. He was first in his officer training class and began a long and distinguished military career. He saw combat duty in Desert Storm, served with various ranger battalions as an officer in Bosnia, and in 2001 Lt. Colonel Banach assumed command of the Third Ranger battalion and led an historic airborne parachute assault in Afghanistan. He was charged with spearheading U.S. combat operations in the worldwide battle against terrorism. He has won numerous awards, including the Bronze Star for valor in combat.

"A lot of what Lou and I accomplished was because of Steve's leadership," said Ed in 2006. "We always looked up to him. He's a colonel now and he's a great leader. Depending on what he's called on to do, he's in charge of anywhere between 4,000 and 5,000 men."

Lou fulfilled his ROTC obligation by serving as an assistant wrestling coach at West Point, then was a graduate assistant coach at Clarion and Penn State while earning a master's degree in business. He embarked upon a successful career in high-level banking in Milwaukee, Wisconsin. But he left a legacy as one of the best heavyweights of all time.

Lou Thesz, a legendary professional star of the 1940s and '50s, wrestled all around the world for decades, facing the best big men on the planet. Watching films of Lou Banach wrestle in college, Thesz was extremely impressed.

"That's the best moving big man I have ever seen," he said with obvious respect. "For his size, he moves like a cat."

Many amateur fans who saw Lou Banach wrestle would agree. They would also agree that Ed Banach was as tenacious a wrestler as ever took to the mat.

Ed coached at cross-state rival Iowa State for four years, but a serious concussion caused him to give up the rigors of the sport. He then entered into the athletic counseling field at ISU. He has worked in the Cyclone athletic department for nearly two decades.

The Banach mat style had a tremendous impact on the wrestling scene in the 1980s at the University of Iowa, as well as the entire state and the nation.

"They energized college wrestling," said Jay Roberts, a three-year Iowa letterman from the 1960s and an attorney. Roberts has been a regular at the Iowa matches and at the NCAA tournament for four decades.

"Their indomitable spirit completely took over the Iowa program – Eddie by his relentlessly aggressive spirit, and Lou by his pure athleticism, going out and whipping much larger men in striking fashion. Lou not only beat great wrestlers who were much heavier, he pinned them!

"Eddie coming back to beat Mike Mann after losing to him three times, and Lou pinning NCAA champions like Bruce Baumgartner and Tab Thacker – that's the stuff that makes legends.

"The Iowa program has been wonderful before and since, but I personally feel the program reached a high point of the energy level when Ed and Lou wrestled. It was brought to the mat by the Banachs and has never been matched since."

Roberts added the final epithet thusly.

"And to top it all off, they are just as outstanding from a personal standpoint. All three of them – Eddie, Lou and Steve – have been extremely successful in their family lives and careers."

To many wrestling fans, the name Banach stood for intensity, excitement, commitment and, most of all, quality.

Ed and Lou Banach

Highlights – Ed Banach was a three-time NCAA champion and four-time finalist. He won four Big Ten championships and posted a collegiate record of 141-9-1, with 73 pins, the all-time Iowa record. He captured the gold medal in the 198-pound class at the 1984 Olympic Games, going 5-0. His overall record is unknown.

Highlights – Lou Banach was a two-time NCAA champion and placed third as well. He had a college record of 90-14-2. He won two Big Ten championships and pinned 40 foes, many of who outweighed him by as much as 200 pounds. He won the gold medal in the 220-pound class at the 1984 Olympics, going 5-0. His overall record is unknown.

Lou and Ed Banach were featred on the cover of a book written by Lou in 1983. Entitled *The New Breed: Living Iowa Wrestling*, It talked about what it took to be a college wrestling champion. Also on the cover were Hawkeye national champions Barry Davis, Jim Zalesky and Pete Bush.

Dave and Mark Schultz
Iron Sharpens Iron

To a casual observer, it hardly seems possible that Dave and Mark Schultz were born of the same set of parents. While Dave had a rather normal physique, Mark looked like he was carved from granite; while Dave was friendly and easy going, Mark was often quiet and aloof; while on a wrestling mat Dave seemed to flow from move to move with ease, Mark's wrestling was characterized by powerfully-executed moves of high precision.

But when competing, they were brothers to the core. They both harbored an intense, fierce pride and a resolute will. They were both national champions, World champions and Olympic champions. They were, in Dave's own words, men of iron, and were sharpened by each other. "Iron sharpens iron," was one of Dave's favorite statements and it certainly described the brothers Schultz!

The proof is in the record book.

Dave was the eldest of the two, born to Jean and Phil Schultz, and raised in Palo Alto, California. It is a city hardly renown for producing wrestlers, or hard-core athletes of the type the Schultzes would eventually become. The hometown of Stanford University, one of the

Mark (left) and Dave Schultz share the honor of being the only brothers to win NCAA, Olympic and World championships. The brothers from California were two of the most dominate American wrestlers of all time. *(Photo courtesy of USA Wrestling)*

Dave Schultz tore through the 1984 Olympics without a close match, winning a gold medal at 163 pounds. He had also won a gold medal in the World Championships the previous year.
(Photo courtesy of Steve Brown)

nation's prize seats of higher education, it is a city that welcomes thinkers, and nurtures intellectuals.

Dave took up wrestling in the seventh grade, at the advice of a teacher who felt it would provide a boost in the area of self-confidence, which he apparently lacked. In a short period of time, he was a fanatic, absorbing information and advice like a sponge. He loved the sport so much that he often wore his singlet under his school clothes, and his feet were constantly adorned with wrestling shoes. He worked indefatigably to learn all he could about the sport, including its techniques and history.

Almost from the start, Dave was more interested in the wide-open freestyle form of wrestling than scholastic style. He didn't set his goals on an NCAA championship but, rather, on World titles. He had a much larger vision than other wrestlers his age, and he was determined to keep improving until the dream came true.

He exploded on the national scene at the Great Plains tournament in Lincoln, Nebraska in 1977. Still a senior in high school, he entered the 149.5-pound class and fought his way to the semifinals, where he found himself facing Chuck Yagla, the defending NCAA champion for Iowa. Yagla took an early 4-0 lead, but then got caught in a Schultz takedown and wound up being pinned. Amazingly, a senior in high school had defeated an NCAA champion, and by pin!

He also defeated Roye Oliver of Arizona State, another All-American, 9-3, and suddenly the entire wrestling world was talking about "that high school kid from California." J. Carl Guymon was one of the first wrestling writers to see the incredible Schultz potential.

"Dave Schultz is such a quiet, mild-mannered fellow that it is hard to imagine his being a voracious predator on the mat. But have no doubt about it. The senior from Palo Alto High School is one of those 'once in a lifetime' athletes coaches dream about.

"Schultz's calm, unobtrusive exterior neatly hides his inward quality of fierce competitiveness – at least it disguises it when he's not competing. When the whistle blows, the business at hand brings out the best in Dave Schultz." *(24)*

Schultz won the California state title at 165 pounds as a senior, without bothering to cut a pound. He also claimed his first senior-level national title as a high school senior when he won the 1977 Greco-Roman AAU title. College recruiters were beating down his door after the Great Plains victory, and he selected Oklahoma

Dave and Mark Schultz

State.

As a Cowboy, he took third in the NCAAs as a freshman; but he wasn't happy in Stillwater and he transferred to UCLA. Shortly after he arrived at the Los Angeles campus, the school announced it was going to drop the sport, and he transferred to the University of Oklahoma. There, as a Sooner, he was second as a junior, and then won the 167-pound title as a senior in 1982. He beat a tough Oklahoma State sophomore, Mike Sheets, in the finals. His overall college record was 88-8-1.

It was on the campus in Norman that Dave met a woman destined to play a huge role in his development off the mat. His affection for Nancy caused him to reassess his life and to settle down. But first she would need to correct her first impression of him.

In a *Sports Illustrated* article entitled "Brothers and Brawlers," by Craig Neff, she related that she first saw "her future husband in a physical ed class in the spring of their junior year, 1981.

"'It was hot out, but he'd show up wearing a parka and his Russian fur hat and sunglasses,' she says. 'He'd just stand at the back of the class and never say anything. I thought he was weird.'" *(25)*

If not weird, he was certainly different, in many respects, from the average Sooner student. All the while Dave was wrestling in college, his true love was the international style. He simply could not get enough, or learn quickly enough. He entered just about any freestyle tournament that was available. The tougher the competition, the more interested Dave Schultz became.

He had found a great workout partner at home. Mark Schultz began his athletic career as a gymnast, and was top ranked in the state for a period of time. But he always had a warrior's spirit locked inside him. When he and Dave got into an argument once, they decided to go out in back to settle the issue. Mark, bigger and stronger, was confident of a quick victory. Instead, Dave took him down and controlled him easily, providing a painful lesson in the value of wrestling as a means of self-defense. Mark said he was so humiliated that he slept in the car overnight, but he was hooked on wrestling as a form of martial art.

The youngest Schultz got off to a slow start in wrestling, losing his first six matches in a row. But then he caught on. He won the California state title as a senior, and signed up at UCLA with Dave. And, like Dave, he transferred to Oklahoma when the Bruins cut the sport. He was more attuned to the collegiate style than Dave, and met with tremendous success. His power and pure athletic ability, coupled with a warrior's heart, were simply too much to be denied.

He won the NCAA championship at 167 pounds in 1981 with a stunning revenge victory over Iowa star Mike DeAnna, a brilliant wrestler. DeAnna had defeated Schultz in the dual meet by a 14-8 score several weeks before the NCAA meet, but in the nationals, Schultz was simply too powerful and too determined for the talented Hawkeye and posted an upset 10-4 triumph.

Mark moved up a weight the following season, forcing a showdown with two-time 177-pound NCAA champion Ed Banach, also of Iowa. What transpired is one of the greatest three-match series in college history. Both men would eventually become three-time NCAA champions and Olympic champions.

Banach won the first meeting at the Midlands, 5-4; Schultz gained revenge in the dual meet in Oklahoma, 9-8. The third confrontation came in the finals of the 1982 NCAA championships, in Ames, Iowa. With a huge crowd waiting in eager anticipation, Schultz and Banach faced each other for the third time.

It was a fabulous meeting between two of the sport's premier champions. Banach took a 4-0 lead on a takedown and near fall in the first period, but Schultz escaped and scored a takedown and near fall of his own to lead 6-5 after one period. Schultz was on top 10-8 entering the third period. The two were locked in a do-or-die, chest-to-chest throwing situation late in the match. In an incredible flurry, Schultz wound up on top, scoring a takedown and near fall, and winning 16-8. He was voted the meet's outstanding wrestler for his sensational victory.

Precision and powerful takedowns were the trademarks of Mark Schultz during his brilliant international career. He won two world championships to go with his 1984 Olympic gold medal and three NCAA championships for the University of Oklahoma. *(Photo courtesy of Steve Brown)*

The next year, Banach moved up to 190 pounds and both he and Schultz won their third titles. The two wrestling stars stood side by side in the NCAA championship photo, Mark the king at 177 pounds and Ed ruling the roost at 190. For the third straight season, Mark defeated a Hawkeye for his title, this time Duane Goldman.

Recalling his gymnastics training, Mark often celebrated his biggest victories with a standing back flip on the center of the mat.

With college behind them, Dave and Mark could concentrate exclusively on the international style that Dave loved, and which Mark was beginning to appreciate more and more. But before he could represent the United States internationally, Dave had to make the team, and standing in his way was Lee Kemp!

Kemp won his first world title in 1978, and defeated Dave to make both the 1979 World team and 1980 Olympic team. Kemp held the spot in 1981 and 1982, while Dave moved up to 180.5 for the 1982 World Championships. There, in Edmonton, Canada, Kemp won his third gold medal and Schultz came home with a bronze medal in the next weight up.

Things were beginning to change for Dave, though. He made the 1983 World team at 163 pounds, and went on to win the gold medal in far-away Kiev, Russia. Schultz went 5-0, winning by scores of 16-4 (Bradford of Canada), 2-2 criteria (Martin Knosp of West Germany), 12-0 (Tamaduiana of Romania), 12-2 (Alexander Nanev of Bulgaria) and, in the finals, 10-4 (Taram Magomadov of the Soviet Union).

Mark also earned a spot in 1983 on the U.S. team at 180.5 pounds, but posted a two-and-two record. He failed to medal, but he gave notice that he was close to the world's best, losing to gold

Legends of the Mat – 139

Dave and Mark Schultz

medallist Teymuraz Dzgoev of the Soviet Union, 5-2.

They both made the 1984 Olympic team, with Dave scoring three straight wins over Kemp in a dramatic showdown of world champions. Mark also made the team, but was stung by comments that he was not as capable as Dave of winning a gold medal. With the Games set in his native California, Mark was doubly determined to prove the experts wrong.

Even though the Soviet Union boycotted the Los Angeles Games, there were plenty of tough customers on hand. Mark drew Turkey's Resit Karabachak, the gold medal favorite at 180.5 pounds, in the very first round. Mark was on a mission. In the first thirty seconds, he caught the Turk in a powerful double wristlock and threw him to the mat for an apparent pin. Karabachak screamed out in pain, his elbow dislocated. An emergency meeting was called by FILA officials, and, after much debate, U.S. coach Dan Gable was told that Schultz had used illegal force in a legal move, and was being hit with four black marks (a total of six meant elimination). Despite American protests, Schultz found himself in a huge hole.

Meanwhile, Dave was drawing attention from his feared leg-lace device. In his opening bout with Saban Sejdi of Yugoslavia, he twisted Sejdi's leg so severely that the Yugoslav wrestler was carried from the mat. The officials were told to watch the Schultz brothers especially close the remainder of the tournament. And they did watch them… as they both won gold medals. Dave compiled a 5-0 record while Mark won his next four matches in a row.

With Olympic championships now on their resume, the Schultz name became one of the most respected in the long annals of wrestling history. They were known all around the globe. Due to his friendly nature and desire to mix freely with wrestlers from other nations, Dave became respected and revered far and wide as a great ambassador of the sport. Not as gregarious by nature, Mark was respected as a fierce competitor who took no prisoners.

The Schultz brothers could have been content to rest on their laurels, but they weren't. With Dave, it was always about learning and growing as a wrestler, and Mark had developed a similar philosophy. Their skills were honed in constant workouts with each other, often leaving them battered and bruised.

In a magazine article in 1999, Mark explained what brothers mean to each other in the practice room.

"They don't get along so well (in workout sessions) because they know they can get away with it," he said. "Brothers know that no matter what they do to each other, they will always be brothers. We definitely worked out with each other more than anyone else. Some times we'd get pretty brutal but we always knew how far to go, He was my best friend and I was his. We understood, so we could go pretty far. Just like most brothers, we were enemies in the room but allies against everyone and anyone else." *(26)*

They both made the 1985 World team, and this time it was Mark who came home with the gold. He was magnificent in tearing through the field assembled in Budapest, Hungary. He turned in one of the most impressive performances in American history, going 6-0 and outscoring the opposition by a wide margin.

"Nobody really scored on Mark, not until he had the match put away and started playing cat and mouse with them," said Greg Strobel, National Teams Coach.

Dave took the silver medal at 163 pounds, losing in the finals to the talented Raul Cascaret of Cuba, 3-1.

They were also on the 1986 World team, which competed in Budapest, Hungary. Battling various injuries, Mark slipped to seventh place at 180.5, while Dave was third again at 163. But both were back in top form at the 1987 World Championships in France; Mark won his second World gold medal and Dave claimed a silver medal.

On his way to the title, Mark beat a former world champion from the Soviet Union in the

Dave and Mark Schultz

semifinals, 1-0, then decisioned the defending world champion, Alexander Nanev of Bulgaria, 3-1. With the victory, Schultz became the only wrestler in American history to win three NCAA titles, an Olympic gold medal and a World gold medal. It's an achievement that still stood alone until Tom Brands matched it in 1996.

Dave won five lopsided matches before losing in the finals to Adlan Varev of the Soviet Union, 3-2.

Mark made the 1988 Olympic team but injuries severely hampered his performance and he finished sixth. He retired from competition in 1988, but Dave was far from finished. He engaged in a series of great contests with future World/Olympic champion Ken Monday, and lost out on bids to make the 1988 and 1992 Olympic teams.

But in 1993, Dave won his third silver medal in World competition. He also won World Cup titles in 1994 and 1995, as well as his second Goodwill Games gold medal in 1994.

Dave had his sights set on the 1996 Olympic team and was coaching the Foxcatcher team when unspeakable tragedy struck. On January 26, 1996, he was shot and killed by John du Pont, owner of the estate where the Foxcatcher team trained. Dave left his widow, Nancy, to carry on, with two children, Alexander and Danielle, and a stunning legacy in the sport he loved so much.

Dave Schultz was a seven-time World medallist, winning gold in the 1983 World Championships and 1984 Olympics. He won a total of 11 national titles, including one NCAA, and two Greco-Roman crowns. He won two Tbilisi tournaments, and the World Cup on five occasions. He was also Pan-American Games champion in 1987.

Perhaps his most impressive national title came at the U.S. Open Freestyle Championships in 1987. He was voted the outstanding wrestler after posting nine straight pins to win the 163-pound title. Among his victims were a pair of three-time NCAA champions – he pinned Jim Zalesky in 1:18 then did away with Nate Carr in 1:59.

Few people have ever impacted the sport of wrestling like Dave Schultz. After his passing, tributes poured in from all around the world. Soviet Union wrestlers were stunned and saddened by the loss of a man they greatly respected and admired.

Alexander Leipold, World champion from Germany, summarized the global reaction to Dave's death: "Wrestling has often opened the door to improved relations among countries. It is the sport of good will and Dave led the way. Wherever he went, he actively reached out in friendship to both the wrestling community and local citizenry."

"Dave was my wrestling mentor and my hero," said Kevin Jackson, Olympic and World champion. "He had the greatest technical mind of any wrestler, and his love of wrestling inspired everyone he met. He has touched so many lives."

"Dave was the most unselfish and giving person I ever met," said his longtime teammate, Bruce Baumgartner. "He was the most devoted father and husband – he loved his kids and his family."

Zeke Jones, 1991 World champion, told of a trip to the fabled Tbilisi in Russia with Dave in 1991: "To say that Dave was a Russian hero is an understatement. Throughout the tournament, Russian spectators would cry out, 'Dave Schultz, we love you! We love you, Dave Schultz!'" He said that Dave injured his shoulder and was tied in the finals 0-0 when the match was stopped. The referee raised the Russian's hand and then was bombarded with boos and items from the stands.

"The officials immediately huddled again (while dodging debris) and within seconds raised the hands of both wrestlers. The crowd went crazy as my teammates and I watched in disbelief. I thought, 'This must be the Twilight Zone.' There is no doubt that Dave could have run for mayor of Tbilisi. Even his opponent saluted and hugged him." *(27)*

If Dave Schultz was spreading good will with his wrestling, Mark Schultz was spreading intimidation. Their styles had always been a con-

Legends of the Mat – 141

Dave and Mark Schultz

trast, both on and off the mat.

"Dave and Mark Schultz were very different people and different athletes," said Gary Abbott, director of media relations at USA Wrestling. "You have to look at each one as an individual, with their own personalities and wrestling styles. The one thing that they shared in common was their love of the sport, and their passion for winning.

"Everybody knows that Dave was a wrestling genius, who made the most of his God-given abilities. Through hard work, intelligence and experience, Dave made himself into an international champion."

Though they had quite different physiques, both were very strong. Mark wasn't an advocate of weightlifting per se, but his gymnastics background helped him develop tremendous upper body strength. In his peak years, he could do over 50 chins with a slight leg kick, and 30 in a row from a dead hang.

Greg Strobel once had to convince the tailor making sports coats for the world team that the measurements he had turned in for Mark were correct. "The tailor kept shaking his head, insisting he couldn't have such a big chest and wide shoulders, and such a narrow waist. I finally convinced him that Mark Schultz was just not your average athlete."

Wayne Baughman, winner of 16 national titles and a member of numerous Olympic and world teams, had the highest praise for Mark in his book, *Wrestling On and Off the Mat*.

"Mark Schultz is definitely one of the greatest, if not the greatest, all-around athletes that has ever participated in the sport of wrestling," wrote Baughman. "As wrestling machines go, his design is close to perfect. His combination of quickness, balance and power is unexcelled." *(28)*

While Mark appeared to be tremendously strong, and was, Dave's appearance was very deceptive. Those who worked on the mat with him knew that he was also very strong, surprisingly so.

"Dave wasn't built like Mark but he was very powerful and that surprised a lot of people," said Strobel. "He also learned how to cope with great strength by necessity through his workouts with Mark."

Iron does indeed sharpen iron!

"Dave was also an important part in the success of Mark as a wrestler and as a person," said Abbott. "Mark was an amazing athlete, with great skills and talent. Some of the things Mark did on the mat did not seem possible for somebody of his size and weight. As different as Mark and Dave were, there was no doubt that they were very close and supportive of each other. You can not tell the story of one without including the other."

Mark agrees wholeheartedly, and is quick to acknowledge what his older brother has meant to him through the years.

"Dave was the greatest influence in my life," he said. "He made me who I am and taught me the most important lessons of life. He taught me humility, how to fight for myself and what it means to be a man. Dave was an extraordinary gift to the entire world and especially to me. He was the most honest and generous person I have ever known."

Mark was named head coach at Brigham Young University in 1994 and was there until 2000, when the school dropped the program. He also moved into the area of combat wrestling, and entered one Ultimate Fighting Championship (UFC). His dramatic victory over a larger man who was a high-degree black belt in karate was one of the highlights of the early years of the UFC, but Mark was eventually forced to stop competing in such events by BYU. Still, his reputation persists throughout the wrestling world and the combat sport world as one of the most respected and successful wrestlers in history

Even many of his Olympic teammates stood in awe of Mark Schultz and his raw talent. Randy Lewis was one of those. Lewis saw him compete against his University of Iowa teams, and was with him during the 1984 Olympic training camps.

"Mark Schultz was probably the most gifted wrestler I've ever seen – strength, flexibility, quickness, and just an unbelievable feel for wrestling," said Lewis. "Looking back, I don't see

Dave and Mark Schultz

how anyone ever beat him!"

Dave's legacy also lives on, primarily in the respect of wrestlers around the world and through the work of his widow, Nancy.

"Dave dedicated his life to sharing his extraordinary passion for amateur wrestling," said Nancy. She has used the Dave Schultz Foundation to "continue in his footsteps to encourage, promote and support amateur wrestling in the United States."

The Schultz name will endure in wrestling for as long as athletes take to the mat to test one another in Mankind's Oldest Sport.

Highlights – Dave Schultz was 1983 World champion and 1984 Olympic champion. He also earned three silver medals and two bronze medals in World competition and won four World Cups. He won the Pan-American Games in 1987 and Goodwill Games in 1986, and twice won titles at the Tbilisi tournament in the former Soviet Union. Dave won 11 national titles - eight in freestyle, two in Greco-Roman and one NCAA crown for University of Oklahoma in 1983. He had a record of 88-8-1 in college but his overall record is unknown.

Highlights – Mark Schultz was a three-time NCAA champion at the University of Oklahoma, with a career record of 97-15. He was Olympic champion in 1984 and World champion in 1985 and 1987. He also made the 1988 Olympic team and World teams in 1983 and 1986. Mark won four national freestyle titles and was Pan-American Games champion in 1987. His overall record is unknown.

Randy Lewis
It's All About the Pin

Randy Lewis won two NCAA titles for the Hawkeyes and won 74 matches in a row but suffered a devastating elbow injury his senior year.
(Photo courtesy of University of Iowa)

When he was a young boy growing up in Rapid City, South Dakota, Randy Lewis received some stern advice from his father, Larry. It was advice he never forgot. The words changed the way he thought about everything, including the sport of wrestling.

"I was about ten, and was wrestling with a boy who was a lot bigger than me," said Randy. "We were in my living room. He got on top of me and held me down. I couldn't get up. He said, 'If you give up, I'll let you up.' So, I said 'I give up.'

"My dad was watching and he took me aside and told me, 'A Lewis never gives up.'"

Randy paused while telling the story, a serious look on his face.

"And I've never given up since. Never. In every workout and in every match, I've always fought for every takedown, and every point. Sure, I've lost takedowns and matches, but I've never given up."

Anyone who saw Randy Lewis wrestle in high school, in college, or in freestyle competition, all the way up through the World Championships and Olympic Games, knows the truth of that statement.

Being born without a right pectoralis muscle didn't make him quit.

Suffering one of the worst injuries ever seen on a wrestling mat, during his senior year in college, didn't make him give up.

A bitter, drawn-out legal battle to earn a spot on the 1984 Olympic team, didn't make him quit.

All those things only made him love the sport of wrestling all the more.

Lewis started wrestling at the age of ten, and quickly enjoyed tremendous success. He won age-group state titles in South Dakota, and nationally. In his final three seasons at Rapids City High School, he was 89-0 with 83 pins. As a sophomore, he won the state title by pinning all 29 of his opponents. At one point, he held the national high school record with 45 consecutive pins.

He won the USA Wrestling Junior Nationals in 1977 at 123 pounds, and one month later, in Las Vegas, won the Junior World championship in dramatic fashion. Trailing Japan's Hideaka Tamiyama in the second period, Lewis

Randy Lewis punishes an opponent during the 1984 Olympics in Los Angeles. The former South Dakota high school and University of Iowa star breezed through the Games without a close match to capture the gold medal at 136.5 pounds. *(Photo courtesy of Steve Brown)*

threw one of his big moves and pinned Tamiyama, who just a year later was world champion at the senior level.

Heavily recruited by college coaches, Lewis selected the University of Iowa to continue his wrestling career. It was a great move, for both the kid from Rapid City and the Hawkeye faithful.

As a pure freshman, Lewis made the Hawkeye team and began delighting Iowa fans immediately. When behind early in matches, he staged dramatic rallies, often pinning his bewildered foe after a flurry of big moves. He rolled up a 30-6 record, and made it all the way to the 1978 NCAA finals at 126 pounds, before losing to a tough veteran from Iowa State, Mike Land.

With the college season over, Lewis turned immediately to freestyle, and pinned his way up the ladder to make the 1978 World team at 125.5 pounds. Among his victims were World bronze medallist Jack Reinwand, and former Olympians Joe Corso and Jimmy Carr. In the final trials, he defeated Nick Gallo, the NCAA's Outstanding Wrestler award winner, twice by lopsided scores. And 1968 Olympic silver medallist Don Behm retired midway through his match with Lewis, trailing by nearly 10 points at the time.

Though he didn't place in the World meet held in Mexico City, it was a big step on the learning ladder for Lewis. He saw Lee Kemp win the gold medal at 163 and John Peterson win a bronze medal at 180.5. Always a keen student of the sport, both its mechanics and its history, Lewis began to form in his mind the concept of what it took to become the world's best.

Returning to college competition, Lewis put together two of the best seasons in collegiate history. In 1979, he posted a 36-0 record as a sophomore at 126 pounds, and made it to the NCAA finals again. Facing another undefeated wrestler, John Azevedo of Cal State-Bakersfield, the two matmen put on a dazzling display of moves and counter moves. When it was all over, Lewis stood on the victory platform, with a 20-14 victory and his first NCAA title.

Randy Lewis

Almost immediately he announced he was moving up to 134 pounds for his junior season, thereby challenging the talented Darryl Burley of Lehigh. Burley had won the 134-pound title in 1979 as a pure freshman by defeating Mike Land in the finals. The Lehigh star was a wrestler who looked nearly unbeatable, a perfect blend of style, grace, speed and strength.

Lewis met Burley in the All-Star meet... and pinned him. Then he defeated the Engineer in the dual meet, 8-4. The 1980 NCAA finals at Oregon State pitted the two champions against one another in the feature match of the tournament. After Azevedo, Lewis's foe the year before, won the title at 126, Lewis captured the 134-pound championship with an 11-3 victory.

That summer, the Hawkeye sensation made the 1980 Olympic team in dramatic fashion, plowing through the competition. He defeated five former national champions and two former Olympians, all but one by pin. But Lewis, and many other top American athletes, was denied the opportunity to show his stuff against the best wrestlers in the world when President Carter announced that the United States was boycotting the Olympics in Moscow as a protest against the Soviet Union's invasion of Afghanistan.

After the bitter disappointment of the Olympics, Lewis entered his final season of college determined to carve out a permanent place in the history of the sport. But fate stepped in and dealt him a cruel blow.

Midway through his senior year and riding a 74-match winning streak, he suffered a crushing injury, one of the worst ever seen on a college mat. Battling Jim Gibbons of Iowa State before a huge crowd at Hilton Coliseum in Ames, Lewis hit the mat with his left arm extended. The elbow bent the opposite way. Onlookers, including both coaching staffs and the referee, were stunned by the severity of the injury.

Though the damage would have ended the season for most wrestlers, Lewis was not about to quit. He wanted to be a four-time All-American, and in order to qualify for the 1981 NCAA Championships just six weeks away, he had to place in the top four of the Big Ten meet. He had won the Big Ten as a freshman, sophomore and junior, but this year his only goal was to qualify for nationals. Wrestling with virtually one arm, he placed second with a courageous performance.

He finished seventh in his final NCAAs and received a long standing ovation from the fans. ABC televised the nationals, and paid homage to Lewis by showing him on the awards medal at the conclusion of the show.

Lewis was fourth in the Worlds in 1982, and always felt he was cheated out of a gold or silver medal. He actually won his semifinal match 13-11 against Simeon Chrerev of Bulgaria, the defending world champion, but the score was overturned while Randy was in the locker room preparing for the gold-medal match. The victory was given to the Bulgarian, 13-13, referee's decision, and the kid from Rapid City wound up in fourth place.

Years later, he said that scoring reversal by officials hurt him far worse than the dislocated elbow injury.

"Facing that adversity (the elbow) made me better in the future, because I learned how to be mentally tough enough to deal with injuries," he explained. "I don't look back on that match and say I wish it never happened. My regrets in my career aren't about that match at all. They are more about the times officials stepped in and changed the outcome of matches, like in the world championships of 1982. That the sort of thing that angers me, not the matches I was injured in." *(29)*

Lewis bounced back to win a gold medal at the 1983 Pan-American Games in Caracas, Venezuela, and in 1984, found himself locked in a tremendous battle for a spot on the Olympic team at 136.5 pound with Burley, Ricky Delagatta and Lee Roy Smith. After considerable controversy, lawsuits and court rulings, Lewis defeated Smith in a special wrestle-off in a closed wrestling room. Then, he had to defeat Delagatta just several days before the Games started in Los Angeles.

Finally on the team, Lewis blew through the weight class. He won the gold medal without a close match, earning tech falls over all five foes. It was a typical finals, with Lewis outscoring Japan's

Randy Lewis

Kosei Akashai by a 24-11 margin. The end came with 1:08 left in the match.

Lewis continued to wrestle for another eight years. Like Rick Sanders a decade earlier, he was also well known for his pursuits away from the wrestling mat. Few wrestlers enjoyed the nightlife as much as Randy Lewis. So, many fans were shocked when he scored a hard-fought 7-5 win over World champion John Smith at the 1988 Olympic trials in Topeka. However, Smith came back to make the team in the final trials.

By the time he decided to call it a career, Lewis had engaged in well over 1,000 matches and won dozens of championships, at nearly every level. Amazingly, he wrestled a total of 27 men who had won medals in either the Olympics or World Championships, and owned victories over 24 of them. In addition, he had wrestled someone from every American World or Olympic team from the years 1968 through 1996, except for the 1975 team. He held victories over 18 American wrestlers who were World/Olympic team members, and he defeated a total of 21 NCAA champions during his career.

And through it all, he gave the fans what they came to see the expectation of a pin or a wild, high-scoring match every single time he went out. Dale Anderson, who won two NCAA titles for Michigan State nearly 15 years earlier, was among those who enjoyed the Lewis style of wrestling.

"I hadn't been to an international meet for years, but went to see a U.S. team wrestle the Soviets," said Anderson. "Lewis was the most exciting wrestler on the mat. He was going full bore all the way, and won in the closing seconds on pure determination. He was fun to watch."

His 64 career pins put Lewis second on the Iowa all-time list, behind only Ed Banach. It is believed he had the highest scoring matches in both the NCAA finals (a combined 34 points) and in an Olympics finals (a combined 35 points).

Though there is no way to prove it, Randy believes he may have been the highest scoring wrestler of all time, per match.

"I'd rather lose a match by a 16-14 score than win 1-0," he said. "You're going out to see 'who the man is,' not to see who can win by the rules and stall your way to a win. At least, that's my philosophy.

"Every tournament I ever entered, I wanted to pin my way through and win the O.W.," he said with a laugh. "I loved to wrestle in front of those large Iowa crowds, and I wanted the fans to have a good show.

"I wrestled for twenty-three years and loved every second of it."

He left his mark on the national and world wrestling scene, and in his home state, as well. In 1999, *Sports Illustrated* magazine ranked the top fifty sports figures of the 20th Century in all fifty states. Randy Lewis was one of the highest regarded wrestlers in the entire poll, ranking seventh among all athletes in South Dakota history.

"I've never met anyone who loves the sport more than Randy Lewis," said Kyle Klingman, associate director of the International Wrestling Institute and Museum in Iowa. "He can talk for hours about wrestling, on any level. He's a walking encyclopedia on the sport, on both America and the international scene."

"He was great for Iowa wrestling and great for the sport overall," said Dan Gable, his coach at Iowa and in the 1984 Olympics. "Randy Lewis was a very unusual, exciting type of wrestler; he wasn't afraid to give you something, anything, really, to see what you could do with it. He came to wrestle every time, every match."

Highlights – Randy Lewis was 89-0 his last three years in high school, and 127-11-1 at the University of Iowa, including a winning streak of 74 in a row. He scored 64 pins in college, good for second place on the all-time Hawkeye list. He won two NCAA titles and was a four-time All-American. He won the 1984 Olympic gold medal at 136.5 pounds, the 1983 Pan-American Games and was silver medallist in the 1982 World Cup. He was Junior World champion in 1977, and fourth in the senior World Championships in 1982. His overall record is unknown.

Kenny Monday
Tough As a Puma

Ken Monday was a four-time state champion in Oklahoma who went on to become a star at Oklahoma State. He also was an Olympic and World gold medallist.

For many years the tournament held in Tbilisi, Russia, was considered by many to be the toughest and most competitive wrestling tournament in the world. It was not uncommon for a weight class at the famed event to include ten or more Russian wrestlers vying for the prestigious title. In the words of Dan Gable, "the Olympics are nowhere near as hard as this tournament".

For Kenny Monday, the 1988 Tbilisi Tournament marked the time and place where he made an international name for himself. Not only did Monday win the tournament by going 9-0 (along with being given the outstanding wrestler award), but it was there where he was given his nickname of "The Puma" by the Soviets.

A puma is described as a large and powerful animal with a long slender body – a definition that fits Kenny Monday well. As a wrestler, Monday used these assets, along with blazing speed and quickness, to win nearly every tournament imaginable. Since the Tbilisi tournament is no longer contested, Kenny Monday will stand as the only wrestler ever to win the Olympic Games, the World Championships, the Tbilisi tournament, the NCAA title, and a Junior National title.

Like a lot of wrestlers, Kenny's career took off early in life. At the age of six, Monday attended an after-school program at the local YMCA in Tulsa, Oklahoma. When his oldest brother, Mike, took up wrestling, both Kenny and his other brother, Jim, followed suit and began participating in the sport.

It was during these formative wrestling years that Monday knew he wanted to achieve greatness in the sport. The wrestling competition during the 1972 Olympic Games in Munich, Germany, gave Monday his first taste of wrestling's premier event.

In the 1996 Olympic trials, Ken Monday battled his way past many of the nation's top wrestlers, including four-time NCAA champ Pat Smith. Monday emerged victorious from the trials to make his third Olympic team at 163 pounds. *(Photo courtesy of Ginger Robinson and W.I.N. Magazine)*

"I caught the Olympic vision when I was ten years old," said Monday. "Watching the 1972 Olympics on television was when I fully understood what the Olympics was all about and what the highest accomplishment was in the sport of wrestling. I knew at ten I wanted to be an Olympic gold medallist and to be the best in the world."

In high school, Monday blossomed into a champion. Wrestling at Booker T. Washington High School in Tulsa from 1977 through 1980, Monday posted a spectacular 140-0-1 record with four state titles and a Junior Nationals freestyle crown in 1977. His lone tie came during his senior year when Monday moved up from 141 pounds to face future Oklahoma State teammate and two-time NCAA champion Mike Sheets at 148 pounds.

When deciding on a college to attend, Monday allowed his options to go as far as the Oklahoma border. Growing up in Tulsa, Monday attended Oklahoma State dual meets and United States Wrestling Federation events held at Gallagher-Iba arena in Stillwater. Attending Oklahoma State became a simple choice.

"My parents would take us down to Oklahoma State meets so I had the privilege to witness some great wrestling and some great wrestling teams that Myron Roderick coached at the time," said Monday. "I got to see a lot of great wrestlers and a lot of tradition growing up. I didn't want to wrestle against the state of Oklahoma and Oklahoma State had the greatest and most storied tradition in wrestling and that kind of drew me into it. I wanted to wrestle for the Cowboys because I watched those guys all my life."

Wrestling at Oklahoma State was also a matter of good timing. The Cowboys retained the services of Lee Roy Smith as an assistant coach, which meant a quality training partner

Kenny Monday

for Monday in the practice room. Smith won the 142-pound NCAA weight class in 1980 as a senior so there was a slot open for Monday to compete in as a freshman. Also instrumental in Monday's choice to attend OSU was head coach Tommy Chesbro, whom he still considers one of the best folkstyle coaches ever.

While competing for Oklahoma State, Monday did not disappoint the Cowboy faithful. During his four-year stint in Stillwater, Monday compiled a 121-12-2 record with 51 pins, winning two Big Eight titles, and an NCAA title in 1984 after placing second the previous two years.

Yet it was his legendary battles with Iowa State wrestler Nate Carr that will be forever linked with the college wrestling career of Kenny Monday. The two conference rivals met in finals of the Big Eight and NCAA tournament in 1982 and 1983 at 150 pounds. Monday defeated Carr both times at the Big Eights, with Carr returning the "favor" two weeks later, both in exciting overtime matches in the NCAA finals.

"We are the best of friends now but in college I don't think we liked each other at the time because I wanted to beat him and he wanted to beat me," said Carr. "Our rivalry was very intense. Kenny Monday is the ultimate competitor and he's going to get right in your face and he will find a way to beat you. It was a war.

"When we went out to wrestle it wasn't like we were buddies. He wanted the bragging rights and I wanted the bragging rights. We disliked each other because of competitive reasons. We took our rivalry on and off the mat. There were a lot of words exchanged between us behind closed doors."

After his college career ended, Monday took a short break before making the transition to freestyle wrestling. Immediately following the 1984 wrestling season, Monday went to Arizona State to assist Bobby Douglas with the Sun Devils program for a year and a half. However, Monday lacked the quality workout partners in Tempe to become competitive internationally.

By the end of the 1986 calendar year Monday decided to make the move back to his home state where Joe Seay had taken over as head coach of Oklahoma State. It was in Stillwater where Monday began his training in earnest for the 1988 Olympic Games.

To make his run toward the gold medal in Seoul, Korea, Monday would need a quality training partner to push him toward greatness. That is when he talked his former Oklahoma State teammate Mike Sheets into trying to make the Olympic team at the 180.5-pound weight class. Practice sessions between the two are now legendary. On one occasion a practice match got so heated that they carried the action all the way into the locker room showers.

"We didn't quit in practice," said Sheets. "It didn't matter if you hit the wall or whatever. It was one of those situations where you were trying to get every advantage you could and if bouncing off the walls was part of it, then that was part of it, there were no time-outs. When it came to training, it was all business. We were friends off the mat but we were all business when we were training. It was high intensity."

Simply making the Olympic team proved to be a huge undertaking for Monday. Standing in the way of his dreams of an Olympic gold medal was the irrepressible Dave Shultz.

Prior to the 1988 Olympic Trials, Schultz had owned the 163-pound weight class in the United States. During the previous five seasons Dave Shultz's international success was remarkable. Not only did he win the silver medal at the 1987 World Championships but he was the 1984 Olympic champion and 1983

Legends of the Mat – 150

Kenny Monday

World champion. He also placed second and third at the 1985 and 1986 World meets.

"If it wasn't for Dave Schultz, it would have been hard for me to win an Olympic gold medal," said Monday. "In '86, I was about 60 percent of Dave. I wrestled him a couple of times in '87 and he dominated me. He was being hailed as one of the best wrestlers we had in the world and I knew I would have to beat him.

"Every day when I woke up and every night before I went to bed I was thinking about how I was going to beat Dave and what did I need to do to beat the rest of the world. I got to the point where if I was working out three times a day I thought that was good enough, but it wasn't, so I had to add another practice. I never imagined that I had to train that hard just to make the team."

At the Olympic Trials in 1988, Monday had finally cut the corner on Schultz. During the final Olympic qualifier, Monday defeated Shultz 3-1 to earn a trip to the finals of the ladder-forming tournament of the Olympic Trials. The two met again several weeks later during the best-of-three series to determine who would represent the United States at the Olympics. Again, Monday was the victor, this time by scores of 6-1 and 5-1.

Even in defeat Schultz showed his championship character. During the team training camp, the defending Olympic champion offered his services to help Monday in his quest for the gold medal. Schultz also provided added incentive as one of Monday's coaches during his gold medal match.

At the Olympics, Monday blazed through the competition, giving up only two points in seven matches leading up to his final match for the gold medal. There, he faced-off against Adlan Varaev of the Soviet Union, the reigning world champion and an opponent who had defeated Monday twice in three previous meetings.

The two were deadlocked at 2-2 heading into sudden victory overtime. In the deciding period, the two exhausted warriors eventually found themselves on their knees in a tie-up position. With 1:30 remaining, Monday locked his arms around Varaev and bear-hugged his Russian adversary straight to his back for three points and the win. The victory represented the first time an African-American had won an Olympic gold medal in wrestling, a fact few people know about Monday's career.

"Both wrestlers looked like they had nothing left," said Bobby Douglas, who was one of the coaches in Monday's corner. "There was a time when Kenny Monday could have accepted the silver but he was determined to win the gold medal. There was nothing but pure determination that won that. It was a magnificent event to see that come out in a champion."

At the conclusion of the match, Schultz gave Monday the ride of his life. When the newly-crowned gold medallist came down from the wrestling platform Schultz hoisted him on his shoulders and paraded him around the mat in a victory celebration.

"That wasn't planned to happen," said Monday. "He asked me if he could be in my corner once I made it to the finals. After I won, he lifted me up on his shoulders and carried me around the mat. It means more now because of Dave's untimely death and his passing. Looking back, that was a very special moment in my life. I have a big picture of that in my house on the wall."

Upset that they didn't win the gold medal at the Olympics, the Soviet Union coaches allowed Arsen Fadzaev to move up from the 149.5-pound weight class to challenge for the 163-pound crown at the World Championships the following year. Considered at the time by many to be the best wrestler in the world, Fadzaev was the winner

Kenny Monday

of the 1988 Olympics as well as the previous four World Championships.

Monday and Fadzaev were placed in opposite pools at the 1989 Worlds so a meeting in the finals was expected. Both wrestlers went unchallenged in their preliminary matches so a showdown between two Olympic champions from the year before became a reality.

However, the potential dream match became a mismatch. Monday overwhelmed Fadzaev with his speed and size and easily won the match by a score of 6-1. After losing to Monday at 163 pounds, Fadzaev went back down to the 149.5-pound weight class and won the next two World Championships and the 1992 Olympics.

"He was tired of cutting weight and he felt like he could go up and win and they let him," said Monday. "They were still kind of mad at Varaev for losing so they let Fadzaev go up but that was a big mistake on their part. I don't think they realized until afterward that he wasn't big enough or strong enough to beat me."

In 1990, Monday missed out on making the world team but came back the next year and placed second at the 1991 World Championships. He made another Olympic team in 1992 and was wrestling well throughout the entire season before blowing out his left shoulder during a practice nine days before the competition was to start.

Despite the injury, Monday reached the finals, winning his first four matches without giving up a point. In the finals against Korea's Jang-Soon, he gave up only one point in the match but it was a crucial one. Jang-Soon scored a late takedown on a Monday shot and won the gold medal by a score of 1-0.

"Honestly, I was about 80 percent with that left arm," said Monday. "I had a good tournament, really. I didn't get scored on until the finals. I got in the semis and I dominated the Russian but it just wasn't meant to be. I went from thinking I wasn't going to compete to having the opportunity to win another gold medal."

After the 1992 Olympics, Monday took a couple of years off from wrestling. He opened up a coffee shop and a Subway shop with former NBA player John Starks and began exploring his professional options. Monday wrestled sporadically throughout 1994 and began training in earnest in November of 1995 in hopes of making another Olympic team the following year.

During Monday's three-year absence, Schultz had taken over the 163-pound weight class in the United States. From 1993 through 1995, Schultz had placed second, seventh, and fifth respectively at the World Championships. Tragically, Dave Schultz would be missing from the 1996 Olympic Trials.

On January 26, 1996, Dave Schultz was murdered at the Foxcatcher Farms near Newtown Square, Pennsylvania, by eccentric millionaire John E. duPont. In an appalling event that shook the nation, one of the greatest ambassadors for the sport of wrestling was gone.

"If I was going to make that Olympic team I was going to have to beat Dave Schultz because he was wrestling pretty well at that time," said Monday. "I went back to training and had a good environment with Kevin Jackson and Melvin Douglas.

"In January, I was coming back from the store and Melvin was in my apartment and he came right out to my car and said, 'It happened.' He said duPont shot him. I just collapsed to the ground. I couldn't believe it. I'm just a wrestler but he was my main competitor. He was the guy I still woke up thinking about. All the wind went out of my sails at that point."

In the face of a heartbreaking personal loss, Monday continued his Olympic pursuit.

— Kenny Monday —

At the 1996 Olympic Trials, Monday defeated four-time NCAA champion Pat Smith in straight matches to make his third and final Olympic team. At the Olympics, the former Oklahoma State star won his first two matches but lost to eventual champion Bouvaisar Saitiev in the semi-finals. Monday placed sixth, in his final wrestling competition.

"He is the ultimate competitor," said Nate Carr, 1988 Olympic bronze medallist. "My hat goes off to him. When I look at Kenny Monday, I see his greatness in the fact that here is a guy that has actually won at every level. I can't say that. You have to give honor where honor is due. He is truly one of the greatest wrestlers ever. That's all there is to it."

"I had a great career and I have no regrets," said Monday. "I won every tournament that there was to win. I don't think there was a tournament I didn't win at some point in time. I had some big wins and I had some big losses and I don't take any of those things back because they made me who I am."

Greatness in the sport of wrestling is based on several things. One of the most important criteria an athlete is judged on is how good his competition was. Kenny Monday not only won every major tournament in the world but he beat the best wrestlers in the world in the process. The man the Soviets call "The Puma" deserves to be recognized as a legend in the sport of wrestling.

Highlights – Ken Monday had a college record of 121-12-2 and was NCAA champion and a three-time All-American. He won four national freestyle titles, and was an Olympic champion, World champion, Olympic silver medal winner and World silver medallist. He also won titles at the Pan-American Games and World Cup. His total record is unknown.

John Smith
Six Times King of the World

John Smith had a common name but a very uncommon devotion to the sport of wrestling. Winning a total of six Olympic/ World Championships puts him alone at the top of the list of great American freestyle wrestlers.
(Photo courtesy of BRUTE)

To win a World or Olympic Championship is the ultimate goal of any amateur athlete. To date, 37 different American wrestlers (men and women) have earned the right to be called "World Champion."

There are even a dozen multi-World champions in American wrestling history. But John Smith stands alone at the top of the mountain when it comes to the total number of World titles won. Unbelievably, the Oklahoma superstar has six World Championship level gold medals sitting in the trophy case at home in Stillwater, Oklahoma.

There are only a few records in the sports world that defy belief, and seem so Herculean in nature that they seem impossible to break. But time has proven that even the loftiest of records are not immortal. At one time, Lou Gehrig's record of playing in 2,130 consecutive games was considered beyond the realm of mortals, as was Babe Ruth's record of 714 career home runs. Both have been eclipsed now, and are only distant second bests.

Tiger Woods has proved that even the most hallowed marks in golf are no longer safe. And in 2003 Emmitt Smith shattered the career NFL rushing record that was held by Walter Payton for fifteen years.

When Cael Sanderson stunned the sports world with his 159-0 record in college, the wrestling fraternity looked at the next record which seemed unbreakable. And at least one long-time national sports writer thinks he's found it.

"I can't imagine anyone breaking John Smith's record of six straight World titles," said the writer. "First of all, they have to make the U.S. team six straight years which in itself is very, very difficult. Then, they have to beat the very best the world has to offer for six consecutive years.

"I don't see it happening any time soon," he concluded.

What John Smith accomplished during his competitive years is indeed remarkable. And yet this amazing career got off to a very rocky start back home in Del City, Oklahoma. The fact is that John Smith lost his first five matches, and all by pin!

However, it didn't take him long to straighten things out. By the time he was in fourth grade, he was city champion. At high school, he was a two-time state champion, and was eager to move on to college and test himself

John Smith sets up the low-single during his college days at Oklahoma State. The move made him famous throughout the world. *(Photo courtesy of Oklahoma State University)*

against the finest collegiate wrestlers in the United States. Years later, John gave credit to his older brother, Lee Roy, for providing the spark that made him work so hard.

Lee Roy was the first of the wrestling Smith brothers. A three-time All-American at Oklahoma State University, he was NCAA champion at 142 pounds in 1980. Three years later, he won a silver medal at the World Championships in Kiev, Russia. In 1984, he and Randy Lewis participated in one of the most heated battles in American history to make the U.S. Olympic team at 136.5 pounds. Lewis finally won the spot and claimed the gold medal in Los Angeles. One of the first comments Lewis made afterwards is that Lee Roy would have won the gold medal, too.

Lee Roy was indeed a fierce competitor, and he showed his younger brothers – beginning with John and continuing through Pat and Mark – how to compete at the very highest level.

"I worked with Lee Roy when he was preparing for the 1984 Olympic trials," Smith told Mike Spence, writing for Olympian magazine. "I learned a lot from him about how to prepare for competition. I saw the fire in his eyes, the determination. He whipped me every day. He worked me over. He rubbed my face in the mat. It taught me what kind of mental attitude you have to have to be a world champion." *(30)*

The mental attitude that John locked onto was a Spartan one, for sure. He learned at an early age to deny himself some of life's greatest pleasures at the dinner table. His discipline and focus was apparent at an early age.

"I saw John in eighth grade and he was so little that he didn't look anything special," said Ron Good, longtime editor of *Amateur Wrestling News*, published in Oklahoma City. "He won state, but he didn't win the Junior Nationals. He didn't have much horsepower, but he was very quick. And he was very determined.

"His dad, Lee Roy, told me a story about his

John Smith

determination. Lee Roy said that he couldn't get John to eat ice cream with the rest of the family. He just told his dad that he wasn't going to eat ice cream, and that was it. I think the turning point for John was his total drive and determination. He never cut much weight during his career because he kept his weight under control all year around. Even at a very early age, he knew what he wanted and was able to focus in on it."

John made the OSU lineup as a freshman, but didn't place in the NCAAs. However, he was second as a sophomore in 1985 at 134 pounds, losing in the finals 7-4 to Wisconsin's Jim Jordan. Disappointed with his performance, John decided to red-shirt the next year and change his style of wrestling. He adopted Jordan's style of constant motion, and then developed his own unique low-style of shooting. The transformation was almost immediate. He captured his first U.S. national freestyle title in 1986 and then won a gold medal at the Goodwill Games.

Returning to college competition after a year off, the "new" John Smith was nearly unbeatable. He won his second Big Eight crown in 1987 and his first NCAA championship. He breezed through the 134-pound field and blistered Gil Sanchez in the finals, 18-4.

He then turned his attention to World competition. He claimed a gold medal at the Pan-American Games championships in Indianapolis, then made the 1987 World team.

Journeying to Clermont-Ferrand, France, Smith shocked the unsuspecting global wrestling community by winning the gold medal at 136.5 pounds in the World Championships! He won his first six matches by scores of 9-1, a pin in 3:51, 6-2, 16-3, 10-2 and 15-2. His only close match came in the finals, where he defeated Khazer Isaev of the Soviet Union, the defending World champion, 5-4. At 22 years and 20 days of age, he was the second youngest American to ever win a world title, just four months shy of Lee Kemp's record.

The next season was even more amazing. John won his second NCAA title at 134 pounds, beating Iowa's tough Joe Melchiore in the finals, 9-2, and closing out his college career with a 90-match winning streak, at that time the second longest streak in collegiate history. A month later, he won his second national freestyle title, and then entered the Olympic trials in Topeka, Kansas. There he met one of his toughest foes, a champion who has since become one of his biggest fans.

Randy Lewis had endured a traumatic struggle with Lee Roy Smith to wind up on the 1984 Olympic team. He won a gold medal at 136.5 pounds in Los Angeles and continued wrestling for the next several years. At the Topeka trials, he found himself on a collision course with another Smith, this one named John.

In a matchup of Olympic and World champions, Lewis won a hard-fought 7-5 triumph at the trials. But John defeated the former Hawkeye two straight matches in the final wrestleoffs to make the 1988 Olympic team. In Seoul, South Korea, Smith proved the 1987 World title was no fluke.

He came back with his first Olympic title, winning the gold medal at 136.5 pounds. He won all seven matches, including a 4-0 finals victory over Stephan Sarkisian of the Soviet Union.

"Right now, I'm still kind of stunned," he admitted afterwards. "It's better than the World championship. A gold medal has been a dream of mine since I started wrestling in the first or second grade."

He received plaudits from just about every source, including from assistant coach Dan Gable: "When he steps on the mat, he floats. He's almost like air, and it's tough to take air down."

Smith's successes continued unabated in 1989 as honors flowed in from all directions. He was named "Athlete of the Year" by USA Wrestling and was presented with the "Master of Technique" award by FILA. Oklahoma State hired him as assistant wrestling coach, and he continued wrestling at the highest level imaginable. He won his third freestyle title and his third World title. His six matches were won by scores of 8-1, 12-3, 8-2, pin, 10-1 and, finally, 6-0, over Gary Bohay of Canada.

In 1990, he won titles at the U.S. freestyle nationals and the Goodwill Games. At the World Championships in Tokyo, he blew through the

Bringing the same intensity to his coaching that he brought to his wrestling has made John Smith one of the most successful college coaches of all time. In 2006, his Cowboys claimed their fourth straight NCAA team title. *(Photo courtesy of Oklahoma State University)*

competition without a close match. He won his six matches, by pin, 16-0, 15-4, 11-0, 6-0 and then 10-0 in the finals over Rousen Vassilev of Bulgaria. Clearly, John Smith was sailing on unchartered waters in the world of American wrestling!

In an event in Pittsburgh, hailed as the main attraction in the World Wrestling Grand Championship, he defeated Soviet Union superstar Sergei Beloglazov, 6-2. Beloglazov owned two Olympic titles and six World titles, five at 125.5 pounds and one at 136.5 pounds.

To close out the year, Smith also won the James E. Sullivan Award as the nation's finest amateur athlete, the first wrestler to ever be so honored. In addition, he was named "Sportsman of the Year" by the United States Olympic Committee.

While many thought that Smith won primarily with his exceptional skills and talents, insiders recognized that he was a very tough athlete, both mentally and physically. He was also extremely focused and determined, two attributes that served him well during his unprecedented march to wrestling glory.

The focus arrived after his sophomore year in college, when he lost in the finals of the 1985 NCAA tournament to Jim Jordan of Wisconsin, at 134 pounds.

"I said to myself, 'That's it, I'm not losing again. From here on out, it's going to be a different story.'" He took a redshirt year at OSU and focused all his energies on getting better, at all levels. He put personal relationships and feelings second to his drive to become the best wrestler possible.

"I made a true commitment," he said. "After I won my first world championships in 1987, I kept raising the bar. I no longer wanted to be just the best in my weight class. I wanted to be considered the best wrestler in the entire world, at any weight. I kept setting the bar higher and working with all I had to get there.

"There are probably a few wrestlers out there who think they make a commitment, but I really made a commitment. Anything that gets in my way, I pretty much eliminate." *(31)*

Legends of the Mat – 157

He admitted that he often would get into slugging matches with workout partners due to the intensity he brought into the room, and that relationships with family and girlfriends suffered. All the while he was growing in the areas of technique and skills, he was also maturing into a very physical wrestler, a fact often overlooked by observers – but not by those who tangled with him on the mat.

"Anyone who doesn't think John Smith wasn't a physical and punishing wrestler never wrestled him," said Tom Brands. "The first time I wrestled him in a freestyle tournament, I was young and unprepared for what hit me. He leg-laced me with such force and power that my legs were sore for a week." *(32)*

By 1991, Smith was recognized as one of the top two or three wrestlers in the entire world. He cemented that claim with another Pan-American Games gold medal, and then traveled to Varna, Bulgaria, to claim his fifth straight World/Olympic title, again without a close match. He defeated his seven foes by a combined score of 78-12. FILA, the governing body for amateur wrestling around the world, recognized his sensational accomplishments by selecting him as the Outstanding Wrestler in the World in 1991.

John suffered one of his very rare losses in the 1992 Olympic trials, to John Fisher, 4-2. But he rebounded to defeat Fisher twice, 3-1 and 6-5, and make the American team. Competing in Barcelona, he dropped a close, overtime match to Cuba's Lazaro Reinoso, but still won the title by virtue of his five victories. He defeated Russia's Gazikhan Azizov 17-1 and Iran's Asgan Mohammadian 6-0 to lock up the gold medal.

He returned home to a hero's welcome, and shortly after was named the seventh head coach in Oklahoma State University history.

Smith made a relatively smooth transition to coaching as the Cowboys captured the NCAA team title in his first full season as head coach, in 1994. Since then, he has stamped himself as one of the nation's finest coaches. In 2006, his Cowboys ran away with the NCAA title, their fourth in a row. They won by a 122.5 to 84 point margin over runnerup Minnesota.

Among his most famous colleges athletes were brothers Pat and Mark. He helped Pat make collegiate history in 1994 by serving as head coach when Pat became the very first wrestler to ever win four NCAA Division I championships.

While Pat eventually became an assistant coach for John at OSU, Mark began his collegiate career and wound up as a three-time All-American. With the achievements of John, Pat, Lee Roy and Mark, the Smith family of Del City, Oklahoma, has won general acknowledgement as wrestling's No. 1 family of all time.

And the lion's share of the credit goes to John.

"John Smith invented his own style of wrestling, using low-level leg shots and finishes that revolutionized the sport during his era," said Gary Abbott, director of media relations for USA Wrestling. "Nobody could stop Smith's offensive attacks effectively. Once they thought they had learned how to stop John, he changed things up and found another way to score.

"Consider that he won a World or Olympic gold medal for six straight years. The rest of the world did everything they could to prepare for him and beat him, but they never could. John retired at the age of 27, still at the age that most wrestlers reach their physical prime. Who knows how long his streak might have gone if he had chosen to go for another Olympic cycle?

"John was so dominant that it is easier to remember the very few times that he lost a match than the hundreds of times that he won with dominance. Most of John Smith's matches, even at the World and Olympic level, were like technique clinics. We may never see another U.S. freestyle wrestler like him, and those who saw him at his best have memories for a lifetime.

"The United States has never had an international wrestler who could rise to the occasion and perform at his best when it counted like John Smith."

Randy Lewis is among those who think John Smith was as good as America has ever produced

The ability to focus intently was one of the many attributes that John Smith had in his arsenal during his legendary career. *(Photo courtesy of Steve Brown)*

on the international level. In fact, Lewis thinks he was the best.

"John was our best technician on his feet, along with being a great freestyler," said Lewis in 2006. "If you shot in on him, he could tilt you, he had real good counters. He was real good on the mat and he stayed in his positions. I have watched him finish and I've never seen another American as good as he was. He's our best takedown guy and our best technician.

"He was always scoring points. You can't win six years in a row by winning matches 1-0. It catches up with you. If you look at the great ones, they all scored a lot of points and they were all good in all positions.

"He's got everything," Lewis concluded. "I definitely think he's our best freestyler ever."

In 1993, a larger-than-life statue of John was unveiled at Del City High School, outside the gym which now bears his name. In 1996, he was voted one of the 100 greatest Olympians of all time. In 2003, he was inducted into the initial class of the FILA International Wrestling Hall of Fame.

Smith moved into the international coaching arena, as well. The 1998 U.S. team under his direction placed third in the World Championships in Iran, and he was one of three head coaches for the 2000 Olympic team. He has been one of the world's top clinicians for a decade and studies the sport like few others ever have.

But most impressive of all, perhaps, is the amazing legacy he has left: He was a ferocious competitor with a new, innovative style that simply was the best of its era. His record of six consecutive World level championships may indeed be the record that stands the longest in American amateur wrestling.

Highlights – John Smith posted a collegiate mark of 154-7-2 at Oklahoma State University, winning two NCAA titles and finishing second once. He also won five national freestyle titles, two Pan-American Games titles and two Goodwill Games titles. He was Olympic champion in 1988 and 1992, and World champion four times. He had an overall international record of 100-5 and his national freestyle record was 77-3, for a combined freestyle mark of 177-8. His overall record is estimated at 331-15-2

Kevin Jackson
Precision in a Singlet

Kevin Jackson presented an intimidating physical presence every time he took to the mat during his highly successful international career. The Michigan native won two world titles and one Olympic gold medal. *(Photo courtesy of Ginger Robinson and W.I.N. Magazine)*

The progression of Kevin Jackson's path to stardom was like no other in the history of American wrestling, but his start in the sport came in a familiar fashion. Like a lot of young boys, the roots of competition often began by watching their siblings compete. Such was the case for Kevin Jackson.

His wrestling career began in sixth grade at the age of 12, a relatively late start considering many kids begin their careers at the age of five. Jackson was already reasonably familiar with wrestling before he ever stepped foot on the mat. Jackson's brother, Leroy Wayne, who was older by a year, was wrestling while Kevin followed him around and watched his matches.

"It kind of came natural to me," said Jackson on the start of his career. "My brother was actually in a tournament my mother had taken him to over the weekend. While he was weighing in she asked me if I wanted to wrestle in the tournament. I ended up wrestling, won the tournament and got a medal. It's kind of funny but she was in my corner for the first several matches of my career."

His mom must have been a pretty good coach. By the time Jackson finished high school at Lansing Eastern in Michigan he had compiled a remarkable career. Over three years of high school wrestling, Jackson posted a record of 95-5, winning state titles his junior and senior seasons. As a senior, he was 31-0 with 29 pins. Adding to his resume was a third place finish at the 1982 freestyle Junior Nationals and first place honors in the Greco-Roman division.

As one of the nation's top prospects, Jackson was recruited by many major wrestling programs. The deciding factor for Jackson wasn't the best program but the best weather, and Louisiana State University was the perfect fit.

"I decided coming out of high school that I wanted to go some place warm," he recalled years later. "I was tired of the cold weather in Michigan and that narrowed down my choices to Arizona State and Louisiana State. I went there for the weather first and the wrestling program second."

Kevin Jackson shoots in deep for a textbook takedown during the 1998 World team trials. Jackson's tremendous athletic talents led him to three national freestyle titles. *(Photo courtesy of Ginger Robinson and W.I.N. Magazine)*

Although Louisiana State was not known as a traditional wrestling power, the situation Jackson stepped into was to his liking. Head coach Larry Schiacchetano was building a quality team that included several Michigan standouts, along with other top stars from around the nation.

Already in the wrestling room was Jim Edwards, an All-American who placed fifth at 134 pounds in 1982 and helped lead LSU to a 20th place finish at the NCAA tournament. Adding to the flavor of the program was Lanny Davidson, a former University of Iowa assistant coach who brought a winning mentality from the Hawkeye dynasty.

The Tigers reached the pinnacle of their program in 1983 and 1984. During his freshman and sophomore campaign, the former Michigan prep standout placed third twice at 158 pounds at the NCAA tournament, leading his team to impressive eighth place finishes both years. The following year Jackson moved up to the 167-pound weight class and was seeded first at the NCAA tournament but finished a disappointing seventh. The team also dropped to a 17th place finish.

Yet the summer of 1986 proved to be an unexpected turning point in the life of Jackson. Already a three-time All-American, Jackson's only mission in his final year of college was to win an individual NCAA title. Unfortunately, he would not get the opportunity to win college

Kevin Jackson

wrestling's most prestigious honor at LSU. In an unexpected turn of events, the Louisiana State wrestling program was eliminated.

When word hit that LSU had dropped its program, Jackson became a hot item on the recruiting market once again. The only difference was that coaches knew they were getting one of the best college wrestlers in the nation with a record to back it up. Regrettably, the school of Jackson's choosing would only receive his services for a year. In the end, Jackson chose to wrestle for first-year head coach Jim Gibbons at Iowa State University.

"I decided on Iowa State because of one summer working J Robinson's camp," said Jackson. "I got a chance to meet Tim Kreiger and Jeff Gibbons, who were wrestling for Iowa State at the time. They became very good friends of mine during that summer and we still remain close. They also had a very diverse team. I really wanted to be on a team that had a chance to beat Iowa."

Unlike his former school, Jackson stepped into a program that was steeped in wrestling tradition. The Cyclones had won six NCAA team championships prior to Jackson's arrival, and had the most dual meet wins in college wrestling history. With the addition of Jackson to the program, Iowa State was in a prime position to dethrone the University of Iowa. After taking a redshirt year in 1986, Jackson wrestled his final collegiate season at 167 pounds in 1987.

That season highlighted Jackson in one of the most intense and talked about rivalries the sport of wrestling has ever known. Standing in the way of Jackson's last chance at an individual NCAA title was cross-state rival Royce Alger from the University of Iowa. Alger, who competed for Lisbon high school, was a homegrown Iowan with an in-your-face style of wrestling that was the epitome of Dan Gable's wrestling teams.

"It was a heated rivalry," said Jackson. "Probably the most heated rivalry that I have ever been involved with, especially with the Iowa/Iowa State angle. The thing about it is that he wanted to win as bad as I did. He was probably paying the same price that I was paying. We both were after something that the other one wanted and that was the NCAA title. We also wanted to go undefeated so it became really competitive."

The two faced each other twice during the season in home-and-home dual meets that excited both the Iowa and Iowa State faithful. When the two wrestlers stepped out on the mat it was nothing short of spectacular. Alger, with his grinding, never-stop attitude, against the fast-as-lightning, well-built Jackson was sure to be a crowd-pleaser.

Jackson met with disappointment on both occasions. In each of their two dual meets the Cyclone star came out on fire and took his Hawkeye opponent down early but faded near the end of the match, succumbing to Alger's now-legendary hand fighting. The only chance for Jackson to defeat Alger was at the final college tournament of the season.

At the 1987 NCAA tournament Jackson fulfilled half of his goal. The Cyclones won the team title by 25 points over the Hawkeyes and in the process stopped them in their bid for 10 titles in a row. Jackson was one of five Iowa State wrestlers to reach the finals but the only one to not win. For the third time that season, he lost to Alger.

"Winning an NCAA team title was very satisfying but it was bitter sweet because I ended up getting beat by the Iowa guy three times," said Jackson. "Royce Alger beat me in both duals and he beat me in the NCAA finals. From my redshirt year at Iowa State we were always in the hunt, we always wrestled Iowa very tough in duals and had a great chance to beat them in '86 as well as '87.

"It was satisfying to go to a team that could actually compete against Iowa's grinding style of wrestling and to win that national title, along with the state title from a dual meet perspective. I hang my hat on that NCAA title, beating Iowa

Kevin Jackson

and stopping them from 10 straight titles."

After five years of college wrestling it was time for Jackson to make a decision about his future. Jackson could end his career as a four-time All-American or turn to freestyle, the international form of the sport where he would pursue World and Olympic honors. After contemplating quitting for good, Jackson chose the latter.

Jackson's first major test was at the 1988 U.S. Nationals in Kansas. Since 1988 was an Olympic year, the former Cyclone entered the competition at 180.5 pounds, one of the toughest weight classes in the country. Although he lost to Mike Sheets and Rico Chiapparelli, Jackson placed high enough to qualify for the final Olympic Trials.

"(The U.S. Nationals) showed me how close I was and that was my first year on the scene," said Jackson. "From there, I threw myself into freestyle full-time to make the World team. I realized there were bigger and greater things out there and Royce Alger was still out there to beat. Royce was a big motivating factor for me because Royce took some things that I definitely wanted to have, like an NCAA title and those dual meets. Him being on the scene motivated me to try and make up for the titles he took from me."

Although he didn't make the 1988 Olympic team, Jackson gained valuable experience in his quest for future gold. But he had his hands full just making world teams over the next two years. Standing in the way of his dreams of Olympic glory were Alger and the always-dangerous Melvin Douglas.

Over the course of the 1989 and 1990 seasons, Jackson missed out on making both world teams, placing second to Douglas and Alger at the world team trials. Both Douglas and Alger represented the United States well. Each placed second at the World Championships after leading throughout most of their championship match. So when the 1991 season began, Jackson's road to World gold would not be easy. He had two World medallists in his weight class to contend with.

Like all great champions Jackson simply found a way to win. During the previous two seasons Jackson notched one win each over Alger and Douglas but dropped seven combined matches to his two rivals. Over the course of the next five years it was Jackson who would do most of the winning.

"I remember one of the first times he beat me was in the finals of the U.S. Open and we went a 15-minute match and neither of us could score," said Douglas "We came back out and the referee gave it to him. From that moment on, Kevin took that step. He knew that he was the world's best. There's something in you that just snaps that tells you 'I am the best,' and I think that's when it happened to Kevin. From that moment on, every match I had with Kevin was tough."

In 1991, Jackson got a crack at the World Championships. After beating Douglas to make his first World team, it was Jackson's turn to prove he was the best in the world.

After posting five consecutive victories, Jackson found himself in the finals against the same Czechoslovakian opponent who had defeated Alger the previous year. The two went scoreless through regulation and the match went into sudden victory overtime. After 25 seconds had elapsed, Jackson shot in on a double-leg takedown and within a matter of seconds Jackson exposed his rival's back for two points and the win. He had now vindicated himself for a loss that had plagued him for the past four years – he was champion of the entire planet!

"I finally got over not winning an NCAA title when I won the Worlds in 1991," said Jackson. "I didn't get over it until then. I'm over it now. You always want to have an NCAA title to go along with your golds. It's kind of the natural progression. If you're good enough to be an NCAA champion then you're good enough to go on and be the best in the world."

The next task was to win the 1992 Olympic

Legends of the Mat – 163

Games held in Barcelona, Spain. USA Wrestling, the governing body for American wrestling, established a situation that all world team members from 1991 earned an automatic bid to the final Olympic Trials in 1992. That meant all Jackson had to do was win his best of three series with the winner of a mini-tournament.

The winner of the mini-tournament was his long-time rival Alger. This time, there was more than an NCAA title at stake; this was for a spot on the Olympic team. The two combatants engaged in two close, hard-fought bouts, but it was Jackson who came away the victor.

At the Olympics, Jackson picked up where he left off at the World Championships the year before, scoring five consecutive wins that placed him in the gold medal finals. His opponent was 1989 World Champion Elmadi Zhabrailov of Russia.

Like his final match from the previous year, Jackson and Zhabrailov were locked in a battle of attrition as neither wrestler could score in regulation. In the sudden-victory overtime, Zhabrailov was in on a single leg but Jackson continued to rotate his position as the two wrestlers went out of bounds. Zhabrailov's coach, two-time Olympic champion Ivan Yarygin, protested the call, claiming that his athlete deserved a point and the win.

After a lengthy argument by the Russian Federation, the match resumed. Within a minute, Jackson hit Zhabrailov with his patented double-leg takedown, placing him on his butt. Jackson looked around to see if he had scored and after several seconds of discussion the point was awarded to Jackson for the win. Not only was Kevin Jackson a gold medallist, but he became only the second black wrestler in the history of the sport to win the Olympics in wrestling.

"I always believed that I was the best guy in the weight class, especially being the defending world champion," said Jackson. "(Winning the Olympics was) the highest sense of satisfaction that I've ever felt. Everything that you sacrifice and put into this sport and the heartbreaks you deal with in this sport were well worth it. It was the greatest sense of achievement that I've ever experienced."

Now that he had won back-to-back titles, Jackson held a spot alongside Dan Gable, Dave Schultz, Mark Schultz, Kenny Monday, John Smith, and Bruce Baumgartner as wrestlers who had won a world and Olympic title in consecutive years. But the 1993 and 1994 seasons ended in disappointment for the reigning Olympic champion.

Victories continued over his domestic rivals during that two-year span as Jackson made both World teams. However, he failed to win a medal at both World Championships, which left some to wonder if his better days were behind him.

But at the 1995 World Championships, Jackson proved he was still at the top of his game. As was his trademark, Jackson wrestled a near flawless tournament and gave up only three points in five matches. In his final match for the gold medal, Jackson scored a 2-0 shutout of Jabrailov, the same Russian he defeated for gold at the '92 Olympics.

With his third World gold medal, Jackson put himself in an even more prestigious category internationally. Jackson had become just the fifth wrestler in the history of the United States to win three or more World or Olympic titles.

"That was a great moment for me to win in 1995 after two years away from the title," said Jackson. "I felt I was the best guy and I felt that I should have been a five-time World champion. Three times was great, I am glad to have that accomplishment. I realized that there were only four other guys who had three World-level titles. I definitely wanted to put my name in that category."

In 1996, Jackson failed in his quest to make his second Olympic team when he was defeated in straight matches at the Olympic Trials by Les Gutches. He also fell short of making World teams in 1997 and 1998 but admitted

— *Kevin Jackson* —

that he was not as prepared mentally or physically as he should have been to compete at a level he had become accustomed to. After the 1998 World team trials, Jackson retired from competitive wrestling for good. But he never forgot the lessons the sport had instilled in him over years of training and competing.

"Wrestling is my life," said Jackson. "I breathe it, I live it, I feel it and it's been a love of my life since I started doing it. I wouldn't be the person I am now, I wouldn't be the father I am now or the husband I am now without wrestling. It's molded me into the person I am and motivated me to be better than the person I am."

He remained in the sport by becoming the National Freestyle Teams coach at USA Wrestling, where he helps lead other freestyle wrestlers on the path to glory. In 2005, he was inducted into the FILA International Wrestling Hall of Fame.

Based on international credentials alone, Jackson is considered one of the top ten American wrestlers of all time. But Jackson's story goes beyond numbers alone. No wrestler has achieved success in wrestling quite the way Jackson has and in this regard Jackson stands alone at the top.

"He has the rightful throne of the greatest black wrestler of all-time because of his performances," said Bobby Douglas.

And it all started with his mom as his first wrestling coach.

Highlights – Kevin Jackson was a four-time All-American in college and had an overall record estimated at 117-19-2. He won an Olympic gold medal and two World Championships. He also won the World Cup three times and the Pan-American Games twice. He captured three national freestyle titles. His overall record is unknown.

Tom and Terry Brands
Twin Tornadoes

There is an oft-quoted adage in sports that goes like this: "In the final analysis, will overcomes skill." If that is the case, nowhere does the proof stand as tall as in the case of the twin tornadoes from Sheldon, Iowa. Tom and Terry Brands may be the two most intense wrestlers to ever step foot on a mat. None of their opponents, or hardly anyone who ever saw them compete, would question their total devotion and commitment to the sport, and to winning. No one could ever question their will.

"The Brands brothers personified intensity," said Randy Lewis, 1984 Olympic champion, and a man who worked out with them on hundreds of occasions. "From the very day they hit the Iowa wrestling room, they gave it all they had, in every practice and in every competition. They are the most intense competitors I've ever seen, no doubt about that. None at all."

The twins were born in Omaha, Nebraska, and raised in tiny Sheldon, Iowa, in the far northwest corner of the state. They loved baseball in their youth, and even tried football. But their size convinced them they would never be able to excel in sports where heft and brawn were prime factors, and at a young age they switched their energies exclusively to wrestling. Soon, their house was a disaster zone, according to their mother, Bonnie.

"They wrestled all over the living room, and everywhere else they could find," she said once. "They never stopped. They banged into things and broke things and just kept going and going."

Terry and Tom Brands were known for their incredible intensity in everything they did – whether it be on the mat, running steps, or lifting weights. They are two of the biggest stars in Iowa wrestling history. *(Photo courtesy of University of Iowa)*

In a key match at the 1996 Olympics, Tom Brands executes a picture perfect single leg takedown on Sergei Smal of Belarus en route to a 5-0 triumph. Tom won the gold medal at 136.5 pounds. *(Photo courtesy of Ginger Robinson and W.I.N. Magazine)*

By the time they reached high school, they had reputations for a very non-stop, aggressive style of wrestling. Terry won two Iowa high school state titles and Tom won one, missing his entire senior season when he and several teammates were sidelined for a prank that got out of hand and prompted disciplinary action from the school. Even many years later, Tom was still angered by the school's action and insisted it was unwarranted because he had not done what was charged.

The twins were not on the prime recruiting lists of most of the nation's college coaches, but Iowa's Dan Gable liked what he saw when the brothers ran onto the mat. Their fire and determination and insatiable appetite for competition caused him to make them offers to attend the University of Iowa. It was a dream come true for the twins, and they quickly accepted.

"I can remember them in the room the first couple of months and they couldn't score a point on anyone," said Lewis. "But they never stopped coming. And they sought out the best training partners. They never wanted an easy workout. They always wanted the best partners in the room, so they could improve."

Improve they did. But the road to the Iowa lineup was easier for Tom than for Terry. Tom made the team as a redshirt freshman in 1989, and posted a 32-4-2 record, winning the Big Ten title at 126 pounds and placing fourth in the NCAA tournament.

Terry was cutting a huge amount of weight to make 118 pounds and couldn't get past senior Steve Martin and was frustrated. They had numerous tryouts, with Martin winning by the narrowest of margins. Terry had to watch from the sidelines as Martin placed seventh in the NCAA that year.

In 1990, both Brands boys were in the lineup, and terrorizing foes all across the nation. They became known for their fierce intensity, and for

Tom and Terry Brands

pushing foes at the edge of the mat, often inciting opposing wrestlers, coaches and fans to an anger almost as intense as the Brands themselves. Their non-stop, in-your-face style of wrestling was loved by the rabid Hawkeyes fans, and despised by fans on the opposite side of the arena.

Even though opposing coaches often complained to the referee and sportswriters, and one even wildly kicked a chair in frustration during a match, Gable and the Iowa coaches were reluctant to tame the Brands boys too much, fearing it would weaken their competitive spirit.

Their sophomore seasons, 1990, both were regulars in the Iowa lineup. They both captured NCAA titles, Terry at 126 pounds and Tom at 134. Terry defeated Nebraska's tough and talented Jason Kelber in the finals by a score of 3-2, and Tom defeated Minnesota's David Zuniga, 9-7. They had arrived on the national wrestling scene and for the remainder of their careers would be two of the most talked about collegiate wrestlers of all time.

In 1991, Tom fashioned a 45-0 record and claimed his second NCAA title, defeating Alan Fried of Oklahoma State in the finals, 5-3. Terry gained the finals for the second straight year, but was upset by Kelber, the same wrestler he had defeated the year before.

Their final collegiate season, 1992, was a great one for the Brands boys. Terry captured his second NCAA title at 126 pounds, and Tom won his third crown at 134, and was voted the outstanding wrestler at the national tournament. Terry's finals foe was Shawn Charles of Arizona State, who he beat 8-5. Tom defeated Fried in the finals for the second straight year, 6-2. Fried won the title two years later, making it to the finals three straight years.

Tom finished his Hawkeye career with a record of 158-7-2, for a winning percentage of .952, good for second on the all-time percentage list at Iowa. Terry's final record was 137-7-0, and he ranks third on the all-time percentage list. Amazingly, he had a .951 mark to Tom's .952!

In addition, Tom is second on the most wins chart with 158 victories, just four behind Barry Davis. Terry is fifth on the victory chart with 137 wins.

Along the way, they had driven Hawkeye fans to a new level of intensity, and stirred anger from fans of other schools across the nation. Many supporters from opposing schools didn't like the constant intensity and in-your-face style they brought to the mat. Writing for *Sports Illustrated*, Frantz Lidz captured the essence of it in an article:

"Tom and Terry's High Noon approach to wrestling – they never back down and they challenge an opponent to the point of humiliation – draws complaints from rivals and their coaches. 'They've got to understand,' Terry says, 'we're just breaking the other guy mentally.'" *(33)*

After college, the twins blasted their way into the demanding world of freestyle wrestling, bringing an intensity that few on the international scene had ever seen before. They both made the 1993 World team, and then battled their way to gold medals at the World championships in Toronto, Terry at 125.5 pounds and Tom at 136.5 pounds. They simply overwhelmed their foes with superior conditioning and intensity, coming from behind in several matches to force their battle-weary opponents into serious mistakes.

"Tom and Terry Brands were among the most intense people our sport has ever experienced," said Gary Abbott, director of media relations at USA Wrestling. "The fact that they could step off the college mats and win the 1993 World gold medals in Toronto, side-by-side, in their first World Championships, was a remarkable feat. The world had not yet experienced the kind of pressure and passion that the Brands brothers brought to wrestling."

Terry scored five straight wins, beating Shim Sang-Hyu of Korea in the finals, 3-0. Tom also won five in a row, but had to rally from a 2-1 deficit to beat Cuba's talented Lazaro Reinoso in overtime, 3-2, in the finals. Reinoso was Olympic bronze medallist in 1992 and even owned two wins over John Smith.

"It's all the same. It's a war out there," Tom

Terry Brands tries to turn a foe during the national freestyle tournament in Las Vegas. A two-time NCAA champion at Iowa, Terry also won two world titles at 127.5 pounds and an Olympic bronze medal *(Photo courtesy of Ginger Robinson)*

said of the close win in the finals. "That's the way I have been coached and that's the way I'll always approach it. Things will take care of themselves if you train hard and prepare properly."

Very few wrestlers have been able to make the transition from the college sport to the international level in such a short amount of time. Years later, in an interview, Tom explained how they were able to make such a quick adjustment between the two styles of wrestling.

"The biggest asset that Terry and I had was we never made excuses because of the difference between collegiate and international," he said. "Wrestling is wrestling and we were able to make adjustments quickly during the transition because of that attitude. Being tough and smart, controlling and moving your opponent, attacking and counter attacking are timeless skills that are universal no matter what the rules are or what the time limit is.

"Of course, I had great coaches and workout partners that were passionate about winning World and Olympic championships also." *(34)*

Despite their successes, there were roadblocks ahead for the indefatigable twins. Neither of the Iowans had a good showing at the 1994 World Championships in far-off Turkey, in some part due to the terribly long flight, poor training conditions and the fatigue factor. They failed to place in the top five.

The 1995 World Championships were held in Atlanta, as a prelude to the coming Olympics, also to be in Atlanta, and Terry was back in top form. He captured his second World title at 125.5 pounds. He pounded on the opposition until they broke. Three of his first four foes were shut out, as he defeated them 10-0, 10-0, 4-1 and 3-0. In the championship finals, he fell behind Giya Sissaouri, who had moved to Canada from the Soviet Union, by a 3-0 score early in the bout. But he turned up the tempo of the match to the degree that Sissaouri simply broke, mentally and physically. Terry tied the match at 3-3 on stalling calls, and with 11 seconds left in the bout, the transplanted Soviet was disqualified.

"I don't panic in matches," said Brands after receiving the gold medal. "They put me down twice and he had the chance to go ahead 5-0 but I blocked it. I don't complain about the officiating, I just keep wrestling hard."

Tom, on the other hand, was struggling. He

Tom and Terry Brands

Weight training played a big role in the Brands's training philosophy.

lost close matches and wound up 9th at 136.5. Back in Iowa City, he took his training to a new level with long, torturous workouts. Though Terry had been on top of the world in 1995 and Tom watched as his brother accepted his second gold medal, the roles were about to be reversed in startling fashion.

Both were favored when the final 1996 Olympic Trials got under way in Spokane, Washington. Tom made the team with a pair of convincing victories over John Fisher, but Terry faltered after winning his opening match against Kendall Cross, an old foe. After losing to Brands 7-2, the former Oklahoma State University champion came back with a pair of incredibly hard-fought, one-point victories (7-6 and 8-7) and won the spot at 125.5 pounds. Though Terry had won the takedown battle with Cross by an 11-1 margin, it wasn't enough. A master at scoring back points with tilts and near-falls, Cross racked up enough points on tilts and near falls to make the team.

"I don't know if I've ever seen a wrestler take a loss that hard," said Dan Gable at the time. "Terry was devastated. But he knew he had to suck it up, and put his life back in order, and act like a champion."

In Atlanta at the 1996 Olympics, Tom wrestled to near perfection. He won all four matches while allowing just one point en route to the gold medal at 136.5. He beat archrival Sergei Smal of Belarus in the second round, 5-0, and then Russian Magomed Azizov, 4-1. In the championship match, he pounded Jang Jae-Sung of Korea, 7-0.

Cross also won the gold medal at 125.5 without a close match. Afterwards, Cross said his toughest bouts were at the Olympic trials with Terry Brands.

"As the matches waned, he got stronger and stronger," said Cross several years later, speaking of his matches with Terry. "I pushed my body beyond my pain threshold during my training so I could get used to that feeling of exhaustion. He still wore me down tremendously. Wrestling Brands was like being in a car wreck." *(35)*

Tom and Terry Brands

Following the 1996 Olympics, Tom retired and continued coaching as a fulltime assistant at the University of Iowa. In 2000, he was named Assistant Coach of the Year by the National Wrestling Coaches Association. He was a member of the U.S. coaching staff at the 2001 and 2002 World Championships, and has coached a number of other U.S. teams in international competition. In 2005, he was named head coach at Virginia Tech and led the team to a 16-4 record in his initial season. In April of 2006, Tom completed a lifelong dream when he was named head coach at the University of Iowa, just the eighth in the college's long and proud history.

Terry served as strength coach at Iowa while he continued to train. Hampered by injuries and the stress of holding his weight near 125 pounds, he retired from competition in 1999. But after a year's rest, he changed his mind and came back a year later to make the 2000 Olympic team.

In Sydney, he won four of his five matches, losing 6-5 to the eventual champion from Iran, Alireza Dabir. Brands had turned Dabir for what looked liked the winning points in their semifinal match, but the judges ruled it was an illegal move. Brands won the bronze medal match over Damir Zakhartdinov of Uzbekistan, 3-2.

He then embarked upon a coaching career, serving as an assistant at several colleges before being named head coach at the University of Tennessee-Chattanooga in 2002. He spent three years building the Mocs into a regional power, then left in 2005 to become a freestyle coach at USA Wrestling.

Their intensity has stamped them, and has made them legends in the wrestling world. Even Gable, known the width of the globe for his intensity, says the Brands stand apart from the crowd in that vital category.

"Today, looking back on their careers, I just can't believe how intense they really were, and still are," said Gable in 2005. "They are just wound so tight. It's very hard to think of anyone – anyone – who would rate above them in that area.

"But I'll tell you something else that not a lot of people realize. They are great people. Tom and Terry Brands are a joy to be around. They are really something extra special. Just don't get them fighting with each other."

"In their international careers, Terry and Tom ended up taking different roads," said Abbott. "Both were World Champions in 1993, then both did not place in the 1994 World meet. In 1995, it was Terry who won the World title, while Tom did not medal. In 1996, Tom was able to step forward and win the Olympic title, while Terry lost in a legendary Olympic Trials.

"Tom was able to retire after the Atlanta Olympics, while Terry had not yet reached his personal goals. Terry's comeback to win an Olympic bronze medal in 2000 was a tremendous effort that showed the kind of heart that he has and the kind of champion that he is.

"Tom and Terry are great people and were a credit to the U.S. program; they were the ultimate warriors in a very demanding sport."

No matter what they accomplish as coaches, the Brands brothers will forever be remembered for their warrior spirit, and for being two of the most intense wrestlers ever seen on a mat anywhere in the world.

Highlights – Tom Brands was a three-time NCAA champion at Iowa with an overall record of 158-7-1 in college. He also won four national freestyle titles. He was World champion in 1993 and Olympic champion in 1996. He won the Pan-American Games in 1995 and two World Cups, as well. His total record is unknown.

Highlights – Terry Brands was a two-time NCAA champion at Iowa and one time runner-up with overall record of 137-7. He also won three national freestyle titles. He was World champion in 1993 and 1995, and won a bronze medal in the 2000 Olympics. He took a Pan-American Games gold medal in 1995 and two World Cup championships, as well. His total record is unknown.

Legends of the Mat – 171

Rulon Gardner
The Impossible Dream

Rulon Gardner used the work ethic taught to him as a youth on a Wyoming ranch to become the No. 1 Greco-Roman star in American wrestling history. He won gold medals at the 2000 Olympics and the 2001 World Championships and attracted world-wide attention.

Despite being worlds apart in age and appearance, Robert Goulet and Rulon Gardner have a lot in common besides the same initials!

The Impossible Dream made them both famous.

With his deep baritone voice, Goulet's version of the powerful song about striving to achieve the impossible, from the hit play "Man of LaMancha," was a huge hit in the late 1960s. And it was Rulon Gardner who actually lived the impossible dream in the late summer of 2000, in Sydney, Australia.

After winning his first four matches in the Olympic Games, the farm kid from Wyoming suddenly found himself face to face with the biggest legend, literally, in the entire history of amateur wrestling. Since exploding on the international scene as a mere twenty-year-old in 1988, Alexander Karelin was the most successful wrestler of all time. He was also the most-talked about and lionized wrestler ever.

With a physique that rivaled that of Arnold Schwarzenegger, the Russian super star tore through the World and Olympic Games in a fashion never seen before. He won nine World titles at 286 pounds, and three Olympics (1988, 1992 and 1996) for a stunning total of 12 gold medals. His patented move, the reverse body lift – where he would grip a hapless foe around the waist, lift him completely off the mat and then send him flying through the air, to land on his neck and back – sent shivers down the back of every heavyweight Greco-Roman wrestler in the world.

What's more, his winning streak was considered to be near the 350 mark. There were stories that Karelin had not even been scored upon for over a decade, which proved to be only a slight exaggeration.

Gardner, on the other hand, brought far less impressive credentials to the match. He had placed fifth in the 1997 World Championships, and had

In the most talked-about wrestling match in amateur wrestling history, Rulon Gardner (right) battles with superstar Alexander Karelin in the 2000 Olympic finals. Gardner's stunning victory made him a superhero around the world. *(Photo courtesy of Tim Tushla and W.I.N. Magazine)*

never made an Olympic team before. Still, he had looked impressive in his first four matches. He defeated Tunisia 7-2 in his opener, then took a 6-0 win over Armenia. He beat a tough Italian 2-1 to enter the medal round. Gardner fell behind the Israeli athlete 2-0 in the fourth match, but fought back to tie match 2-2 and send it to overtime. There, he won when the exhausted foe was penalized for stalling.

Short pep talks from two Dans – Greco coach Dan Chandler and freestyle coach Dan Gable – helped get him in the right frame of mind. He even looked confident as he took to the mat on September 27, 2000, to face Superman.

What transpired next is a key part of wrestling folklore. And it made Rulon Gardner an international sports celebrity overnight the likes of which wrestling has seldom, if ever, seen before!

The two men battled to a 0-0 tie in the first three-minute period. After the break, they started in the clinch position, each wrapping his arms around the other, and locking their hands in back. By the rules of the clinch and the flip of the coin, Karelin was under pressure to score a point in the first minute, or lose a point. If his grip came undone in the first minute, he would lose a point by penalty.

About halfway through the first minute, the

unbelievable happened. Karelin's hands parted, but quickly came back together. The mat official blew the whistle and the wrestlers paced nervously as a brief conference ensued. The officials awarded a penalty point to Gardner, and the match resumed with a stunning intensity.

As the seconds clicked away, Gardner seemed to grow even stronger. He had trained extremely hard for this moment, emerging from a very tough Olympic trials in Dallas just three months earlier.

In the final seconds, Karelin dropped his hands and gave a half-hearted shrug. It was over. The young rancher from Afton, Wyoming, had defeated the greatest wrestler on earth! Swarmed by coaches Steve Fraser and Dan Chandler and by fans, family members and media, Gardner seemed stunned in the pressroom.

"I didn't actually think I could beat him," he said candidly. "All I knew is that I'd go out with my head down and work forward. I grew up on a farm and I always learned that when you worked you go forward. I didn't think I was going to win but I was going to work as hard as I could."

One person who did believe that Gardner had a real shot at winning was his coach, Steve Fraser. In 1984, Fraser became the first American to ever win an Olympic gold medal in Greco-Roman wrestling and he had studied Karelin for years. In a visit to the International Wrestling Institute and Museum in Newton, Iowa, with his family just several months before the Olympics, Fraser made a startling prediction.

"We can beat Karelin in Sydney," Fraser said softly. "I really admire Karelin and all he has done for the sport. He's a tremendous athlete, and very friendly to us. But we want to beat him, just like we want to beat anyone else.

"Rulon is made to order for him style wise. Rulon is hard to score on and in great shape. We feel Karelin is past his peak and we have the strategy to beat him."

Gardner had the mental toughness and physical ability to make the impossible dream come true. News of the monumental upset sent shock waves around the wrestling world and brought an avalanche of recognition to the sport in the United States. Prior to departing from Sydney, Rulon was given a huge honor by his Olympic teammates when he was selected to carry the American flag in the closing ceremonies.

Back home, the celebrity drum was beating at a tremendous scale. Gardner was invited to appear on a number of national television shows alongside such stars as Jay Leno, Conan O'Brien and others. He even appeared on the hugely-popular show "Who Wants To Be a Millionaire" with Regis Philbin.

Perhaps the best moment came on the "David Letterman Show." As Gardner sat talking to the television icon, the huge picture screen behind him began to show the gymnasium at his old high school in Afton, packed with family, friends and coaches. Rulon turned around to survey the scene and had to fight back the emotions. A few days later, over five thousand fans were on hand in Afton (population 1,865) to greet the new Olympic superstar in his first trip back to his hometown.

Over the next few months, Gardner's list of honors grew to an astonishing level. Among the awards he was given were:
- USOC SportsMan of the Year;
- ESPY award winner for
  Male U.S. Olympic Athlete of the Year;
- USA Wrestling Man of the Year;
- USOC Male Wrestler of the Year;
- USA Wrestling Greco-Roman Wrestler
  of the Year;
- USA Today 2000 Sports Award winner;
- James E. Sullivan Award winner, presented by the AAU to the greatest amateur athlete of the year.

"Gardner won the major amateur sports awards during an Olympic year, which is almost unheard of for a wrestler," said Gary Abbott, media relations director of USA Wrestling, the sport's national governing body.

"During an Olympic year, the award usually goes to an athlete who received tremendous

Rulon Gardner

amounts of television time in one of the most prominent sports in the Olympic movement. These awards have a popularity contest factor in them, especially during the Olympics. Yet Gardner emerged as the athlete with both a great achievement and a great personal recognition and popularity.

"There was a consistent theme we have heard about Rulon from those who dealt with him at public appearances, those who gave him awards, and from the toughest critics out there, the journalists who interviewed him. Almost without exception, these people say how much they like Rulon as a person and how well he represents the sport of wrestling and the Olympic movement. They talk about how sincere and honest he is, and how much they enjoyed dealing with him.

"This may have been Rulon's greatest achievement. He became a national public hero as a person, and has educated the world about wrestling along the way."

He was in demand as a public speaker, and also became a major endorsement figure. His "Got Milk" ad put him on the same level as movie stars and comic book heroes, and the advertisement of him holding a pail of milk while attired in a wrestling singlet was seen coast to coast. It was rumored that he made close to one million dollars in endorsements and appearances the year after his incredible victory.

As the honors came pouring in and his fame exploded, many fans around the world wondered if the giant American could ever focus enough to win another major title. He silenced any doubters with a tremendous showing at the 2001 World Championships in Athens, Greece. He won all five matches, including an amazing come-from-behind triumph over Russia's newest star, Yuri Patrikeev. Trailing Patrikeev 3-0 late in the match, Gardner threw him for a pin, and left for home with another gold medal.

He had come a long way since his early start in wrestling. Growing up in a hard-working farm family, Rulon and his siblings learned early the necessity for a tough mental outlook. Work, work and more work was the order of the day, from early in the pre-dawn until late at night, seven days a week, in boiling hot temperatures and frigid cold weather.

And then there was school. Rulon had a learning disability and it would plague him for the next fifteen years or so.

"I wasn't at the same level as kids my age," he wrote in his book, *Never Stop Pushing*. "The other students always seemed smarter, faster. Everyone was a better reader than I was. I couldn't spell simple words, couldn't keep up in most of the learning exercises. I had a hard time absorbing and applying what the teachers were telling us." *(36)*

Though he matured slowly as an athlete, he really hit his stride his senior year. He was a state wrestling champion in high school in Wyoming in 1989, and was all-state in football and the shot put. At Ricks Junior College, he began to show he had national-level talent. He was third in the national junior college wrestling championships as a freshman, posting a record of 50-5. He went 42-1 and won the heavyweight title his second year.

Those accomplishments earned him an athletic scholarship to the University of Nebraska. He had several options for college but chose Nebraska largely because of the respect he developed for the coach, Tim Neumann. His first season, he finished 24-10-2 and qualified for the NCAA tournament, failing to place.

The next year he went 34-5, and finished fourth in the 1993 NCAA tournament. He won his first two bouts, then dropped a 7-3 match to Michigan State's Don Whipp, the eventual runnerup. Rulon battled back to gain the third place match, but lost a hard-fought 8-7 decision to John Oostendorp of Iowa.

He tried out for the Nebraska Cornhusker football team, coached by the legendary Tom Osborne, that spring and enjoyed the experience. But when a coach told him he probably wouldn't see much playing time the next season, he decided his future was with wrestling.

He won a Greco-Roman tournament in Colorado Springs, earning a trip to Cuba. On his

Rulon Gardner

way out of the USA Wrestling offices, he spotted for the first time a famous poster. It was called "Train Like A Madman" and showed Alexander Karelin in all his glory, gritting his teeth, muscles bulging, throwing an opponent. The image stuck in Gardner's mind for years.

He won the tournament in Cuba and returned to Lincoln, Nebraska, to finish up his academic work to get his degree. He thought he was sitting near the top of the world at the time. But he experienced very negative feedback in the educational system. He was baffled at the roadblocks that kept being placed in his path; it seemed to him that some officials were going out of their way to try and defeat him in the classroom.

"Certain teachers at Nebraska tried to wear me down, get me to quit and, short of that, to fail," he wrote. He kept plugging away, he said, determined to "do everything I could to excel, even though I knew certain people were working against me." *(37)*

With the help of some good people, Gardner eventually overcame all the obstacles and earned his degree. He had also begun a true education in wrestling by joining the Sunkist Kids Club in Phoenix, Arizona. The wrestlers there were so good that Gardner felt he improved dramatically in his practice sessions with the team.

He won national Greco-Roman titles in 1995, 1997 and 1998. He was fifth in the 1997 World Championships, losing a 5-0 match to Karelin. He also won the 1996 World Cup and major tournaments in Cuba, Poland and Hungary. Despite a severe groin injury, he was able to win the gold medal in the Pan-American Games in 2000, defeating Cuban star Hector Milan along the way.

He had to defeat friend and mentor Matt Ghaffari, a two-time Olympian and 1996 silver medallist, to make the 2000 Olympic team. And then it was on to Sydney… and his moment with destiny.

After the Impossible Dream victory, life seemed almost perfect for Rulon Gardner. But a snowmobile trip on February 14, 2002, abruptly changed all of that, almost permanently. He and two friends started out on a trip in the Bridger-Teton National Forest. In mid afternoon, the trio became separated and the other two men turned back. Despite sub-zero temperatures and deep snow, Gardner forged on ahead in the same fearless style that had carried him to victory in Sydney, and soon found himself in serious trouble.

He became lost and ran into a gully, with no easy way to turn around. At one point he drove his snowmobile off a fifty-foot cliff. He eventually gave up the 650-pound machine and struggled on in the growing darkness, wet and cold. A large search party began looking for him, but had no luck. He drifted in and out of consciousness during the night and at one point even felt he saw Jesus and Rulon's older brother, Ronald, who had died years earlier.

"The cold was consuming me," he wrote in his book. "No doubt in my mind I was now in this for the long haul. Life or death. Sudden death. Overtime. Think about it: the bout of my life, this time for my survival.

"But the cold. I had been cold before, freezing at times. But never had I been as frozen to my core as I was now." *(38)*

A search plane spotted him at seven the next morning, but it took another two hours for a rescue helicopter to get to him. By that time, his body temperature was about eighty degrees, twenty below normal. His boots were frozen to his feet and had to be cut off by doctors. His toes were all suffering from severe frostbite.

The story of his harrowing escape made front-page news all over the nation, and was carried on all three national networks. As the weeks slipped by, he eventually lost a toe (it had to be amputated) and the others were slow to heal from the severe frostbite. He endured pins in his toes, several operations and skin grafts, and incredible pain. The reports sent a tremor of apprehension through the American wrestling community, fearful their sudden superstar might be finished forever as a world-class competitor.

He began a long convalescence program and

Rulon Gardner

his first competition since the tragedy came October 26, 2002, in a new format. Wrestling in Los Angeles on the RealPro Wrestling program, he scored a 3-0 decision over Billy Pierce, one of the same men he had to defeat in Dallas in 2000 to make the Olympic team. He had started on the long road back.

But standing directly in his path was a huge roadblock, Dremiel Byers. In order for Gardner to even make the 2004 Olympic team, he had to defeat Byers – who had won the World Championship in 2002! Gardner defeated Byers to make the 2003 World team, and placed 10th in 2003.

Gardner had to defeat Byers again the following year to make the 2004 Olympic team. The matches were as close as could be, with the two warriors battling for every inch of mat space and for every point. Gardner emerged victorious again, but soon after he suffered two more major injuries, including a badly-damaged wrist while playing basketball.

In Athens, Greece, the birthplace of the Olympic Games, Gardner showed the world what he was made of. He won four matches and lost just one, in overtime, to claim the bronze medal. Following his 3-0 overtime victory over Sajad Barzi of Iran for third place, he sat down on the center mat and took his shoes off, announcing that he had officially retired.

Several months later, on Sept. 31, 2004, he entered the world of mixed martial arts and was one of the main attractions on the Pride show in Japan. He entered the ring in front of nearly 60,000 fans to face Hidehiko Yoshida, a former Olympic gold medallist in judo. Rulon took the challenge to heart and became the aggressor, pounding out a three-round decision.

Returning home to the United States, he engaged in another round of talk shows, where he once again helped to spread the gospel of his chosen sport through the media. Gardner had proven a second time his value to the entire sport of wrestling. He was a sought-after guest for clinics and speeches of all kinds, and with the publication of his biography, *Never Stop Pushing*, in 2005, he was a frequent guest at book signings around the country.

"He is simply our best Greco-Roman wrestler of all time, in a class by himself in this country," said Steve Fraser, national coach at USA Wrestling and an Olympic champion himself (Los Angeles, 1984). "No one has ever brought as much attention to this sport in this country. He is a true legend."

Highlights – Rulon Gardner was junior college national champion in 1991 and posted a 94-6 record at Ricks Junior College. He was 58-15-2 at the University of Nebraska, placing fourth in the 1993 NCAA championships. His total college record was 152-21-2. He was fifth in the World championships in 1997, and Olympic champion in 2000 and World champion in 2001. He won the bronze medal at the 2004 Olympics in Athens. His total record is unknown.

Cael Sanderson
All-Time College King

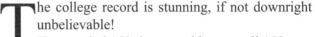

The college record is stunning, if not downright unbelievable!

He wrestled 159 times, and he won all 159.

He entered four NCAA championships and won four times.

He was named the Outstanding Wrestler at all four NCAA tournaments, the first wrestler to ever win more than two O.W. awards.

He won three Dan Hodge Trophies, wrestling's version of the Heisman Trophy. No other wrestler owns more than one.

Along the way, he signed thousands and thousands of autographs.

And he did it all with style and grace and class.

"I never saw him turn down anyone for an autograph," said his head coach, Bobby Douglas. "Sometimes, he signed for over two hours. He was just as amazing off the mat as he was unbeatable on the mat."

What Cael Sanderson accomplished in his four seasons of college wrestling is so amazing that *Sports Illustrated* magazine called it the second most impressive achievement in the entire history of college sports. Only the performance of legendary sprinter Jesse Owens was rated above him. On one sultry afternoon in 1935, Owens entered four races in the Big Ten Championships, winning all of them and setting four world records along the way!

One only has to look at the other sports heroes ranked behind Cael Sanderson in the SI Top Ten poll to see how impressive his college career was: In third place came Barry Sanders and his 1988 record year at Oklahoma State, when he rushed for the all-time record

Wearing the long red robe of Iowa State, Cael Sanderson brought everlasting fame to himself and the Cyclones by winning 159 straight matches and four NCAA titles. He also was 2004 Olympic champion. *(Photo courtesy of Iowa State University)*

Legends of the Mat – 178

Cael Sanderson seldom had a close match during his four-year career at Iowa State University. Not only did he finish his collegiate career undefeated, he won the Dan Hodge Trophy, given annually to the top college wrestler in the United States, three times and was also named college athlete of the year by ESPN. *(Photo courtesy of Iowa State University)*

of 2,629 yards, scored an NCAA record of 39 touchdowns and ran away with the Heisman Trophy. Also ranked behind Sanderson on the list were football's Jimmy Brown, fourth, and basketball's Oscar Robertson, fifth.

"How can you get any better than Cael was in college?" asked Bryan Van Kley, publisher of Wrestling International Newsmagazine (WIN). "He is, simply, the best there ever was in college wrestling."

Cael Sanderson first began wrestling at the age of eight in Heber City, Utah. He won numerous kids titles, and was extremely successful at Wasatch High School. With his dad, Steve, a former wrestler at BYU, coaching him, and his mother, Debbie, providing motivation at home, he and his two older brothers were the talk of the state.

His older brother, Cody, won three titles, blazing the path that other brothers would follow. Cole, just a year younger than Cody, won four state titles. Cael, two years behind Cole, gave the family a total of eleven state titles when his hand was raised as a senior in his final scholastic match. He won championships at 119, 135, 145 and 171, closing out high school with a 122-3 record. Cyler won three state titles, his last coming in 2005, giving the Sandersons a grand total of 14.

Because Cody and Cole had selected Iowa State University, Cael was inclined to follow them. Heavily recruited, he narrowed the field to Oklahoma State and Iowa State, then chose the Cyclone program run by Coach Bobby Douglas. At that time, no one – including Cael and Bobby – had any idea what was in store for them.

"I knew he was going to be good," said Douglas after Cael's first two seasons, "but we had

Cael Sanderson

no idea he was going to be this good."

Even Cael admitted his expectations were not too lofty at the outset of his college career. At the Cyclone banquet his senior year, he told the huge crowd that his initial goal upon taking to the mat as a freshman was to not get pinned. Later, in a newspaper article, he confided he thought about perhaps winning a championship ring as a member of a national championship team.

But the story turned out to be far, far more than he or anyone else could have ever imagined. By the time his run was over at Iowa State University, the young man from Utah was being called the best collegiate wrestler of all time!

Cael took a redshirt season his first year, and posted a 10-1 record, losing one match to Iowa's Paul Jenn while wrestling unattached. In his first year on the varsity, the 1998-99 season, Cael went 39-0 at 184 pounds and won the NCAA title without a close match. He defeated Brandon Eggum of Minnesota 6-1 in the finals and was voted the meet's outstanding wrestler, the first time a freshman had ever been so honored.

His sophomore year was a repeat as he went 40-0, defeating Vertus Jones of West Virginia in the finals, 19-6. He was voted the O.W. award again, and was also selected winner of the Dan Hodge Trophy, presented annually by the International Wrestling Institute and Museum and W.I.N. magazine to the top collegiate star in the nation. He also won his second straight Midlands Championship, and that summer won a gold medal at the World University Championships.

The victory train kept rolling his junior year, even though the pressure began to mount. Everywhere Iowa State appeared, the focus was the long winning streak. He was constantly compared to Dan Gable, who won 117 straight matches as a collegian before suffering a loss in his final match for Iowa State. Cael posed for endless photos and signed thousands of autographs en route to another 40-0 record, including his third NCAA title and second Dan Hodge Trophy. His finals victim was Daniel Cormier of Oklahoma State, by a score of 8-4.

Sanderson also increased his pinning ability. While he scored 10 pins as a freshman he had 11 as a sophomore and 18 as a junior, despite the fact that most foes were trying more to keep the score close than to actually win the match.

As Cael approached his senior year, everyone around him was beginning to feel the pressure. Collegiate wrestling had not seen such a major attraction since the 450-pound Chris Taylor came back from the Munich Olympics in 1972 with a bronze medal to start his senior year, also at Iowa State.

Following his third NCAA title, he captured the 187.25-pound title at the freestyle nationals and then won the World Team trials. He was also named O.W. at both events! He was set for his first crack at the best senior-level wrestlers in the world, but the 2001 World Championships scheduled for New York City were postponed due to the tragic events of September 11. The event was later moved to Sofia, Bulgaria, but he passed up the opportunity since the date conflicted with the season schedule at ISU.

Riding a winning streak of 119 in a row, Cael moved up to 197 pounds for his final season of collegiate wrestling. He was the subject of mounting curiosity and interest everywhere. Iowa Public Television produced a special documentary on him, as did ESPN. After one Iowa State meet, the autograph procedure took nearly two hours, with Cael sitting patiently as hundreds of fans, young and old alike, streamed past.

All the pressure came to a stunning climax at the NCAA Championships on March 23, 2002, in Albany, New York. Cael won four straight matches to find himself in the finals on Saturday night against Lehigh sophomore Jon Trenge. He scored a 12-4 triumph to take his solitary place in the record books with four NCAA titles, four Outstanding Wrestler Awards, a record of 159-0, and his third straight Dan Hodge Trophy.

His senior season was a fitting climax to the entire career. He finished 35-0, with 20 pins, 11 tech falls and three major decisions. Only one match ended with a normal victory!

"What could be harder than coping with the pressure of staying undefeated?" asked writer Mark

Cael Sanderson

Bechtel of *Sports Illustrated*. "That pressure lasted so long with Sanderson that it should have been paying him rent. The attention the streak brought him was unprecedented for a college wrestler." (39)

When he wasn't put on the cover of that issue of *Sports Illustrated*, the magazine was flooded with emails and letters from irate wrestling fans. He didn't make the cover, but SI did publish a photo of what the cover would have looked like had Cael been on it.

However, he was on the front and backside of a Wheaties box, the first wrestler to be honored by the legendary cereal company since Terry McCann in 1960. Also, a bobblehead doll in Cael's likeness became a hot seller. Though originally sold by the ISU athletic department for $15, it was soon going for as high as $150 on ebay.

The HyVee grocery store chain created a life-size standup figure of Cael in full color holding a can of soup, and distributed it throughout the state of Iowa. Meanwhile, the accolades continued to flow. He was invited on various national television shows, led the fans in singing "Take Me Out to The Ballgame" at a Chicago Cubs game, was named College Male Athlete of the Year by ESPN and was a finalist for the AAU's Sullivan Award.

A two-time academic All-American, he earned a bachelor's degree in art and design at Iowa State. On May 1, 2002, he accepted a position as an administrative assistant within the Iowa State University athletic department. The position included community relations, fund-raising and administrative responsibilities, allowing him the flexibility to continue to train in Ames and work toward the Olympic Games of 2004.

"This position will help me reach my goals of being a world champion and an Olympic champion while still allowing me to train in Ames with the wrestlers in the Iowa State wrestling program," Sanderson said. "It will also give me valuable experience in areas that will help me during my competitive career and long after my career is over. I feel comfortable at Iowa State, it is home and I'm proud to represent ISU around the world."

"We are excited that Cael is going to continue his career in Ames as a Cyclone," ISU athletic director Bruce Van De Velde said. "The only thing that has exceeded Cael's accomplishments is the grace with which he has handled himself. I don't know that Iowa State could have a better ambassador. His reputation is growing worldwide."

"There has never been anyone like Cael Sanderson, his record speaks for itself," said ISU head wrestling coach Bobby Douglas. "His presence in our wrestling room and as a representative of our program can't be underplayed. He is already a legend."

But the legend had more to accomplish. He made the World team again, then had to watch from the sidelines as the United States decided not to attend the 2002 competition in Iran due to threats of violence. For the second straight year, he could not test himself against the best in the world.

In 2003, he gained valuable international experience. He won a major tournament in Russia and earned a bronze medal in the Pan-American Games, losing to Cuban star, Yoel Romero. He earned a silver medal at the World Championships in New York, wrestling in the famed Madison Square Garden. He won his first four bouts and then dropped a thriller to a young Russian wrestler, Sazhid Sazhidov, when he was taken down in a wild scramble near the end.

Cael was learning from the new adversity. He had to survive a severe challenge from former University of Iowa star Lee Fullhart to make the 2004 Olympic team. Fullhart defeated the former Cyclone 5-2 in the Senior National freestyle meet, and Cael had to work his way up through the challenge ladder to even earn a berth on the U.S. team. In the final trials, he defeated Fullhart in the first match, 3-1, but lost the second one, 2-2 criteria. With everything on the line, he and Fullhart squared off for the final match, and Sanderson scored a very hard-fought 4-1 decision. Both men were drenched in sweat and speckled with blood from time to time.

"He's real physical," said Sanderson after the final match. "It's more of a fight than a wrestling match against him. That last match wasn't real pretty but it didn't have to be. I was just trying to get on that team."

Cael Sanderson

There was considerable talk before the trials that Cael had lost his zest for competition, that the last two years of college wrestling and the constant pressure had worn down his enthusiasm for the sport. It was even said that he had considered not trying out for the Olympics at all. But the triumph at the trials changed all of that.

"It's crazy to make an Olympic team because you dream about it for years and years, but it seems so far away," he said in the press interview. "It is strange to finally make it after thinking about it for twenty years. But it is pretty neat."

With the trials behind him, Sanderson kicked his training program into high gear and stayed last after nearly every practice, working on technique and pumping the stationery bike, hour after hour. He enjoyed the long workout sessions, and working with coaches like Kevin Jackson, Bobby Douglas and Tom Brands. His workouts were etched with determination and a renewed sense of purpose.

That set the stage for his final competition. In Greece, the homeland of the ancient and modern Olympics, Cael won five straight matches to claim the Olympic gold medal, but it wasn't easy. He started out well with 4-2 and 9-1 victories over Kazakhstan and Belarus, respectively. In the third round, he found himself trailing Iran's Majid Khodaei 5-3 early in the second period. He tied the match at 5-5 on a takedown with just 22 seconds left, and then scored a takedown in overtime for a 6-5 win.

"Having to come from behind made that match special," said Sanderson afterwards. "I was having fun, even when I was down. It's been a few matches since I felt like that."

His semifinal foe was Yoel Romero, the 1999 world champion from Cuba who owned a 2-0 record against the American superstar. But Sanderson came out with a 3-2 win to move into the championship bout against Korea's Eui Jae Moon. The Korean had scored a shocking upset over the defending world champion, Sazhid Sahidov, on the other side of the bracket.

Sanderson and Moon battled to a 0-0 first period, then Sanderson fought back with two takedowns and an exposure for the 3-1 win and the gold medal.

"I see the medal but it's still hard to believe," he said shortly after.

He returned home to a hero's welcome and tremendous publicity, then accepted a job as assistant coach at Iowa State University, secure in his position as one of the greatest wrestlers in American history. Among his thousands of fans are some of the greatest champions from out of the past.

"He's as smooth as I've ever seen on his feet, especially for a big man," said Gray Simons, who won seven national collegiate titles during his great career at Lock Haven State in the early 1960s. "He has great reflexes and timing. I'm very impressed with him, in every respect."

Bill Smith, who was undefeated in college (52-0-2 for Iowa State Teachers College) and was an Olympic champion, feels much the same.

"There's no doubt that he's one of the all-time greats," said Smith, who has seen all of America's top wrestlers since the mid 1940s. "His biggest asset – beside being a great technician – is that he seemed to be able to improve all the time. He was always improving from year to year, and even when he faced some difficulties with freestyle at the outset, he was able to improve.

"Also, I think there is something else that a lot of people miss. Cael doesn't look really powerful, but I think he had strength that people weren't aware of. A bunch of us would watch from the stands when he'd shoot in on something, and his opponent would just fall down. We'd wonder how Cael could make it look so easy. Well, I think he was probably stronger than most people realize, that he could finish those moves because he had great natural pulling power."

Those closest to him have come up with their own idea of what made him so successful on the mat.

"Since the day he stepped on the wrestling mat, he's been good," Cody told a reporter in 2002. "He's always had an understanding for what is going on. Physically and mentally, he was right there the day he started."

Legends of the Mat – 182

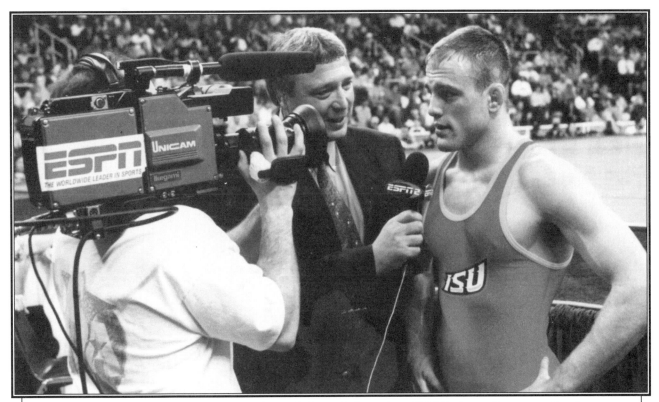

Moments after becoming the only undefeated, four-time NCAA champion ever, Cael Sanderson is interviewed by ESPN commentator Jeff Blatnick (center), who was 1984 Olympic champion. *(Photo courtesy of Ginger Robinson and W.I.N. Magazine)*

Bobby Douglas summed it up this way: "You can talk all you want about talent, but the reason Cael Sanderson is an Olympic champion is he has the heart of a champion."

In April of 2006, Sanderson was given another huge honor when Iowa State named him the sixth head coach in the history of the program. In an emotional press conference Sanderson faced the huge media turnout and expressed his feelings for his coach and the Cyclone family he had become such a part of. The era of Cael Sanderson, wrestler, was officially over and the career of Cael Sanderson, coach, was under way.

In a meeting in Des Moines during the summer before his first year as coach, he told a group of former Iowa State wrestlers that the Cyclones would be aggressive and in the condition to go all out, all the time.

"We won't be backing up, and we'll be fighting all the way," he said. "That's the type of wrestling that I like, and that I believe in. That's the kind of wrestling Iowa State stands for and that we will work very hard to give to the fans."

As an athlete, Cael Sanderson was one of the brightest spots in the long history of amateur wrestling. As a coach, he may have an equally large impact on the sport that he loves, and that loves him back.

"He's the right man in the right job at the right time," said Frank Santana, a NCAA champion for Iowa State at 190 pounds in 1977, and a three-time NCAA finalist. "As a Cyclone faithful, I'm very proud that he is our coach; as a supporter of wrestling as a whole, I think he's going to be terrific for the entire sport. He's one of a kind, really."

Highlights – Cael Sanderson was 122-3 in high school and 159-0 in college (10-1 in redshirt year) at Iowa State University. He won an Olympic gold medal in 2004, a World silver medal in 2003, and a Pan-American Games bronze medal. He also won three national freestyle titles. He had a combined scholastic record over nine years of 292-4, but his overall freestyle record is unknown.

About the Author

Author Mike Chapman (center) stands with two of the legends featured in this book, Doug Blubaugh (left) and Dan Gable.

Mike Chapman is one of the nation's leading wrestling writers and historians. He has written over 600 columns on the sport and has been named National Wrestling Writer of the Year five times, by four different organizations. He is the founder of W.I.N. magazine, the Dan Hodge Trophy, the WIN Memorabilia Show and the International Wrestling Institute and Museum. He has appeared on nearly a hundred radio talks shows and several television programs and documentaries, including for ESPN, A&E, Fox Sports and Fox and Friends.

Mr. Chapman has attended 36 NCAA wrestling tournaments, two Olympic Games and two World Wrestling Championships. He is a member of four halls of fame, including the National AAU Wrestling Hall of Fame. This is his 19th book, and 13th about the sport of wrestling.

He and his wife, Bev, live in Newton, Iowa.

Bibliography

1. *From Milo to Londos*, by Nat Fleischer, 1935, Press of C.J. O'Brien, Inc, NYC

2. *A Distant Flame*, by Jack VanBebber as told to Julia VanBebber, 1992, New Forum Press, Inc., Stillwater, Oklahoma

3. *Wrestling: On and Off the Mat*, by Wayne Baughman, 1987, Wayne R. Baughman, Colorado Springs, Colorado

4. *From Gotch to Gable: A History of Iowa Wrestling*, by Mike Chapman, 1981, University of Iowa Press, Iowa City, Iowa

5. *Coaching Wrestling Successfully*, by Dan Gable, 1999, Human Kinetics, Champaign, Illinois

6. *Little Men in Sports*, by Larry Fox, 1968, Grossett and Dunlap, New York

7. *Wrestling Tough*, by Mike Chapman, 2005, Human Kinetics, Champaign, Illinois

8. *The Last Takedown*, by Bobby Douglas, 2004, McMillen Publishing, Ames, Iowa

9. *Sports Wars*, by David Zang, 2001, University of Arkansas Press, Fayetteville, Arkansas

10. *Wrestling Is A Man's Game*, by Sergei Preobrazhensky, 1981, Progress Publishers, Moscow

11. *Gifford: On Courage*, by Frank Gifford, 1976, M. Evans and Company, Inc., New York

12. *Mat Snacks*, by Jack Spates, 1989, Oklahoma Gold, Oklahoma City, Oklahoma

13. *The New Breed: Living Iowa Wrestling*, by Lou Banach with Mike Chapman, 1985, Leisure Press, West Point, New York

14. *Never Stop Pushing*, by Rulon Gardner, with Bob Schaller, 2005, Carroll & Graff Publishers, New York

15. *Great Jews in Sports*, by Robert Slater, 1992, Jonathon David Publisher, Inc.

16. *Victory*, by Steve Fraser, 2005, International Wrestling Institute and Museum, Newton, Iowa

17. *Alumni News*, The Iowa State magazine, 1988

Footnotes

1. *From Milo to Londos*, page 199
2. *A Distant Flame*, page 18
3. Ibid, pages 62-63
4. Ibid, page 159
5. Ibid, page vii
6. *Wrestling: On and Off the Mat*, page 11
7. Newspaper article by Doug McDonald
8. *From Gotch to Gable: A History of Iowa Wrestling*, page 127
9. *Alumni News*, The Iowa State magazine
10. *Wrestling: On and Off the Mat*, page 16
11. *Little Men in Sports*, page unknown
12. *Wrestling: On and Off the Mat*, page 43
13. *Sports Illustrated*, Man of the Ash, March 9, 1992
14. *Sports Wars*, page 49
15. Ibid, page 33
16. From article by Leo Davis in the *Oregonian*, August 30, 1971
17. *Wrestling Is A Man's Game*, page 64
18. *Gifford: On Courage*, page 178
19. Interview with Kyle Klingman
20. Thewrestlingmall.com, interview by Mat Krumrie
21. Interview with Kyle Klingman
22. *The New Breed: Living Iowa Wrestling*, page 24
23. Ibid, page 63
24. *The Young Wrestler*, March-April, 1977, J. Carl Guyman article
25. *Sports Illustrated*, July 16, 1984, page 38, story by Craig Neff
26. *GAIN*, page 11, Vol 1. No. 8, Sept/Oct 1999

27. *Mat Snacks*, pages 1, 2

28. *Wrestling: On and off the Mat*, page 28

29. *Wrestling Tough*, page 134

30. *The Olympian* magazine, November 1990, page 17

31. Ibid, page 34, 35

32. Ibid, page 65

33. *Sports Illustrated*, Wrestling Mania, article by Franz Lidz, page 65

34. *USA Wrestler*, Profile, July/August 2006 issue

35. *Winning Ways: America's Masters of the Mat Reveal Secrets of Their Success*, coordinated by James Birk, page 20

36. *Never Stop Pushing*, page 9

37. Ibid, page 121

38. Ibid, page 139

39. *Sports Illustrated*, issue April 1, 2002, article by Mark Bechtel

To order additional copies of *Legends of the Mat* or any other books published by Culture House, call 641-791-3072 or write: Culture House, PO Box 293, Newton, IA 50208.